THE EXODUS
You Almost
Passed Over

THE EXODUS
You Almost
Passed Over

BY

Rabbi David Fohrman

ALEPH BETA PRESS
2016

The author invites feedback.
He can be reached at info@alephbeta.org.

The Exodus You Almost Passed Over
Published by Aleph Beta Press
Text Copyright © 2016 by Hoffberger Institute for Text Study

First edition March 2016
Second printing April 2016
Third printing January 2017

Hardcover ISBN: 978-0-9973476-0-9

Email: info@alephbeta.org
Website: http://www.alephbeta.org

Printed in the United States of America.

Contents

PART IV

Joseph and the Phantom Exodus

APPENDIX A

APPENDIX B

The Hoffberger Institute for Text Study

BOARD OF GOVERNORS

Acknowledgments

Shortly after *The Queen You Thought You Knew* was published, some good friends, Alan and Fran Broder, approached me about any plans I might have for writing a third book. I had mentioned to them that I was working on researching the story of Joseph, and anticipated that this would probably be the subject of my next writing project. They eagerly asked to dedicate a book on that topic, and we agreed to embark on that project as partners.

At various Pesach retreats over the years, I had wonderful conversations with Alan and his family about the hidden delights of Torah texts. As a computer scientist, and later as a professor at Yeshiva University, Alan has specialized in data mining—finding and analyzing hidden, often nested, patterns in seemingly random bursts of data. We quickly felt each other to be kindred spirits. Those patterns exist in our sacred texts, too, and we each shared a sense of elation at finding them and setting about the task of discerning what they might mean. This book, especially its second part, is an attempt to do just that with the latter part of Genesis and the first part of Exodus. This book has had a long gestation period, and Alan and Fran have waited patiently for it. I hope in its pages they will find something of the delight of those conversations we've had around the Pesach table.

Speaking of that long gestation period, there's a story behind that, too. As I mentioned, I had initially planned with Alan and Fran to write a book focusing on Joseph themes. Time, though, has a way of confounding our best-laid plans. I devised an outline for a book that would begin with Exodus themes, and then show how aspects of the Joseph story related to those themes. But I started, and abandoned, several drafts. I wasn't pleased with how the ideas looked on the printed page. The whole plan didn't seem to be working out.

Throughout it all, Alan and Fran were patient and more than encouraging, but it didn't look like their hopes for a Joseph-related book would pan out. I finished the Exodus-related sections of the book I had outlined, and pretty much intended to end things there. And that's the way things stood, until a cold Shabbat afternoon in December, when another good friend, Stephen Wagner, approached me to share a thought.

Steve had noticed that the text of the Torah, at the end of the book of Genesis, seemed to devote an inordinate amount of attention to the child-care arrangements that were put in place for Jacob's funeral. He noted that it seemed evocative, in a way, of events that would later transpire in the Exodus. I looked at the text Steve was talking about and it struck me that he was on to something. Steve's insight about Jacob's funeral, I became convinced, was the tip of a grand iceberg that lay just under the surface of the biblical text. Over the next days and weeks, I ran some of these ideas by Immanuel Shalev, our COO at Aleph Beta, and together, we began to discern some of the edges of the rest of the iceberg. That iceberg ended up being the second half of this book. As it turns out, the story of Joseph, and his interaction with his father Jacob, was tied to the Exodus in breathtaking ways. The connection was deeper than I ever suspected.

This would all have passed me by without Steve's little nudge. And, in all likelihood, it all would have passed me by if it weren't for Fran and Alan. Their gentle hope for a work that would speak of the inner meaning of the Joseph story helped change my view of the Exodus and Joseph stories in dramatic ways. I am grateful for Fran and Alan not only for the support that made this book possible, but for helping to spark the ideas that made this book worth writing in the first place.

This book owes a great deal to many others, too.

LeRoy Hoffberger, *z'l*, has been a real source of blessing in my life. He was my student at the Johns Hopkins University, close to twenty years ago. He was the first to really believe in me, and to see what might come if I devoted myself to the study and teaching of Jewish texts as a full-time occupation. He created a foundation to make that dream a reality, and this book, the two that preceded it, and hundreds of hours of audio and video content available on alephbeta.org, are all the fruits of that dream. His love, enthusiasm, and vision for what can yet be achieved–all this is a constant treasure to me. LeRoy has recently passed away; may this book, and the other works of AlephBeta, continue to give him *nachas* in the Heavenly spheres.

Over the years, as I moved to the New York area, others joined Roy's vision. They banded together to create what has become Aleph Beta, an organization that has helped distill much of my work, and the methodology behind it, into video presentations that speak to a new generation of Torah students. Aleph Beta has its sights on cultivating a new generation not only of students, but of teachers and scholars as well, and I'm proud to say that it has taken its first steps in that direction. I cannot wait to see what the future has in store for this organization, but I do want to acknowledge some of the people who have been instrumental in making it into what it has already become.

The board of Aleph Beta has helped shape the vision for what we could achieve together. In the process of our working together, each has also become a friend. They are: Etta Brandman, Donny Rosenberg, Robbie Rothenberg, Dan Schwartz, Kuty Shalev, and Stephen Wagner. Officers of the board include Jeff Haskell, Josh Mallin, Searle Mitnick, and David Roffman. Mayim Bialik serves in an advisory capacity to the board.

Terri and Andrew Herenstein have been fast friends. They are fierce supporters of original and spiritually meaningful Torah scholarship, and I'm proud to recognize them as those who've made possible *The Queen You Thought You Knew*—first in English, and now in Hebrew as well.

Stephen Wagner's insight on that Shabbat morning in December wasn't just a passing fluke; he consistently anticipates the direction of my thinking more often than I care to remember. Sharing Torah with him has become a regular highlight of my week. Steve, also a founding member of Aleph Beta, has been a forceful advocate for having Aleph Beta maintain a focus on day-school education, which has blossomed into a relationship that the company now maintains with hundreds of schools and scores of teachers.

Kuty Shalev is a close friend. His mortal enemy is small-mindedness, and that has been one of the great gifts he has brought to me. Our bond goes back to a scintillating discussion we had over coffee at Central Perk Cafe, where we ruminated about harnessing technology to create captivating and truly individualized adventures in Jewish learning. That discussion became a kind of touchstone for us, and as Aleph Beta gradually came to take shape, we plucked more and more of that vision out of the rarefied realms of our own imagination and brought it into the real world. Scores of Torah learners are the beneficiaries of his vision, passion, and relentless focus on results.

Robbie Rothenberg describes himself as a disciple of mine, but for all his familiarity with my work—and he really does know most of it cold—he is really more of a trusted partner. He is one of the formative forces behind Aleph Beta, and his vision, support, and leadership continue to help drive it forward. Aleph Beta is a personal mission of his, as much as it is my own. He and Helene are a great audience for many ideas that I'm first taking for a spin. They appreciate the good, and gently point out the rough edges. Their friendship means the world to me.

I want to thank the incredibly talented team at Aleph Beta. It has been truly thrilling to work so closely with capable and creative folks who write, research, design, develop, illustrate, animate, produce, market, and help bring Torah to life. Ramie Smith acted as producer for this book, offering valuable insight and commentary–especially bringing to life how an outside reader might relate to what I was writing. I want to thank Carly Friedman for her skill, passion and enthusiasm in marketing and distributing this book, as well as for her strategic vision surrounding this and other Aleph Beta projects. Rabbi David Block provided valuable feedback on the book's first draft, helping to make it cleaner and more readable.

There are others who participated even more directly in the creation of this book.

Many read and commented on the manuscript. These include: Jason Botvin, Michael Fellus, Daniel Fried, Etta Brandman Klaristenfeld and Harry Klaristenfeld, Elinatan Kupferberg, Michael Levy, Searle Mitnick, Shimmy Rosenberg, Robbie Rothenberg, Yair Saperstein, Robert Schechter, Davina Shalev, Josh Shpayer, Hillel Silvera, Stephen Wagner, Barry Waldman, and Shlomo Zuckier. Thanks also to Jerry Stulberger for graciously printing review copies of the manuscript.

Yosef Abraham served as research editor on this project and contributed much valuable material that augmented the footnotes.

Carol Wise helped make this book shine. As the erstwhile editor of both *The Beast that Crouches at the Door* and *The Queen You Thought You Knew,* Carol knows the traps I often fall into as a writer. I am grateful to her for detecting those little foibles and helping smooth the way for the reader.

I want to especially thank Rivky Stern for her contributions to this book. Rivky has a unique ability to ruthlessly spot, and excise, the extra embellishment that really does not need to be there; the clause that just creates a little bit more fuzz in the reader's mind. Had I allowed her to edit these very lines, she would certainly have deleted the second half of the previous sentence. That the book is as concise as it is owes itself, in large part, to Rivky. She spent countless hours, nights, and weekends painstakingly reviewing the book and making sure it was in perfect shape. She did all this on a tight timetable and with great skill. I am deeply grateful.

I wish I had some sort of neat title to describe the contribution to this book made by Immanuel Shalev, but his influence exceeds such language. He acted tirelessly as a kind of hybrid between editor, *chevrusa* and producer, alternately wearing one hat, then another—and sometimes all three. But Imu wears a fourth hat, too, maybe more important than all three—that of a friend. His enthusiasm and boundless energy have lifted me up; his humor has brought a wry smile to my face at the end of a long day of writing. Imu is someone who cares deeply about the ideas in this book, and he helped shape many of them, especially in the second half of the work. He is probably as much of a creator of this as I am. If this book touches your life in any way, you are in Immanuel's debt.

Rabbi Hershel Billet, a mentor and friend, has graciously invited me to serve as resident scholar at the Young Israel of Woodmere, where I've been privileged to teach and interact with a wide swath of eager and excited adult students. The Nusach Sefard Minyan at the YIW, in particular, has been a proving ground for many of the ideas in the book. My thanks go to Shaul Schwalb and the other officers of both the *minyan* and the larger shul.

My family has been a real anchor for me. I came into the Wolfson family as a teenager, and it means so much to me to have been embraced, with so much love, by them all, as we gradually became one large family. My siblings and their spouses have been there for me at every turn: Avreimi and Tovi Wolfson, Rabbi Motti and Rifky Wolmark, Rabbi Shlomo and Bella Gottesman, Moishe and Arielle Wolfson, Yanky and Aliza Safier, Aaron and

Ellen Wolfson, Joey and Sarah Felsen, Daniel and Estie Wolfson, and Yossi and Elisheva Oratz.

The unity of our family is a tribute to my mother, Mrs. Nechama Wolfson, who has showered love on child and stepchild alike, as if there were no tomorrow. As a beneficiary of that love, I am immensely grateful. She does what moms get paid to do, and more: she's always happy to listen to my lectures, even if she's heard that one four times before. The material I've developed on Joseph has always been close to her heart, so I hope she will find this book particularly meaningful. My mother's presence in my life has meant everything to me.

My children have brought me great joy, and have also helped out with this book, each in their own way. Moshe, who is on his way towards becoming a serious Torah scholar in his own right, has batted around ideas with me from his perch in Jerusalem. Shalva's quick wit and wisdom has enriched this book. She harbors great passion for the messages in these pages and for their ability to transform lives. She has encouraged me to write with a broad audience in mind, so that the book's message be carried beyond just the audiences it would most easily reach. Avigail thoughtfully and happily parried ideas with me; her keen input helped reassure me that the outline of it all really *did* hold water. Shana holds the distinction of being the earliest reader of the book's first draft. When she felt it passed muster, I breathed a palpable sigh of relief. While writing, Yael's graceful ballet, executed at the barre in our living room, helped soothe my heart. Her dance, and her presence in my life, puts me at ease in a way that is hard to convey in words. Ariella has a running homework assignment to read for fifteen minutes a night, and it touched my heart that she chose to fill her evenings with my manuscript. Her delight in those chapters is a source of great happiness to me. Avichai has the distinction of being named for the material in this book. His sweet innocence constantly reassures me that the world really is a good place.

And here it is, late at night, after many late nights devoted to writing this book. I'm still at my office, trying to reach a publication deadline. At home is the greatest gift I could ask for: my loving wife, Reena. Her presence in my life, and in the life of my family, has meant, and continues to mean, more than I can put into words. While I was busy writing, she was busy studying Tanach with Ariella, helping her take her first steps towards competition in the Chidon HaTanach. Together, we have raised children and weathered life's storms. She laughs at my jokes; she knows my flaws and accepts me anyway. She shares a vision of life with me that has only deepened over the years. I hope that this book is a credit to the love and faith she has placed in me.

To some extent, this book is about what it means for a son to relate to a father—and sometimes, to more than one father. That is a topic that is dear to my heart, for I have been the grateful beneficiary of more than one father's love. My own father, Moshe Fohrman *z'l*, died before I became a *bar mitzvah*, but in the short time we had together, he taught me so much about life and how best to live it. He possessed great psychological and spiritual acumen; he was a teacher to many—and I count myself as not just a son but a student. I hope this book would do him proud. Certainly, much of his wisdom can be found in its pages.

Later, another father would come into my life. My mother married Zev Wolfson *z'l*, a man who embraced me as his own, as did the rest of his loving family. Over the years, my stepfather gave of himself deeply to me; he took a heartfelt interest in fostering my welfare and growth as a student and teacher of Torah. He was my regular *chevrusa*—sometimes by phone, sometimes in person—for almost two decades, and in our learning sessions, we would find ourselves held rapt by the mysteries of the Exodus and the Joseph narratives. Those sessions, too, helped nurture the ideas that would appear in this book.

Still later, one more special man would come to occupy an important place in my life—my father-in-law, Yitzchak Dinewitz, *z'l*.

His quiet and gentle manner, coupled with his vast knowledge of Tanach and commentaries, has made him a wonderful partner. He relished nothing more at a Shabbat afternoon meal than the chance to engage in fierce debate and discussion with me, his wife Vivian, and the rest of the family, over the finer points of the weekly Torah portion. I have learned so much from him over the years. He has recently passed away, and I miss him greatly.

Finally, if writing this book has taught me anything, it is that we all have a deeper father than our earthly ones. Part of life is learning to accept the love of our fathers, even as the mystery of their ways sometimes seem inscrutable. If that is true for the earthly variety of fathers, it is true for our Heavenly Father, too. My thanks go to our Heavenly Father for His love and beneficence in my life. I hope this book will do honor to Him.

Preface

What Kind of Book is This?

I once read a fascinating book by Mortimer Adler, entitled *How to Read a Book*. In it, Adler argues that one of the first things a reader needs to ask themselves is: what genre does this book in front of me belong to? What *kind* of book is it? The reason this question is important to ask, he argues, is that if I do not know the kind of book I am reading, I am likely to misinterpret it. I am likely to ask the wrong questions about the book.

Imagine you are reading Carl Sandburg's poetry—but you think you're reading a meteorology textbook instead. The first line you encounter is: "The fog comes on little cat feet." You become indignant at that silly statement. Fog doesn't have feet. And it's not a cat. You conclude that you are reading a ridiculous book.

Bottom line: knowing the genre of a book makes a difference. In that spirit, let me try to clarify for you, the reader, the kind of book I've intended to write.

The Kind of Book This Is Not

This book may seem a little different than some other books of biblical commentary you might have encountered. The easiest way to describe its genre might be to describe, first, what kind of book it is *not*. Contemporary biblical commentary comes in three different varieties, more or less. This book does not neatly fit into any of them, though I think you'll find that it does include elements of all three.

One kind of biblical commentary that can be found on today's bookshelf is what we might call critical academic scholarship. While the book in your hands does make evidence-based arguments, it does not fit neatly into the academic genre. I am writing for a lay audience as much as a scholarly one, and I am also seeking to explore questions related to *meaning*: how are we meant to relate to these texts? How can they, and how should they, inform our lives? What spiritual meaning does the Torah wish us to derive from them? Academic writing is typically silent on these questions. I believe, however, that the serious student of the Bible needs to consider them.

At the other end of the spectrum lies another genre of English-language biblical commentary that focuses more directly on questions of personal relevance. This sort of commentary, however, sometimes seems less interested in rigorously examining the biblical text than in offering nuggets of inspiration for the benefit of the reader. It tends to use the biblical text as a springboard to discuss ideas the author deems to be of spiritual or religious value. While this book is not indifferent to questions of meaning, it tries to allow meaning to arise organically from a close examination of the biblical text itself. As such, it does not really belong to this genre, either.

A third kind of biblical analysis available in today's marketplace is the anthology. In today's Jewish world, such works aggregate the ideas and analyses offered by the classical commentators of the medieval era—such greats as Rashi, Ramban, Seforno, and the even earlier Sages who composed the Midrash. Such works are certainly of immense value, but this book does not belong to that genre, either. While the reader will certainly find many of these commentators cited in the pages ahead, and while the wisdom of the Midrash serves as a guidepost for me at various crucial points, this book is not, principally, an anthology of earlier commentary.

The Kind of Book This Is

What kind of book is this, then?

It is, perhaps, a guidebook. This book offers the reader a journey–a journey that I myself have taken. It is a travelogue, of sorts, of my own personal attempt to grapple with the Torah's account of the Exodus, and with the meaning of that story. I am sharing with you, a reader of the Torah, how things seem to me, a fellow reader of the Torah.

At the core of this journey is an attempt to engage with the original Hebrew text of the Torah. Everything else will revolve around that. Our journey will begin with a number of questions about the biblical text–basic questions that the average person might ask, were they encountering the stories we are looking at for the very first time. I'll introduce these questions not in the spirit of skepticism but in the spirit of genuine inquiry. By grappling with these questions, and by paying attention to cues in biblical language, we will find our way to deeper and deeper layers of meaning embedded in the text.

There is nothing new or novel in trying to engage the Torah's text directly. Truthfully, *any* classic commentator–from Rashi to the Ramban, to Seforno, to Samson Raphael Hirsch and the Ha'emek Davar–is writing to you based on the assumption that you have already made a serious attempt to understand the text. If you have not tried to do so yet, you are not yet ready to read the commentator–for indeed, you have not yet read the text that he or she is commenting upon.

Making an attempt to read the text closely is not something new in the Jewish tradition. It is something I personally learned from my *rebbe*, the late Rosh Yeshiva of Ner Israel, Rabbi Yaakov

Weinberg. Rabbi Weinberg believed that, when it comes to the Torah, the choice between meaning and evidence-based learning is a false one. To simply use the Bible as fodder for sermonics is to disregard its depth and sophistication. To confine the Torah to the realm of sterile intellectual curiosity is to similarly mis-understand and devalue it. Rigorous, evidence-based study and spiritual meaning must not only coexist in our study of the Torah, but the former must be a bridge to the latter.

I have written this book in an informal style, eschewing the detached air of academic impartiality or tendentious prose that pervades many scholarly works. My hope is that the reader can spend his or her time figuring out what the Torah means to say, rather than what Fohrman means to say. As befits a guidebook, in these pages, I have opted to engage the reader directly. If it feels like I'm talking to you in this book, that is by design. I am opening up my own personal journey through biblical texts and their mysteries to the reader who cares to join me on a re-creation of that journey. If you accept my invitation, I will do my best to provide you with a guided adventure that hopefully will kindle in you some of the excitement and thrill of discovery that I my-self have found in the sacred words of the biblical Exodus saga.

PART I

Taking Apart
the Exodus Story

CHAPTER ONE

The Angel in the Back
of the Room

In Hebrew, it is *Pesach*; in English, it is Passover. But either way, it seems like an odd name for a holiday. Would *you* have named it that?[1]

Imagine it is 3,000 years ago. You are an angel in heaven, and you have been invited to join God's Nominating Committee for the Naming of New Festivals.[2] One day, you and your fellow angels on the committee get word that the Master of the Universe would like to make a shiny new festival that celebrates His miraculous deliverance of the Israelites from slavery in Egypt.

---

1. The biblical text often calls the seven-day holiday that we know of as Passover *Chag ha-Matzot*, "The Holiday of Matzot," and seems to reserve the name *Pesach*, or Passover, for the first night (Leviticus 23:5–6 and elsewhere). However, the use of the name Pesach to characterize the entire holiday seems to reach back to the days of King Josiah (see, for example, 2 Chronicles, chapter 35). Moreover, the Talmud regularly calls the entire holiday Passover. At the very least, starting with the Rabbinic Sages long ago, Jewish tradition has ensconced Passover as the name by which this holiday is known. It is this tradition that we will be wondering about below.

2. This is a variation on a thought experiment I first posed in my previous book, *The Queen You Thought You Knew*.

You immediately get down to work with your colleagues to brainstorm some possible names.

The angel on your left nominates *Independence Day*. Most everyone nods in agreement: it's nice, it's short, it gets right to the point. Someone else says, "We could call it *Freedom Day*; how about *Freedom Day*?" A bunch of angels concur. You put *Freedom Day* up on the whiteboard, right below *Independence Day*.

But then imagine some angel in the back of the room raises his hand and says, "I have a great idea. Much better than those names. Let's call it *Passover*. Passover is a really wonderful name."

So you say, as politely as you can, "Can you clarify a bit? That seems like a strange name. Why should we call it Passover?"

The angel at the back of the room speaks up again: "See, it's kind of a pun." He looks disappointed at having to explain his little joke. "You know how God made all these plagues to let the Israelites go, and then there was this tenth plague, right? And in the tenth plague, all of the firstborn children of the Egyptians were killed. But the Israelites? They were saved. So you could say that God sort of 'passed over' their firstborn children that night, when He didn't kill them. You get it? He *passed over* their firstborn? So let's call it Passover!"

You'd assume that few of your fellow angels would be impressed. What kind of name is that? Look, it's all very nice that our firstborn were saved from destruction that night, but in the scheme of things, that's just one particular detail about one particular plague. Yes, it's an important detail–no one wishes that our firstborn were killed–but still, it's a detail; it doesn't address what the holiday is *really* about, in the big picture. It doesn't speak of freedom, independence, redemption, or the birth of a nation.

But then imagine that, yes, God decides to go with that back-of-the-room angel's suggestion: the name Passover wins the day. You'd be left incredulous. And, of course, this isn't really a thought experiment at all; it's more or less real life. The Torah *does* ordain a holiday to celebrate our Exodus from Egypt, and, of all things, that holiday ends up being called Passover!

Remarkable. What are we to make of that?

Perhaps the name suggests that we should adjust our sights somewhat. We tend to think of Passover the way I've just described it to you, as the holiday on which we got our freedom.[3] And yet, the Torah's *own* name for the night we went free doesn't emphasize the "free" part, it emphasizes being "passed over." Could it be that, somehow, the essence of the holiday really *does* revolve around the mysterious salvation that our firstborn experienced that night?

There might well be reason to believe it does. One gets the sense that the role of the firstborn children in the Exodus story is anything but peripheral. What happened to the firstborn on the night Israel went free seems to represent something more, as if their experience was a crucible, of sorts; as if their experience pointed to some kind of larger idea or mission.

We can demonstrate that with a second thought experiment...

The Little Black Boxes

Let's imagine that one day, you decide to create your very own religion (don't try this at home). You put together lots of commandments for your band of followers, along with a bunch of theological tenets you'd like them to embrace. You write it all down in this really long book. Then you have a wonderful idea: why not create ways your adherents will be able to express their fealty to the tenets of this book? So you decide to create some rituals. In one of them, your followers will fashion for themselves

---

3. Indeed, even later Rabbinic characterizations of Passover suggest as much; in our prayers, we regularly refer to the holiday as *zman cheiruteinu*, "the time of our freedom."

little black boxes. In these boxes, they will place a scroll on which they will inscribe representative sections of the book. The scroll will contain the most basic tenets of their new faith. Your adherents will show their devotion to these tenets by literally strapping the boxes onto their arms and heads at least once a day.

As it happens, Judaism has just such a ritual device. The little black boxes are known as *tefillin*, and they contain scrolls with short sections of the Bible inscribed upon them.

So back to our thought experiment: let's talk about what you would put in those boxes. If the book with all those laws was the Five Books of Moses–what short selections from the Five Books would you choose to put in those boxes?

Well, you might nominate the short text known as the Shema. The Shema proclaims one's basic belief in God, and is generally seen as the credo of the Jewish faith: "Hear O Israel, the Lord is our God, the Lord is One." That would be a good thing to put in the boxes, right?

One might go further, and add the next paragraph of the Shema declaration. This next paragraph instructs people to love God with all their hearts and with all their souls. That would be good to put in the boxes, too.

What else would you put in the boxes? Remember, there's not a lot of room on the little scroll. You have to choose carefully.

To borrow our earlier image, imagine that our friend, the angel in the back of the room, is back. He raises his hand and suggests the following:

"Why don't we include the law of *peter chamor*, the law of the broken-necked donkey?"

"Excuse me?" you respond, somewhat confused.

"Sure," he says, "you know the law. It's right there in Exodus, chapter 13. See, the Bible says that whenever the Children of Israel have a firstborn male–whether human or animal–they should consider it sanctified to God. If it's a human child, it needs to be redeemed with money, to take ownership of it back from God, so to speak. If the offspring is an animal, then it depends. If it's an animal that can be offered on the altar, like a sheep, then the firstborn is slaughtered as an offering to God. If it's an animal that is not kosher for sacrifice, like a donkey, then the owner can redeem it with money, and use the money to buy an animal that *can* be offered, like a lamb. And for a donkey in particular, there's a special law—if you don't redeem your firstborn donkey, then it must be killed; the Bible says its neck is to be broken."

The angel takes a deep breath, and comes to his emphatic conclusion:

"So I say we include *that* law in the little boxes!"

If you were in charge of the ritual committee, you'd probably ask this angel to find himself another job. Look, you might tell this fellow, it's a fine law, this idea of redemption of the firstborn and all those permutations about the donkey and everything. It's great for putting in the book of Leviticus somewhere. But we only have so much room in the little boxes. We must save the space for what's really essential, for the laws and ideas that define the essence of what it means to be a Jew. There's no room for that law in the boxes.

But lo and behold, there *is* room for his law in the boxes; for when we exit our thought experiment and rejoin real life, we find that tefillin, as described by the Torah, do contain, of all things, the law of the broken-necked donkey. Surprisingly, the Torah mandates that tefillin must include these laws. Why? Because they are meant to recall the way God spared our firstborn the night we left Egypt and went free (Exodus 13:14-16).

So there you have it. The threat to the firstborn on the night we went free, and their redemption from that threat—these ideas are evidently more fundamental than we might have supposed. Passover gets its name from them. And these ideas make their way onto the ultimate short list—the tefillin scroll that contains the basic tenets of the Bible. How might we explain that?

Beyond Biblical Poetry

I mentioned above the possibility that the Torah is using the idea of firstbornness as a kind of shorthand, perhaps, for a larger idea. I want to call your attention to a strange statement that seems to confirm this. It appears at the very beginning of the Exodus narrative, before even the first of the ten plagues has struck Egypt:

וְאָמַרְתָּ אֶל־פַּרְעֹה כֹּה אָמַר יְקֹוָה בְּנִי בְכֹרִי
יִשְׂרָאֵל: וָאֹמַר אֵלֶיךָ שַׁלַּח אֶת־בְּנִי וְיַעַבְדֵנִי

And you shall tell Pharaoh, Thus says God: My firstborn child is Israel. And I say to you: Send out my child that he may serve Me... (Exodus 4:22–23)

If you stop to think about it, what the verse says here is puzzling. Evidently, God had instructed Moses to go to Pharaoh and to use those exact words, "My firstborn child is Israel," in phrasing his demand that Pharaoh set Israel free. But the words are so hard to understand; what does it mean to claim that Israel is the firstborn child of God?

Maybe calling Israel firstborn is nothing more than a flourish of biblical poetry. In that case, it simply indicates that God sort of likes the Children of Israel, and that's the end of it. Anyway, we might argue, no one really takes biblical poetry all that literally. The Bible speaks of a land flowing with milk and honey, but no one traveling to Israel packs galoshes so they can wade through the honey-filled streets more easily. So too, when one encounters a biblical phrase like "Israel is My firstborn child," a first reaction might be to see it as some sort of flowery, non-literal turn of phrase.

But while this might seem a handy explanation, the rest of the verse simply does not allow for it. After calling Israel the firstborn child of God, the verse continues:

וַתְּמָאֵן לְשַׁלְּחוֹ הִנֵּה אָנֹכִי הֹרֵג אֶת־בִּנְךָ בְּכֹרֶךָ:

And if you refrain from sending him out, behold, I will kill your firstborn child (Exodus 4:23)

The Almighty makes a direct comparison between Israel, His firstborn, and the actual firstborn children of the Egyptians. On the basis of this comparison, He states that if the Egyptians fail to send out God's firstborn, they will ultimately suffer the demise of their own firstborn—a prophecy that comes to its chilling realization when the tenth plague eventually strikes.

So let's be clear: people will die because of this firstborn-to-firstborn comparison. *You take my firstborn; I'll take your firstborn!* Now, you'll excuse me, but this doesn't sound much like poetry. This sounds real. It sounds like God is quite serious about the notion that Israel is a firstborn nation. But why? Israel was not the first nation ever to come into existence. Lots of others were around before Israel came on the scene. In what sense are they firstborn?

A Nation, First Born

At this point, we don't know much, but we do know one thing for sure: the firstborn theme is everywhere in the Exodus story. The story begins with God's statement to Moses that Israel is His firstborn. It ends with the Smiting of the Firstborn. It is commemorated by tefillin and by rituals such as the redemption of the firstborn. The holiday that celebrates it all is named for what happened to our firstborn. The firstborn theme is the fabric out of which this story is woven. To know the Exodus is to know firstbornness.

Maybe, then, the Exodus story is about more than we ever suspected. Is it about freedom? Yes, it surely is. Independence and the birth of a nation? Yes, that, too. But it is about more than this.

In this book, I want to argue that the Exodus story tells us who we are. It is a story that tells us not just about our past, but about our future. It speaks not only of our birth, but of our destiny. It speaks of *why* we are here and what we are meant to achieve. The story is about what it means to be a firstborn nation.

In the pages that follow, we are going to examine the Exodus story and try to unpack some of its mysteries—among them, the meaning of the firstborn theme. We will try to read the story with fresh eyes, and taste its newness. I invite you to come along with me on that journey, so that together, we may thrill in the discovery of unseen delights, uncovering the hidden secrets of this ancient and sacred saga.

CHAPTER TWO

The Exodus Game

A remarkable thing about the Exodus story is that the three most important figures in it—God, Pharaoh, and Moses—each act in ways that defy our expectations. Taken together, their unexpected actions suggest that the story may have some hidden dimensions to it.

Join me, if you would, in a little thought experiment. We might call it The Exodus Game. Let's imagine that we could occupy the position of each of these three different players. What choices might we make? How would our choices have compared to theirs?

Let's start with God.

Let's Play Exodus!

Imagine you are God (again, don't try this at home). As the deity in charge, here's your challenge: An entire people has been unjustly enslaved in the ancient Land of Egypt. You want to deliver the slaves from bondage and take them to the Land of Canaan, making good on a promise you made to their forebears. Your opponent is a nasty and recalcitrant Pharaoh, who has no intention, thank you very much, of letting his fine slaves go free.

Take a moment to ponder your strategy: how are you going to accomplish this task? Now, don't get all nervous; it's not as hard as you think. Remember, you are playing God, the ultimate power in the universe. Any and all conceivable weapons are at your disposal: lightning, earthquakes, tidal waves, you name it. There's simply nothing you can't do. So how might you, as quickly and efficiently as possible, achieve your objective?

What It Takes to Win

Do you think you would need *ten different plagues* to set your people free? Probably not. Surely you could come up with a scheme that would accomplish your goal more quickly and efficiently than that.

Perhaps you could have skipped the first nine and gone straight to the tenth plague, the Smiting of the Firstborn. It probably would have brought Egypt to its knees all by itself.

You probably could have done it without any plagues at all, if you liked. Maybe you could load all the Hebrews onto magic carpets, departing at noon from Gate C-15 for the Holy Land. Or even easier: freeze the Egyptians in place and let the Israelites simply walk to freedom, right before their oppressors' eyes. For added measure, you could erect a magical force field around your people to protect them from any wayward spears or arrows cast in their direction by the hapless Egyptians.

When you really think about it, the above scenario could have been implemented without too much trouble in the real Exodus; all the elements needed for it were already in place.

Consider, for example, the ninth plague, the plague of darkness. In that plague, an unnatural pitch-black darkness descended upon the Land of Egypt. The blackness was so profound that no Egyptian dared venture outside for a full three days (Exodus 10:23).[4] But, the text tells us, the blackness affected Egyptians

---

4. Generally, we think of darkness as an absence of light. Ramban, in his commentary to Exodus 10:23, however, suggests that this darkness was different. Its cause was not an absence of light but a physical *presence* of darkness, almost palpable. Hence, the Egyptians could not circumvent the

only. The Israelites could see perfectly.[5]

Can you imagine a better opportunity? The Egyptians can't see a blasted thing. The Israelites are enjoying full lighting privileges. Why not just walk right out of Egypt? The Hebrews have three whole days to make their escape, plenty of time to gather their possessions and go.

Why didn't they do it? Was it, perhaps, too dangerous? Were the Children of Israel worried that sightless Egyptians would randomly hurl arrows and projectiles their way, some of which might find their mark? Well, let's talk about that protective force field for a moment. As it turns out, that too was a feature of the real Exodus. At the Splitting of the Sea, the text goes out of its way to tell us that God employed a pillar of cloud as a kind of protective barrier between the pursuing Egyptian army and the fleeing Israelites. So again, all these elements really *were* used by God in the real-life Exodus. They were just used differently.

For some reason, in the real Exodus, God uses darkness and protective pillars of cloud—but does not employ them to quickly allow the Israelites to leave. Instead, a long, laborious process ensues, involving no less than ten distinct plagues. Why did God dismiss these marvelous alternative possibilities, and insist on doing it the long way? Was He simply trying to be dramatic?

---

effects of the plague by kindling light for themselves. In a room merely devoid of light, one can light a candle and see, but in a place covered with the mysterious *presence* of darkness, lighting a candle is of no use at all.

5. In Goshen, where the Israelites lived, the sun continued to shine. According to tradition, it wasn't only in Goshen that the Israelites were provided light; they could see perfectly well *anywhere and everywhere* in Egypt. In other words, in some mysterious way, the ninth plague was a subjective phenomenon: the same landscape that might appear utterly dark from an Egyptian's point of view would appear full of normal light and color to an Israelite.

Was He worried that future generations wouldn't find the story intriguing if He got it over with too quickly?

None of these explanations seem particularly compelling. Does the fact that God eschewed the quick and easy road to freedom indicate that there was some other agenda at work in the Exodus events, that we've not yet picked up on?

Getting to Yes

The outline of some larger divine agenda is suggested by other aspects of the story, too. Leaving aside the question of whether the Exodus could have happened more efficiently, there are other things we probably would have done differently had we been the ones in charge, had this been our little "Exodus Game" version of events. Consider, for example, the seemingly duplicitous request that Moses makes for a three-day work holiday.

In the very first encounter between Moses and Pharaoh, Moses asks the Egyptian king to "please" let the Israelites go into the desert "for three days" so they can worship God and offer sacrifices to Him (Exodus 5:3). Would you have done this, if you were playing Master of the Universe in our Exodus Game? Why talk about three days when you really mean forever? Phrasing your "request" in these terms makes you seem unnecessarily weak and waffling, not to mention dishonest.[6] God has all the power in the world. There's no need for a charade. Just declare: *Let My people go!*—and leave out this silliness about three days.

In the movies, by the way, that's the way it always goes. From Cecil B. Demille's *The Ten Commandments* to Steven Spielberg's *Prince of Egypt*, Moses's interaction with Pharaoh looks very different. In these Hollywood portraits of the Exodus, a stern-faced Moses sets forth a no-holds-barred ultimatum to Pharaoh: *let*

---

6. Cf. R. Yaakov Kaminetsky, *Emet L'Yaakov*, 255.

my people go! Somehow, the rest of Moses's speech–the word *please*, and the part about the three-day vacation–always gets left on the cutting room floor. And it's no wonder why. It's not the way we would expect the Lord to play His hand. But for some reason, there it is, black and white, in the Torah: "The God of the Hebrews has called to us; let us go, please, for three days in the desert to sacrifice to him, lest he strike us with the sword or with pestilence" (Exodus 5:3).

Pharaoh and the Persian Bazaar

The truth is, why Moses needed to ask for just a three-day work holiday is really part of a larger question: why did Moses need to ask Pharaoh for anything at all? Over the course of the Exodus, Moses bargains with Pharaoh repeatedly, seeking his consent to let the slaves go. Moses exhibits extraordinary patience as the Egyptian king gives in partially, retracts his consent, and then gives in just a little more next time.

For example: a plague occurs in which wild animals are unleashed into Egyptian homes and marketplaces. Pharaoh tells Moses that he will allow the Hebrews to worship for three days, but *could they please do it right here, in the Land of Egypt, rather than out there in the desert?* (Exodus 8:21) Moses refuses, on grounds that the Egyptians wouldn't react kindly to Israel slaughtering these animals, since the Egyptians hold them sacred (Exodus 8:22). Pharaoh concedes the point and says that Israel can leave the country for three days–but then he adds, almost hopelessly:

רַק הַרְחֵק לֹא־תַרְחִיקוּ לָלֶכֶת

Just make sure you don't go too far away! (Exodus 8:24)

It all seems faintly ridiculous, the squabbling back and forth. One wonders: Isn't all this a little beneath Moses's dignity? Isn't it beneath God's? God doesn't need to bargain with Pharaoh.

God doesn't even need Pharaoh to say yes at all! The Master of the Universe is perfectly capable of delivering His people to the Promised Land, whether Pharaoh agrees to the plan or not. So why go through all of this?

An Unwritten Rule

One thing seems clear. For some undetermined reason, there appears to be an unwritten rule throughout the Exodus narrative, a rule that God is *choosing* to adhere to: the Israelites aren't going anywhere unless Pharaoh says they are.

Why is Pharaoh's consent so important to God? Why would God go to such lengths to secure that consent, even to the point of asking Pharaoh–seemingly deceptively–for just a three-day holiday? What was God's agenda? What was He really after?

Catch-22

Whatever God was trying to accomplish, it involved something more than just setting Israel free. Seemingly, it involved obtaining Pharaoh's *consent* to let Israel go free, too. But that's not quite it either. For just when you think Pharaoh's consent is everything, it turns out to be nothing at all.

Consider the following: any reader of the Exodus story will pretty quickly notice a familiar pattern. It goes, more or less, like this: A plague hits Egypt. Soon enough, Pharaoh summons Moses and asks him to call off the pain and hardship. Moses asks that, in return, the Israelites be set free, and Pharaoh agrees. But once the plague comes to a halt, Pharaoh reneges and decides to keep the Hebrews enslaved after all. Another plague strikes Egypt, and the cycle repeats.

But here's the thing: at a certain point in the development of the Ten Plagues, this familiar script shifts. Instead of Pharaoh changing his *own* mind, God seems to step in and do the mind-changing for him. In the words of the Torah, the Almighty "hardens Pharaoh's heart" (Exodus 9:12). This happens pretty consistently through the later plagues, like *arbeh*, Locusts, and *choshech*, Darkness. In these cases, Pharaoh's mind changes–but God appears to cause it.

Turning Yes to No

Now, there are two problems that can be raised here: a moral problem and a tactical one.

Here's the moral problem: To the extent that Pharaoh's free will was compromised by God Himself, how can this same God hold Pharaoh responsible for his actions? It seems axiomatic that people are responsible for their choices only if they are the ones making those choices. Take away our autonomy, and you also take away our responsibility. So if God deprived Pharaoh of free will, say, in Plague Eight–where's the justice in inflicting Plague Nine upon him? Why is Pharaoh punished by God for recalcitrance that wasn't really his fault?

To be sure, we aren't the first readers to notice this difficulty. The problem is debated vigorously by the classical commentators, and they offer various solutions.[7] This is an issue we shall return to later in this book. But for now, put this problem out of your mind, and let's consider a related difficulty. Leaving aside the

---

7. *Ramban* to Exodus 7:3 (based on Exodus Rabbah 5:6), for example, suggests that Pharaoh, by virtue of his barbarism toward his slaves and his free-willed refusal to let them go, richly earned a good deal of divine retribution. Thus, God at a certain point withheld from Pharaoh the possibility of repenting, and any plagues that afflicted Pharaoh after this point were justified as punishment for his prior refusals. Other commentators offer different solutions. For a fuller exploration of this topic, see Appendix A, *God, Moses, and the Worst-Case Scenario*.

question of whether it is ethically justified to change Pharaoh's mind—why would God even want to?

From a tactical standpoint, it just doesn't seem to add up. Here God is, sending Moses repeatedly to Pharaoh, enduring endless bargaining sessions with the Egyptian monarch, even coming up with a dubious three-day vacation offer—all in the interest of getting Pharaoh to say yes. Finally, it actually happens! Pharaoh says yes, and it really *is* yes; he's not going to back down and change his mind. Why, at that very moment, would God interfere with Pharaoh's free will and make him say no? Wasn't this the moment we had all been waiting for?

God's decision to harden Pharaoh's heart seems inexplicable. Instead of allowing Pharaoh to release the Israelites, instead of bringing the whole Exodus story to a nice, satisfying conclusion—the Israelites head off into the sunset, bound for the Promised Land, and everyone lives happily ever after—instead of all that, the Almighty sees fit to harden Pharaoh's heart, and suddenly, we're all back to square one. Why would God do that?

Indeed, we can go even further and ask the question this way: if *that's* what the Almighty had been planning to do all along—turn a long-awaited yes from Pharaoh into a no—then why bother asking Pharaoh for his consent in the first place?

At the end of the day, it's a catch-22. Does God care about Pharaoh's free-willed consent, or not? If He does, then once Pharaoh gives that consent, the game should be over. And if the Almighty doesn't care about that consent, why needlessly ask for it to begin with? Either way, the story as we have it doesn't seem to add up.

Taking Stock

Let's take stock of where we are. In the Exodus, God takes the long way: ten plagues replace a simple magic carpet exit. And God, for some reason, seems interested in securing Pharaoh's consent to Israel's departure–except when God is not interested in it, and makes Pharaoh say no.

It certainly is not the way we would have done it if we were God, playing the Exodus game. But as it turns out, it is not only the Almighty's actions that defy expectations in this story. The actions of Pharaoh do, too. Let's now take *his* position in the Exodus game, and see just how surprising the Egyptian king's actions really are.

CHAPTER THREE

Power and Precision

Pharaoh's behavior over the course of the Exodus story is a rich source of evidence for understanding the larger significance of the Exodus events. The Sages of the Talmud and Midrash seem to say as much. They observed Pharaoh's behavior carefully, and, almost as if these Sages were themselves playing our Exodus game, they highlighted some of the ways the king's decisions departed radically from expectations.

Calculated Ambiguity

Just before the tenth plague, Moses warns Pharaoh about the coming devastation:

כֹּה אָמַר יְקֹוָה כַּחֲצֹת הַלַּיְלָה אֲנִי יוֹצֵא בְּתוֹךְ מִצְרָיִם:
וּמֵת כָּל־בְּכוֹר בְּאֶרֶץ מִצְרַיִם מִבְּכוֹר פַּרְעֹה

Thus says the Lord: At about midnight, I shall go out into the midst of Egypt; and all firstborn in Egypt shall die (Exodus 11:4–5)

The ancient Sages (*Berachot* 4a) were bothered by the language of the verse. Moses had said *kachatzot halaylah* (כַּחֲצֹת הַלַּיְלָה), which can be rendered literally as "at *approximately* midnight." Why, the Talmud asks, does Moses need to fudge it like that? After all, God knows when midnight is. So just say outright that the plague will occur at midnight! Just a few lines later, when the plague actually strikes Egypt, the text is very clear about the timing:

וַיְהִי בַּחֲצִי הַלַּיְלָה וַיקוָה הִכָּה כָל־בְּכוֹר בְּאֶרֶץ מִצְרַיִם

*And it happened **at midnight**, that God struck all the firstborn in the Land of Egypt* (Exodus 12:29)

When the plague descends upon Egypt, the narrator says it happens *at midnight*. It seems odd that Moses would be imprecise about this when forecasting the events to Pharaoh.

The Sages propose an answer. They say that, yes, God obviously knew the precise moment at which midnight would occur, but who says Pharaoh knew this—or if he thought he knew, who says he was correct? Say that Pharaoh's palace astrologers were off by a few minutes in their calculations. Had that occurred, the Talmud continues, Pharaoh might have summoned Moses the morning after the plague, and scornfully accused him of lying: *You said the plague would occur at midnight—and you were wrong!* Thus, to prevent any possible mix-up, Moses avoided pinning the plague down to a precise time. Better safe than sorry.

CNN and the Prophet

Now, here's the problem with all this. Just stop for a moment and think about the scenario the Talmud suggests here. Are things really likely to have played out like that?

Imagine if something similar were to happen in contemporary times. One day, the CNN newsroom receives a faxed message from a self-proclaimed prophet, containing an outlandish prediction. "Tomorrow, at exactly 4:03 PM EST," it warns, "simultaneous lightning bolts will descend from heaven and destroy the seats of governments in all world capitals represented in the United Nations General Assembly." *Right.* CNN routinely gets occasional messages from crackpots like this. The clerk who first sees the message rolls his eyes, then files it away. The message doesn't even get reported. Everyone goes about their business, just as before.

But then imagine that the very next day, at exactly 4:01 PM EST, *it really happens*. Simultaneous lightning bolts really do descend and wipe out all the seats of government. What would the headlines be in the next day's papers? Would they be PROPHET IS A LIAR? PROPHET SAYS DESTRUCTION WILL HAPPEN AT 4:03; IT HAPPENS AT 4:01? We all know that's not the headline! What, then, are the Sages telling us here? That Moses had to pull his punches and say *kachatzot halaylah*, it's going to happen at *approximately* midnight, to forestall these ridiculous headlines in the Egyptian papers? On the morning after the tenth plague, whether Pharaoh thought it happened precisely at midnight or not, the last thing on his mind would be calling Moses a liar about a tiny detail in the plague!

I want to suggest that the Sages of the Talmud didn't concoct some half-baked theory out of thin air. They really believed this is how Pharaoh would react, and they had good reason to believe this. They looked at the evidence—Pharaoh's reactions to prior plagues—and they discerned a pattern. They then extrapolated the next obvious step in the pattern and concluded that Pharaoh would have reacted to the tenth plague in precisely the way they described. Let me show you what I mean.

A Frog-Free Tomorrow

The pattern begins with Pharaoh's reaction to the second plague, the plague of frogs. To set the scene, there are frogs everywhere: under tables, in beds, in ovens. He is so desperate to get rid of them that he is willing, at least for the moment, to trade his Hebrew slaves for relief from the amphibian onslaught. So the king calls Moses in for an audience, and says to him:

הַעְתִּירוּ אֶל־יְקֹוָה וְיָסֵר הַצְפַרְדְּעִים מִמֶּנִּי וּמֵעַמִּי
וַאֲשַׁלְּחָה אֶת־הָעָם וְיִזְבְּחוּ לַיקֹוָה:

Beseech YHVH,[8] *that he take away the frogs from me and my people;*
I will let the people go, that they may sacrifice to YHVH (Exodus 8:4)

And now listen to Moses's reply:

הִתְפָּאֵר עָלַי לְמָתַי אַעְתִּיר לְךָ וְלַעֲבָדֶיךָ וּלְעַמְּךָ
לְהַכְרִית הַצֲפַרְדְּעִים מִמְּךָ וּמִבָּתֶּיךָ

Glorify yourself over me: exactly when should I beseech
God, on behalf of your servants and your people, to
rid you and your houses of frogs? (Exodus 8:5)

It sounds like Moses is taunting the Egyptian king with those
words. "Glorify yourself over me," Moses says. Rashi interprets
Moses as having issued a challenge to Pharaoh: *Give me something*
you don't think I can do. You pick the time, and we'll see if I can call off
the frogs precisely when you want them to be gone!

Now, if you were Pharaoh, how would you react to that?

I don't know about you, but if I were Pharaoh, I would probably say something like: *Now would be good. Yesterday would be even*
better. Can we dispense with this silly game and just get rid of the frogs?
But look at Pharaoh's actual response:

וַיֹּאמֶר לְמָחָר

And he said: Tomorrow. (Exodus 8:6)

Tomorrow? Is this for real? The frogs are everywhere, and Pharaoh
can't stand it anymore. He'll do anything to be rid of them—but
now he is willing to endure another twenty-four hours of frogs,
just to see whether Moses can turn off the frogs at exactly the
moment Pharaoh picks?

---

8. Throughout this book, I will adopt the convention of transliterating
the divine name spelled ה-ו-ה-י as YHVH. I will treat the significance of
this name and its possible implications later.

He took the bait Moses cast out to him. It's as if Moses spread
out a deck of cards, asked the king to *pick a card, any card*—and
the king, suddenly oblivious to the stench and aggravation of
the amphibian infestation, complies! Pharaoh draws a card from
the deck, just to see whether Moses really *can* guess his card.

When Pharaoh asks for the frogs to go away "tomorrow,"
Moses replies:

כִּדְבָרְךָ לְמַעַן תֵּדַע כִּי־אֵין כַּיקֹוָה אֱלֹקֵינוּ:

*As you wish! So that you should know, that there is
none like the Lord, our God!* (Exodus 8:6)

In a way, Pharaoh and Moses appear to be on the same page here.
Moses taunts Pharaoh with an odd challenge, and he seems to
know that this is exactly the kind of challenge Pharaoh is likely
to take him up on. And he was right; Pharaoh *does* take him up
on it. Moreover, once the challenge is set, Moses wraps up the
dialogue by saying that his winning the bet will prove "that there
is none like the Lord," which in itself is kind of strange, once you
really think about it. Why would whether Moses can turn off the
plague precisely when Pharaoh wants it turned off become—in
both Pharaoh's eyes and Moses's—*the* most important indicator
here of the might of God? It's as if turning off the plague is
somehow even more impressive than its miraculous onset in
the first place! Strange.

But there is no denying that Moses understands how Pharaoh
will see things. For some reason, the sheer power of the plague—the
discomfort and stench of the frogs, as overwhelming as this is—is
less impressive to Pharaoh than whether Moses can turn off the
frogs precisely at the moment Pharaoh picks.

That's the first instance of this kind of behavior on the part
of Pharaoh. Now, one instance does not a pattern make—but
there's a second, too.

The Wrong Question

A few plagues later, the fifth plague strikes Egypt's cattle and livestock. Let's return to our little role playing game and imagine how we might react in the situation the Torah describes.

You are the sovereign of Egypt. You've been battling Moses over this thorny slavery issue for a while. One fine day, you are sitting in your throne room, when the first reports start to trickle in from some of the provinces. *Sire, there's been a plague; it seems to be hitting the livestock. It happened in Heliopolis, maybe in Nabata, too. We don't understand what's happening, or why, Sire. We'll keep you posted.* Five minutes later, you're getting reports from a third city and a fourth.

If you are a responsible Egyptian sovereign, what's the first thing you do? You want to assess the damage; you need to know how bad it is. Any captain would do that following a strike on his vessel. Any leader would do that following a strike upon his land. But look at Pharaoh's actual response:

וַיִּשְׁלַח פַּרְעֹה וְהִנֵּה לֹא־מֵת מִמִּקְנֵה יִשְׂרָאֵל עַד־אֶחָד

And Pharaoh sent—and, behold! Not one of Israel's animals had died! (Exodus 9:7)

Pharaoh doesn't even bother looking at his own losses! The only thing he looks at is how many head of cattle the Children of Israel lost (and, of course, he finds that they didn't lose any). *That's all he cares about.* It's the strangest damage report of all time.

Precision vs. Power

For some reason, Pharaoh seems more interested in the precision with which God wages a plague against the Egyptians than in the raw power of the plague itself. In the plague of frogs, Pharaoh and Moses wrangled about precision in time: *If I pick 'tomorrow' out of the hat, can you turn the frogs off tomorrow?* And now, in the plague of dying livestock, Pharaoh's concern focuses on precision in space: *How precise are the spatial contours of the affected area?*

If you or I were the sovereign of Egypt, we wouldn't care a whit about precision; we would care only about how powerful the plagues were. But for some reason, that's not true for Pharaoh. He *is* interested in precision. We can debate why, but that's the way Pharaoh seems to look at things. The Sages of the Talmud saw this, and it led them to their theory about why Moses chose to be ambiguous about when the climactic tenth plague would strike. Moses preferred to say it would happen at "about" midnight, they suggest, because had he specified midnight, *that* would become the focus of Pharaoh's attention. As crazy as it sounds, there would have been hundreds and thousands of dead Egyptian firstborn all around Egypt, yet the obsessive focus of Pharaoh's mind would be on the precision with which the plague had descended. In Pharaoh's mind, if the plague were off by three minutes, the whole thing wouldn't have seemed nearly as impressive anymore.

Now, this sounds crazy, but there is method in his madness, as Shakespeare might say. There was clearly a test of wills going on between Pharaoh and God, but maybe the test of wills wasn't entirely about what we thought. We tend to assume Pharaoh was battling God exclusively over the release of the enslaved Hebrews. But maybe that wasn't the only agenda. Maybe he was battling God over something for which precision, strangely, counts even more than power. What could that be?

Moses

We have seen how, in various parts of the Exodus story, both God and Pharaoh seem to defy our expectations. Let us now turn to the third key figure in the Exodus story, Moses. We will find that he, too, behaves in ways that seem inscrutable.

CHAPTER FOUR

A Tale of Two Speeches

One fine day, after centuries of unremitting Egyptian oppression, Moses and his brother Aaron show up at Pharaoh's palace and makes a demand on behalf of Israel. It is Moses's opening salvo in what will soon become a protracted battle:

כֹּה־אָמַר יְקוָה אֱלֹקֵי יִשְׂרָאֵל שַׁלַּח אֶת־עַמִּי וְיָחֹגּוּ לִי בַּמִּדְבָּר:

Thus says YHVH, God of Israel: Send out My people, and let them rejoice before Me in the desert (Exodus 5:1)

Let's freeze the action right here, and imagine that we can walk back in time and inhabit that moment. Pretend you are Moses and you have just said these words to Pharaoh. Pharaoh is about to respond to this demand you have made, and when he does, you will need to figure out what to say next. So listen carefully, and plot your next move accordingly. Here is what Pharaoh says to you:

מִי יְקוָה אֲשֶׁר אֶשְׁמַע בְּקֹלוֹ לְשַׁלַּח אֶת־יִשְׂרָאֵל לֹא
יָדַעְתִּי אֶת־יְקוָה וְגַם אֶת־יִשְׂרָאֵל לֹא אֲשַׁלֵּחַ:

Who is YHVH that I should listen to his voice to let Israel go? I do not know YHVH, and what's more, I will not let Israel go! (Exodus 5:2)

Okay, Moses, your move. How are you going to respond to this? Pharaoh is being pretty direct here; there's not a lot of ambiguity in his position. He doesn't know your God. He's not interested in letting Israel go. End of story. What are you going to say to him?

You seem to have two options.

The first is simply to accept Pharaoh's answer, throw up your hands, and go back to God for further instructions. Remember, God is the one who sent you to deliver this message to Pharaoh. You fulfilled that mission. You went to Pharaoh just like God asked you to, and you said what you were supposed to say. So you're done. You just go back to God and say: *Look, I did what you wanted. Here's what Pharaoh replied.* The ball, as it were, is back in God's court. The Master of the Universe will have to figure out how to handle things from here.

Your second option is to do the exact opposite. Instead of retreating, you could up the ante: *Look, Pharaoh, you don't realize who you're provoking here. It's the Master of the Universe, and trust me, you don't want to get Him angry. If you back down now and let your slaves go, I think you'll be able to work something out with this God. But if you don't—look, I don't know how much of Egypt is going to be left after God is done with you.*

Either of those responses would have made some sense: retreat, or up the ante. But what seems to make absolutely no sense is what Moses actually says.

An Inexplicable Plea

Here are Moses's *actual* words to Pharaoh at this juncture:

אֱלֹקֵי הָעִבְרִים נִקְרָא עָלֵינוּ נֵלֲכָה נָּא דֶּרֶךְ שְׁלֹשֶׁת יָמִים בַּמִּדְבָּר וְנִזְבְּחָה לַיקֹוָה אֱלֹקֵינוּ פֶּן־יִפְגָּעֵנוּ בַּדֶּבֶר אוֹ בֶחָרֶב:

The God of the Hebrews happened upon us. Let us go, please, for three days in the desert and sacrifice to our God; otherwise, he might hurt us with pestilence or with the sword. (Exodus 5:3)

Now, did Moses really think this would work? It's as if he's saying: *Pharaoh, we're really scared of our God. Who knows what he might do to us if we don't take a long weekend in the desert to offer sacrifices to Him? Please, can't we just go? You wouldn't want your loyal slaves to get hurt or anything...*

Did Moses believe this had a *chance* of working?

Why would Moses think that Pharaoh would react favorably to this? Pharaoh had already said he didn't know who God was. The Being in whose name Moses is speaking is a nonentity to Pharaoh. So why should Moses have any hope that Pharaoh would agree to his proposal? Is Pharaoh going to be worried that his slaves might feel the wrath of their fairy-tale god?

And, of course, it *doesn't* work. This second speech of Moses seems to backfire terribly. Pharaoh accuses Moses and Aaron of needlessly distracting his precious slaves from their work (Exodus 5:4-5). He dismisses them, and tells his taskmasters to double down on the Hebrews' workload. From now on, the slaves will not be provided straw for making bricks; they will need to gather their own—but their daily quota of bricks will remain the same (Exodus 5:6-9). Pharaoh accuses the people of being lazy—*why do they have so much time on their hands to dream about a vacation in the desert to serve their god?*—so he dispenses the ultimate "cure" for laziness: crippling, backbreaking work (Exodus 5:17-18).

What was Moses thinking? What was the point of that second speech? Pharaoh had already said no, in clear, unambiguous terms. If Moses had retreated back to God, or alternatively, upped the ante—fine, maybe those are risks worth taking. But don't provoke Pharaoh with an appeal that has virtually no chance of success. *Um, Pharaoh... remember that God you say you don't believe in? Well, we're worried He might get really mad at us if you don't let us go for three days to sacrifice to Him.* Why even bother with a second speech that seems destined from the get-go to infuriate the Egyptian king?

If Pharaoh's response to the various plagues seemed peculiar to us, Moses's tactics now, in this discussion with Pharaoh, seem equally mind-boggling. Surely, though, Moses must have had some sort of rational plan. What was it?

A Study in Contrasts

It might be possible to discover the plan if we look carefully at the two speeches of Moses and compare them side by side. The tale of these two speeches is told not just in the generalities but in the specific, granular details that distinguish each speech from the other. In general terms, the first speech feels confident and bold and the second feels weak and waffly–but we need to drill a bit deeper and examine exactly *why* each speech feels the way it does. What are the details that combine to form our impressions of these speeches?

The speeches differ in maybe a half a dozen different ways, from the name used to describe the Israelites, right down to the consequences that might ensue if Israel doesn't go into the desert to serve the Lord. I invite you to take a moment and go through the speeches on your own. As you read, you might want to jot down a brief list of the discrepancies as you see them.

SPEECH 1	SPEECH 2
Exodus 5:1	Exodus 5:3

כֹּה־אָמַר יְקוָֹה אֱלֹקֵי יִשְׂרָאֵל שַׁלַּח אֶת־עַמִּי וְיָחֹגּוּ לִי בַּמִּדְבָּר:	אֱלֹקֵי הָעִבְרִים נִקְרָא עָלֵינוּ נֵלֲכָה נָּא דֶּרֶךְ שְׁלֹשֶׁת יָמִים בַּמִּדְבָּר וְנִזְבְּחָה לַיקוָֹה אֱלֹקֵינוּ פֶּן־יִפְגָּעֵנוּ בַּדֶּבֶר אוֹ בֶחָרֶב:

Thus says YHVH, God of Israel: Send out My people, and let them rejoice before Me in the desert.	*The God of the Hebrews happened upon us. Let us go, please, for three days in the desert and sacrifice to our God; otherwise, he might hurt us with pestilence or with the sword.*

Discrepancies

Here is a quick summary of some of the main differences I've found between the speeches:

WHAT ARE THE ENSLAVED PEOPLE CALLED? In Speech 1, Moses refers to them as *Israel* and God calls them *My People*. In Speech 2, the enslaved people are referred to as *the Hebrews*.

DIRECT OR INDIRECT COMMUNICATION? In Speech 1, Moses portrays God as communicating a message directly to Egypt: *Thus says God: Let my people go...* In Speech 2, however, God is not portrayed as communicating directly to anyone—neither Egypt nor Israel. Moses instead tells Pharaoh that God "happened upon us" (*nikra aleinu*), a phrase suggesting a kind of haphazard, unplanned encounter. And in that encounter, God didn't actually say anything to the Hebrews. In this speech, the request comes from the people, not God: *and now, let us go three days...*

CELEBRATION OR SACRIFICE? In Speech 1, Moses says that the people are leaving in order to *celebrate* with God in the desert. In Speech 2, he says they are going to *sacrifice* to God.

WHAT HAPPENS IF ISRAEL DOESN'T GO? Speech 1 doesn't suggest any untoward consequences for Israel if they don't go. There's simply a demand to Pharaoh to let them go. Speech 2 mentions that bad things might happen to the Hebrews if they don't offer the sacrifices.

Faced with these differences, the next logical question to ask is: do these discrepancies add up to something? Are there any patterns here, clues that would help us understand the underlying dynamic of each speech? Can we look at this list, above, and say: *Speech 1, it's all about x. Speech 2, it's all about y*? I think we can.

X and Y

It seems to me that, in Moses's two speeches, two radically different conceptions of God are being portrayed.

The God of Moses's first speech is a God who wants His people to celebrate with Him. This God will address humans directly and convey His desires and expectations to them. He is a God who views the enslaved people as *Israel*—a special name, denoting a covenant He made with their forebears. This God seems to evince a personal connection to the people, calling them *My people*. He doesn't intimidate His people with threats of retribution if they don't serve Him. People serve this God because they actually want to. That's the God of Moses's first speech.

The God of Moses's second speech is a very different being. He doesn't address human beings directly; at best, He might "happen upon" them now and then. The people that are enslaved are not "His" people. They are just Hebrews (*Ivrim*)—a generic term denoting folks that migrated from across (*me'ever*) the river. No one has a very clear idea exactly what this Being wants from them—but the people surmise that they'd better sacrifice to Him, just to be safe. He can be vindictive if not appeased. Celebration with this Being would be out of the question. Fear-driven sacrifice would be the limits of service to Him.

Why, exactly, does Moses open with one conception of God and then transition to another? Which of these two visions is the real one? These are very good questions, and in time, we will get back to them. But for now, I want to call your attention to one last way in which the two speeches of Moses contrast. Of all the differences between the two speeches, this is perhaps the most mysterious. It has to do with the names of God.

In his first speech to Pharaoh, Moses spoke of God using His ineffable name, spelled in Hebrew יְ-ה-וָ-ה, or, as we've rendered it in English, YHVH. In the second speech, Moses did not introduce the Almighty this way. He instead spoke of the Lord as אֱלֹקֵי הָעִבְרִים, the God of the Hebrews.

Was this a random, haphazard switch–or was there a reason Moses invoked one name rather than the other in each speech?

There was indeed a reason.

We speculated that Pharaoh had another agenda in his battle with God, over and above keeping his slaves. And God, who uses ten plagues rather than magic carpets, and insists on securing Pharaoh's yes (only to change it to a no)–perhaps He has another agenda. Maybe Moses–whose two speeches seem inexplicable–had another agenda, too.

What do all three figures know that we don't?

The key might well lie in the divine names that Moses has begun to use in his two speeches. It is time to try and figure out what Moses might have meant by invoking one name rather than the other, to try and discern what these names might signify.

CHAPTER FIVE

Much Ado about Names

It turns out that, just after Moses made those two "failed" speeches to Pharaoh, God appeared to Moses and talked to him, of all things, about His names. Let me try to give you a sense of how unusual that is.

If you've read more than a few chapters of the Bible, you probably know that there are a few different names by which God is called. Sometimes it's one, sometimes it's another. As a reader, you become accustomed to that pretty quickly, and soon enough, you don't give the issue a second thought. You stop paying attention to the particular name of God used at any given junction.

And it's not just you, the reader, who doesn't give the issue a second thought. For the most part, God Himself doesn't make such a big deal about these names, either. Whatever name a biblical personality happens to call God at any particular point in time, seems to be just fine with Him. In all the many pages of *Tanach*, for example, where do you ever find the Deity interrupting someone like Moses or Miriam mid-sentence to say *look, I hate to bring this up, but you just called me by the wrong name*? That never happens. Or, to be more accurate, it *almost* never happens.

When Names Start to Matter

Strangely, in the course of the Exodus narrative, God *does* make a big deal about His names. All of a sudden, it starts to matter.

37

To my knowledge, it's the only place in the Bible where the Deity Himself wants to make sure everyone is on the same page about His name.

It happens twice in the Exodus story: once when God first encounters Moses at the Burning Bush, and again, just before the Ten Plagues begin. I want to explore both of these episodes with you. Let's start with the second.

To set the scene, Moses has just made his two speeches to Pharaoh, and Pharaoh has responded cruelly. The Egyptian king has utterly rejected Moses's request for a three-day respite. Instead, he's saddled the Children of Israel with an even more burdensome workload than before, and has deafened his ear to their cries. At this point, God tells Moses that, although He has not acted yet, Moses will now witness what He is going to do to Pharaoh. The Almighty shall secure the freedom of His people with a mighty hand. And the very next thing God does is tell Moses about His names:

וַיְדַבֵּר אֱלֹקִים אֶל־מֹשֶׁה וַיֹּאמֶר אֵלָיו אֲנִי יְקֹוָה: וָאֵרָא אֶל־אַבְרָהָם אֶל־יִצְחָק וְאֶל־יַעֲקֹב בְּאֵל שַׁדָּי וּשְׁמִי יְקֹוָה לֹא נוֹדַעְתִּי לָהֶם:

And God spoke to Moses, and said to him: I am YHVH. I appeared to Abraham, Isaac, and Jacob as El Shaddai, but My name YHVH I did not make known to them (Exodus 6:2–3)

Taken at face value, this seems like a very strange divine pronouncement. It appears to deal with relative trivialities–and really, at the least opportune time. We are perched at one of the most suspenseful moments in the entire Exodus story. Everything has been going wrong. Pharaoh is being especially cruel, and he seems to be getting away with it. The people are desperate. The leaders of the Hebrews complain that Moses has only made things worse by going to Pharaoh; those two speeches he made to the king are starting to seem like a really bad idea. Moses himself complains to God. Everything seems to be collapsing.

In the face of all this, God assures Moses that he has no idea, yet, of the divine might that will be unleashed against Egypt. Moses cannot fathom, in his wildest dreams, what is about to happen to Pharaoh and to Egypt.

The first-time reader of the story is on the edge of his or her seat. What will happen next? Will God make good on these promises? A showdown is brewing and the action is set to begin. The first of the plagues, you would imagine, is about to strike.

But it doesn't strike. Not yet. Instead, the Deity takes us on an excursion through some theological arcana concerning His names. It feels almost like a badly-placed commercial break, brought to you, strangely, by the Master of the Universe Himself: *Did I happen to mention to you, Moses, anything about these names of Mine? No? Well, I happen to have one that is shiny and new! Abraham Isaac and Jacob never knew about it. Let Me fill you in...* It seems quite strange indeed.

Not as New as It Seems

Truth be told, it's not just the placement of this declaration about divine names that is puzzling. What God is actually saying here is hard to understand, as well. The Lord seems to be telling Moses that He is revealing a new name to him—one that his forebears, Abraham, Isaac, and Jacob, were not aware of. That name, which I have been rendering YHVH, is spelled with the four Hebrew letters ה-ו-ה-י, and is sometimes known in English as the tetragrammaton. The problem—and this is plain for any reader of the Bible to see—is that this name is not really new at all. It is used constantly throughout the book of Genesis, oftentimes to characterize the Lord in conversation with Abraham, Isaac, and Jacob—the very people who, according to God's declaration here, were not supposed to know about this name. So in what sense is this name *new*? Where's the novelty here?

What's perhaps even stranger is that God had an earlier opportunity in the Exodus story to reveal this "new" name to Moses–and God let that opportunity slide. I am referring now to the *other* time in the Exodus story that God places emphasis on His names, when God was speaking to Moses at the Burning Bush. There, too, names were suddenly an issue. But the name YHVH didn't seem to make it into the discussion.

The Burning Bush Conundrum

The Burning Bush is when God first meets Moses. At the Bush, God introduces Himself, and tells Moses about His plan to free the Children of Israel from Egyptian slavery. It is also the moment God first enlists Moses to help execute that plan. What better time than now to tell Moses who He truly is–and, concomitantly, to introduce Moses to the name by which He wants to be called?

And wouldn't you know it–at the Burning Bush, the perfect moment for God to make such a revelation readily presents itself. In the course of the conversation, Moses puts a question to this God who has appeared to him. He wants to know how to introduce Him to the Children of Israel:

וַיֹּאמֶר מֹשֶׁה אֶל־הָאֱלֹקִים הִנֵּה אָנֹכִי בָא אֶל־בְּנֵי יִשְׂרָאֵל וְאָמַרְתִּי לָהֶם
אֱלֹהֵי אֲבוֹתֵיכֶם שְׁלָחַנִי אֲלֵיכֶם וְאָמְרוּ־לִי מַה־שְּׁמוֹ מָה אֹמַר אֲלֵהֶם:

And Moses said to God: Here I am, coming to the Children of Israel, and I am going to tell them 'the God of your ancestors sent me to you.' They'll say to me, 'What's His name?' What shall I tell them? (Exodus 3:13)

What a wonderful segue! One could imagine God's response going something like this: *Well, Moses, I'm really glad you asked. As a matter of fact, I have this wonderful new name I'd like to tell everybody about. It's YHVH. Please let them know.*

But that is not what God says:

וַיֹּאמֶר אֱלֹקִים אֶל־מֹשֶׁה אֶהְיֶה אֲשֶׁר אֶהְיֶה וַיֹּאמֶר
כֹּה תֹאמַר לִבְנֵי יִשְׂרָאֵל אֶהְיֶה שְׁלָחַנִי אֲלֵיכֶם:

And God said to Moses: I Will Be That Which I Will
Be. Thus you shall say to the Children of Israel: 'I
Will Be' sent me to you (Exodus 3:14)

A mysterious reply, indeed. As a matter of fact, it seems to be no
reply at all. God almost seems to be evading the question. After
all, what kind of name is *I Will Be That Which I Will Be*? Is it really
a name at all?

As if this weren't enough, the conversation between Moses
and God at the Burning Bush becomes even more baffling. Just
after telling Moses that He wants to be known as *I Will Be*, the
Lord seems to change His mind:

וַיֹּאמֶר עוֹד אֱלֹקִים אֶל־מֹשֶׁה כֹּה־תֹאמַר אֶל־בְּנֵי יִשְׂרָאֵל
יְקֹוָה אֱלֹקֵי אֲבֹתֵיכֶם אֱלֹקֵי אַבְרָהָם אֱלֹקֵי יִצְחָק וֵאלֹקֵי
יַעֲקֹב שְׁלָחַנִי אֲלֵיכֶם זֶה־שְּׁמִי לְעֹלָם וְזֶה זִכְרִי לְדֹר דֹּר:

And God further said to Moses: Thus you shall say to the
Children of Israel: YHVH, the God of your fathers—the God
of Abraham, God of Isaac and God of Jacob—sent me to
you. That is my name forever, and this is my remembrance
from generation to generation (Exodus 3:15)

The confusion is now complete. If you were Moses, walking away
from this conversation, and someone asked you: *So, God appeared*
to you today. How interesting. What's His name? What would you
tell him? *Well, He Will Be What He Will Be. Or, actually, maybe He*
just Will Be. But, you know, on second thought, forget all that. He's the
God of our fathers, that's who He is. Sorry for the mix-up there, but I
think that would be right.

At this point, the reader of the Torah could be excused for
asking: why does something as simple as a name have to be so
complicated? It's hard enough to get straight what the Almighty

was trying to say at the Burning Bush. It's doubly hard to get straight what He was trying to say later, when after Moses's two speeches to Pharaoh He reveals to Moses this "new" name, YHVH. And it is even harder than that to somehow mesh the two, and figure out how these two discussions about names dovetail.

But we should not abandon the struggle to understand these dialogues about divine names. They seem to be an integral part of the story, a lynchpin of sorts. Moses, at the Burning Bush, seems to want to understand God's name before accepting the leadership role God is thrusting upon him. And, just before the Ten Plagues begin, the Almighty seems to want to "introduce" Himself, via His name, to Moses, Egypt, and perhaps the world. These names *are* important. The rest of the Exodus seems to ride upon them.

What are we to make of them?

PART II

The Exit Strategy

CHAPTER SIX

What's in a Name?

To bestow a name on someone, or something, is to begin to grapple with the identity of the one you are naming. We do this with our newborn children. A child is born. Who is this little soul? We don't know them yet. Our first attempt to reach out and begin to understand who they are, or perhaps express our hopes for who they might become, is to name them.

In the Exodus story, the Torah tells of God seeking to help humans find a name it would make sense to call Him. But that is a tall order indeed. A name gives us a way of comprehending someone. What could a human hope to comprehend about God?

The discussions about divine names at the Burning Bush, and then later, before the plagues begin, are discussions about identity. At the Burning Bush, Moses asks God about His name. What he is really saying is: *The people will want to know who You are; what shall I tell them?* And later, just before the Ten Plagues begin, God comes back to the issue of names. He tells Moses that He is revealing Himself to the world using a new "name," as it were. A new facet of His identity, earlier hidden, will now, in the Exodus, start to become clear. It is bound up in the name YHVH.

To discover what God was saying at that moment, let's go back to the language of the text and see if we can decipher it. God had said that He appeared to Moses's ancestors as El Shaddai, and only now would He become known as YHVH. What do these two names signify?

A Strategy

I'd like to suggest a simple and straightforward strategy for figuring that out. Let's take these names of God and pretend, for
a moment, that they aren't names, but words. As words, what
would they mean? Some of these names for God have a double
life as ordinary words in the Bible; maybe the meaning of the
name borrows from the meaning of the word.

Let's start by applying this strategy to *El*, a shortened form
of the divine name *Elohim*. God had told Moses that this is how
He had revealed himself to the forefathers, as *El* Shaddai. What
does that first part, *El*, or its longer form, *Elohim*, mean? More
precisely, what do these terms mean when they are words, and
not names? Consider how *el* is used in the following verse:

יֶשׁ־לְאֵל יָדִי לַעֲשׂוֹת עִמָּכֶם רָע

I have it within my power to do harm to you (Genesis 31:29)

That was the warning Laban gave to Jacob upon catching up
to him after Jacob's sudden departure from his home. In that
verse, *el* is the Hebrew word for "power." That seems to be the
connotation of *El*, or *Elohim*, when it is used as a divine name,
too. The Deity is being denoted as a powerful force.[9]

---

9. Thus, the Torah even uses the word *elohim* on occasion to refer to
people in positions of power. Speaking of certain disputes that might
arise between two parties, the Torah states: עַד הָאֱלֹהִים יָבֹא דְּבַר־שְׁנֵיהֶם,
"to the judges shall come the matter of the two of them" (Exodus 22:8). In
that verse, *elohim* was the word for "judges." Inasmuch as they hold great
power over litigants whose fate they decide, judges can be known as *elohim*,
too. Indeed, in rabbinic literature, when the term *elohim* is used for the
Almighty, it is often seen as denoting a particular divine "trait"–God as a
doer of justice. *Elohim* thus describes both human judges and the Divine
Judge of All.

This explains something that, taken at face value, is quite puzzling. The second of the Ten Commandments is oddly worded: "Thou shalt not have [allegiance to] any other gods before Me." The statement seems almost self-contradictory. Here the Torah insists on an absolute devotion to monotheism, faith in the one and only God—and then, in the selfsame statement, the text seems to take for granted the existence of *other* gods, saying only that we shouldn't have allegiance to them. But what other gods *are* there? Isn't the Torah's whole point that there is only one?

The problem falls away, though, if you go back to the original Hebrew and read it carefully. The second commandment states: "Thou shalt not have [allegiance to] any other *elohim* before Me." Just plug in our working definition of *elohim*, and suddenly it all starts to make sense: the text adjures us not to have allegiance to other "powers" besides God. For, indeed, there *are* other great sources of power one might choose to worship. The sun is powerful, there's no denying that. It provides light and heat, and without it, we die. Nevertheless, the second commandment tells us that the sun is off-limits for worship because we may not have allegiance to any power other than the Almighty.

As such, it emerges that *el* is more a generic descriptor than a name for a particular divine being. To the extent that we relate to God as a powerful being, it is appropriate to call Him an *el* or *elohim*.[10] God is the *el* of the Hebrews, the power to whom the Hebrews have allegiance, as Moses will tell Pharaoh in his

---

10. To refine this idea, inasmuch as *el* connotes "power," calling God *El* might denote that He is the supreme power—or the source of all power. In his *Shulchan Aruch*, R. Joseph Karo suggests that this is what one should bear in mind when vocalizing the world *Elohim* in the context of a blessing (*Shulchan Aruch, Orach Chaim* 5). Once God is identified as Creator and the one true source of existence, speaking of God as an *el* would now seem to convey this sense of "ultimate" power.

second speech (Exodus 5:3). But this is only to say that He is a being to which the Hebrews attribute power. Other powers can and do exist.

In short, *el* or *elohim* may describe God, but it does not *uniquely* describe God. *Elohim* can just as easily denote any force believed to be powerful, even if it is not divine. Again, it is more a generic descriptor than a name.

Saying "Enough!" to the Expanding World

Let's consider the next part of God's declaration to Moses about His names, past and present. God tells Moses that, in the past, He had appeared to the forefathers not just as El, but as El Shaddai. What does *that* mean?

As it happens, the term *Shaddai* doesn't have a life in Biblical Hebrew outside its use as a divine name—so we can't directly apply our strategy to this name. We can, however, apply it indirectly—for although *Shaddai* itself is not a word, the Sages of the Midrash (Genesis Rabbah 5:8 and elsewhere) saw the name as a kind of contraction of *several* words. As they put it, *Shaddai* is the name given to *Mi she'amar le'olamo 'dai,'* or "the One who said to His world 'Enough!'" As the Midrash goes on to explain, the heavens and the earth, after first coming into being, were not static and motionless. Rather, they were expanding rapidly—they were "stretching" or "swelling," in the words of the Midrash. And were it not for God declaring "Enough!" and reigning in that process of expansion, the expansion would have careened out of control over infinite stretches of time—leaving us with a universe very different from the comparatively nice and tidy one we inhabit today.[11]

---

11. This comment of the Sages about the God "who says to His world 'Enough!'" eerily dovetails with, and seems to presage, some of what modern physicists tell us about various limiting forces imposed upon the universe

WHAT'S IN A NAME?

Returning to our particular verse, when God says that he had once, in the days of Moses's ancestors, been known as El Shaddai, it might mean that God had revealed Himself, earlier, not just as an *el*, a power, but as a *very significant* power. God had publicly displayed great power in the days of the forefathers–think, for example, of the destruction of Sodom and Gomorrah in the days of Abraham. People would thus have spoken of God as *El Shaddai*–a very significant power, a Being possessing great might.

The Name of Names

What God was now telling Moses, though, was that describing God in this way–as "powerful," even "powerful in the extreme"–isn't the whole picture. Power is an attribute of God, but it is not His identity. It is not His true name. *Back then, I never revealed Myself for who I really was,* as God goes on to tell Moses:

וּשְׁמִי יְקֹוָה לֹא נוֹדַעְתִּי לָהֶם:

My name YHVH I never made known to them (Exodus 6:3)

Now, though, in the Exodus, that would change. Just as the Ten Plagues are about to begin, God seems to be saying: *Before we go any further in this process, there's something I need to tell you. You need to know who I truly am.* And to that effect, God tells Moses His name: it is YHVH.

There is a subtle irony in this. Right now, at the moment God is set to unleash the greatest expressions of sheer power ever seen in human history, the Ten Plagues, God makes clear to Moses

---

in the first moments after its inception. For a closer look at how modern science might further articulate this notion of the God "who says to His world 'Enough!'" watch *Seeing God in Science,* a short video presentation I created with the team at Aleph Beta. It can be found at alephbeta.org.

that *power is not His name.* It is not who He is, fundamentally. God will *make use of* power, as He is about to do—but it does not define Him. Instead, the essence of God is about something else. It is about being YHVH.

What *that* means, is what we need to explore next.

CHAPTER SEVEN

Do You Believe in Parker?

YHVH. In Hebrew letters, י-ה-ו-ה. In trying to figure out what the name means, we can't really turn to the Hebrew language for guidance—as we did with the word *el*—because, aside from the name of God, there *is* no word in Hebrew spelled י-ה-ו-ה. That combination of letters doesn't mean anything other than "God." But we can try another thought experiment. This will require some imagination, so bear with me. To begin, let's ask:

If י-ה-ו-ה *were* a word, what would it mean?

Imaginary Words

I know, it sounds preposterous to imagine a word and then ask what it might mean if it existed. *If it doesn't exist, why bother asking about it?* But bear with me. If י-ה-ו-ה *were* an actual word in the Hebrew language, and we had to hazard a guess as to what it meant, what would we guess?

Well, י-ה-ו-ה may not spell a word, but these letters do seem very close—related, if you will—to a certain *family* of words. Consider the last three letters of this name of God. They spell הוה, the Hebrew word for *is*, or *to exist*. Moreover, three out of four of the י-ה-ו-ה letters spell היה, the Hebrew word for *was*. And finally, this entire י-ה-ו-ה name seems suspiciously close to the Hebrew word for *will be*, which just happens to be spelled יהיה.

51

To summarize: this name of God is close, but not exactly equiv-alent to, each one of the three Hebrew words that denote past, present, and future existence. But here's the really remarkable thing: Try taking those words for existing in the past, present, and future and *overlay* them, one on top of the other.

Start with היה. Lay הוה on top of that—and the composite word will look like הוה (the י disappears into the ו). Now take the composite word you just formed, and overlay יהיה on top of *that*. What do the four letters in front of you look like now?

Congratulations. You just formed the name YHVH.[12]

More than Eternal

The correspondence is eerie, and hardly seems coincidental. But what, exactly, are we to make of it?

The immediate temptation is to suggest that the name YHVH conveys the idea that God is eternal: God was, is, and always will be. And, indeed, some English translations render the YHVH name exactly this way, as *the Eternal One*. But such a translation, I believe, is not entirely accurate.

You see, if I exist eternally, I might exist for a very long time, but the way I'm existing at any given moment is what we might call "ordinary." When I existed in the past, I *was*; when I'm ex-isting now, I *am*—and when I exist in the future, I *will be*. These states don't overlap. But YHVH seems to convey something else entirely. Comprised of an overlay of the Hebrew words for *was*,

---

12. Indeed, R. Joseph Karo writes (*Shulchan Aruch, Orach Chaim* 5) that when one vocalizes the name YHVH while making a blessing, one should keep in mind the idea that God exists in past, present, and future. He writes also that this name YHVH connotes the idea that God is Master of all. Later in this chapter, we will suggest that these two ideas are two sides of the same coin.

is, and *will be*, it seems to denote the simultaneous experience of all three of these states. It is *was*, *is*, and *will be*–experienced all at once.[13] That's not just being eternal; that's a whole new way of being altogether. Which is why, after all, י-ה-ו-ה is not an actual Hebrew word. It's not a word because what it would mean if it were a word, just doesn't exist in our world.

Who experiences time like that? Where would you have to be, to experience time like that?

You'd have to be outside our world.

Inside, Outside

In our world, we humans experience time as if it were some long tunnel through which we travel. We make our way through it, but at any given moment, we are located at a distinct point in the tunnel. The only way to experience all states of time simultaneously is to be, somehow, *outside* the tunnel; only from that vantage point could one look at time "all at once." That, the name YHVH implies, is how God experiences time.

But what about God makes Him experience time that way? How did God get outside of time?

The answer is: *He exists outside of time because He is the creator of time.*[14]

While imagining the way God would experience time seems like a mind-bending thing to do, it's not as difficult as it first appears. We just need to bear in mind a fairly intuitive principle–namely, that a creator naturally exists outside the system he or she creates.

A little story might help illustrate that.

---

13. Cf. *Ohr Hachaim* to Exodus 7:17, from *Zohar* 3:297.

14. See Rambam, *Moreh Nevuchim* 2:30, cf. *Tosafot Yom Tov*, Avot 3:15

Little Hat and Little Shoe Go for a Walk

A few years back, I was having a conversation with a friend of mine who proudly considered himself an atheist. He was making one of his favorite points: "Where is God?" he wanted to know. "If God really exists, how come you and I don't see more of Him?"

I told him he reminded me of Little Hat and Little Shoe, wondering about the whereabouts of Parker.

I was referring, of course, to tokens in Monopoly—the real estate trading game made by Parker Brothers. If you've ever played the game, you know that there are all sorts of tokens by which a player can choose to represent him or herself. You can be the automobile, the thimble, the little hat, or the little shoe. Imagine a discussion between Little Hat and Little Shoe, who are faithfully going around the Monopoly board for the umpteenth time. As Little Hat passes a hotel belonging to one of his opponents, he says to Little Shoe:

"Say... do you believe in Parker?"

Little Shoe looks at him quizzically.

Little Hat explains: "You know—look over there, on the side of the board. It says in big black letters, MADE BY PARKER BROTHERS. So, do you believe in that? *Do you believe in Parker?*"

Little Shoe replies: "Yes, I suppose I do. What about you?"

So Little Hat responds, with an air of weary frustration: "Look, I've been around here a long time. Every week, I pass GO, and I collect my $200. I've been to TENNESSEE AVENUE, ST. JAMES PLACE, BOARDWALK, you name it. I've seen it all. Heck, I've even been to JAIL. And I'll tell you something. *I ain't never seen Parker.* This whole time, I've just *never* bumped into him. So no, I don't believe in Parker. I'm a Parker atheist."

If you could interject at this point in the conversation, what would you say to Little Hat? You'd say: "My dear Little Hat, you're looking for Parker in all the wrong places. Parker doesn't live on the board. He *made* the board!"

The maker of a system doesn't live inside that system. As a creator, you can *interact* with the system you made: you can make the rules by which it functions. You can decree that every piece collects $200 on passing GO, and that when a player picks the chance card that says GO DIRECTLY TO JAIL, then yes, that player really has to go directly to JAIL. All that, a creator can do. But the creator doesn't *live* on the board. That's not his natural place. The board is the environment put in place for the created, not the Creator.[15]

In the case of humankind, the board is the universe, the world of space and time in which we find ourselves. When we look around the universe demanding to touch, feel or see the Creator—we are looking in the wrong place; we are treating the Creator as if He were one of us. The universe is the place made for creatures; it's not the natural domicile of the Creator.[16]

---

15. All this is not to say the Creator is cut off from His creation. Although the Creator does not have spatial or temporal qualities, He can interact closely with us. Indeed, one of the ways He interacts is that He makes the "rules of the game." Some of those rules are reflected in the way the environment is set up; we call these the laws of physics, chemistry, and biology. Some of the rules are more like the little folded sheet that comes with Monopoly. Those are the rules that govern how players should play the game, what they should do and what they ought not do. We sometimes call these moral laws. All of these rules are brought to us courtesy of the Creator of the system.

16. Despite all this, the mysterious fact remains that God asks humans to create a place for Him in this world: וְעָשׂוּ לִי מִקְדָּשׁ וְשָׁכַנְתִּי בְּתוֹכָם, "Make a sanctuary for Me, and I will dwell among you" (Exodus 25:8). This world is not the "native place" of God, as it is a world of time and space, and God has neither spatial nor temporal qualities. Nevertheless, He asks humans to create a dwelling for Him in the world He created for them—and, paradoxically, He commits to inhabiting that dwelling. For more on the

Place Holding

These ideas may sound novel, but they aren't new. Take away
the Monopoly board analogy, and you'll find that they were
articulated centuries ago by the Sages of the Midrash. It turns
out that, aside from the biblical names for God, the Sages added
one of their own. They would sometimes call God "The Place,"
or in Hebrew, *Hamakom*. By way of explanation, they said:

מִפְּנֵי מָה מְכַנִּין שְׁמוֹ שֶׁל הַקָּדוֹשׁ בָּרוּךְ הוּא וְקוֹרְאִין אוֹתוֹ
מָקוֹם? שֶׁהוּא מְקוֹמוֹ שֶׁל עוֹלָם וְאֵין עוֹלָמוֹ מְקוֹמוֹ

*Why do we call God The Place? Because He is the place of the
world... and yet the world is not His place* (Genesis Rabbah 68:9)

To discern what they meant by this brainteaser of an explanation,
think of what the word *place* suggests. A place is where something
exists, its spatial environment. When it comes to God, the Sages
were saying, the world is not His place. The universe that you and
I live in is not His environment. It doesn't hold Him; space and
time are not His confines. Asking where God is, the Sages were
saying, is fruitless. Where is His place? If anything, He *is* the place
of the universe, the vessel that contains it. In other words, take
all the *stuff* in the universe, take space and time, as well; now ask
yourself, what is the environment in which all *that* exists? The
answer is God. He is The Place of the World.[17]

---

implications of this paradox, watch the following videos at alephbeta.org:
Terumah: Is There a Face Hiding in the Tabernacle?, *Tetzaveh: Where is God in a
Physical World?*, and *Vayakhel-Pikudei: God in Space, God in Time*.

17. The precise implications of this Midrash and the exact meaning of
the associated Kabbalistic concept of *tzimtzum* (divine contraction) are
debated by masters of the Chassidic and Mitnagdic traditions. See, for
example, *Tanya, Sha'ar Hayichud V'Ha'Emunah*, ch. 3 and 4; *Likkutei Moharan*
I, 64:1; Vilna Gaon: *Likutim* at end of *Safra de-Tzneuta*; *Nefesh HaChaim* 3:7.

To make it short and sweet, the Sages simply called God *The Place*.

The Definition that Wasn't

So, getting back to God's speech to Moses just before the Ten Plagues begin, God was saying that in the past, He had been revealed as a powerful force (an *el*), perhaps even an ultimately powerful force (*el shaddai*); but now, through the Exodus, He would be revealed for who He really was: YHVH, the one who is "off the board," outside of time and space; the Maker of time and space.[18] Parker. The Creator.

In a way, that was what God had been saying to Moses earlier, at the Burning Bush–or at least, God had been alluding to it. We were puzzled, then, as to how God's various declarations concerning His Names jibe with one another. Why did He say one thing to Moses at the Burning Bush, and another just before the Ten Plagues? In reality, God may well have been saying the same thing both times, just in different words.

Let's revisit what God said at the Burning Bush, the other time in the Exodus narrative that God's name occupies center stage. Back then, Moses told God that the people would want to know the name of this God that supposedly had appeared to him. What should he tell them? To which God answered: אֶהְיֶה אֲשֶׁר אֶהְיֶה—*I Am That Which I Am*.

Earlier, we found this "name" rather puzzling: *'I Will Be That Which I Will Be?'* What kind of name is that? Indeed, if God is trying to help the people understand His identity, this seems to be no help at all. The first rule of definitions, the rule most of us learned back in grade school, is that a dictionary definition of a

---

18. Or, in the language of the Sages who spoke of God as "place," God is the "environment" in which space, time, and the universe find a home. Paradoxically, He transcends space and time but in some way incorporates them.

certain word can't include that same word as part of its definition. You can't define something in terms of itself. But that seems to be exactly what God is doing here. *I Will Be That Which I Will Be* is a definition of self that is a non-definition.

But maybe that's exactly the point. *You want to know who I am?* God is saying. *The best I can give you is this: I am that which I am. There is no other way to define Me other than in terms of Myself.* And if you stop to think about that for a moment, you'll realize why that *has* to be true. Think about how definitions work. Define, for instance, the word *castigate*. You say to yourself: *Hmm, you don't know what 'castigate' means? Well, how would I explain that to you?* And then you try to come up with two or three ideas that, when you put them together, get you *castigate*. You say something like: *Well, do you know what 'reprimand' means—when you tell someone off? Okay, good. And do you know what 'severely' means—when you do something in a very stern and strict way? Okay. Well, to castigate is to reprimand someone severely.*

To define something is to break it down into its more familiar and simpler parts. *You might not know x, but you know the things x is made of.* But there's the rub. When it comes to the Creator, that's just not possible. God is "off the board." He is, strange as it may be to say, the ultimate extraterrestrial being, in that He is not of this world. So there's nothing in this world that would give you an approximation of God. There are no "simpler elements" with which you are familiar, such that if you would just add them up, you would get God. God is what He is.

I Knew Your Dad

All of this, however, does present something of a problem to a human being. For if God is not understandable in this-world terms, if you can't touch Him and you can't feel Him—then how are you supposed to relate to Him? That problem accounts for the very next thing God said to Moses back at the Burning Bush. Having declared Himself to be undefinable, God continued speaking to Moses, and told him to tell the people something else: He was the God of their forefathers.

וַיֹּאמֶר עוֹד אֱלֹקִים אֶל־מֹשֶׁה כֹּה־תֹאמַר אֶל־בְּנֵי יִשְׂרָאֵל יְקֹוָה אֱלֹקֵי אֲבֹתֵיכֶם אֱלֹקֵי אַבְרָהָם אֱלֹקֵי יִצְחָק וֵאלֹקֵי יַעֲקֹב שְׁלָחַנִי אֲלֵיכֶם זֶה־שְּׁמִי לְעֹלָם וְזֶה זִכְרִי לְדֹר דֹּר:

And God further said to Moses, Thus you shall say to the Children of Israel: YHVH, the God of your fathers—the God of Abraham, God of Isaac and God of Jacob—sent me to you. That is my name forever. And this is my remembrance from generation to generation (Exodus 3:15)

It's as if God is saying: *You're worried about whether we can have a relationship? Don't worry so much. I knew your parents. We go back a long way, you and I.*

In the end, what God said earlier to Moses about being *That Which I Am*, about being unknowable—it's true, but it's not the whole truth. It is equally true that God has a history of interaction with us. You don't have to understand someone to have a relationship with them. That's true not just between humans and God, it's so even among humans. You never *really* know someone outside of yourself. Much as you might try, you can never directly perceive, much less understand, their innermost thoughts and experiences. But you forge a relationship anyway. Mystery can be good for a relationship. It keeps things intriguing.[19]

---

19. If you can't access or know the essence of another human being, one of the ways we *do* relate to other humans is through their actions. People's actions help us size them up; they give us clues through which we seek to understand them.

Similarly, we can relate to God through His actions. Indeed, the Torah itself is a record of divine interaction with humans, helping us in our quest to understand what we can of the Divine.

What the Exodus Would Demonstrate

To summarize, then: as the redemption from Egypt was about to begin, God told Moses something about what this event would reveal. It would be a process through which He would come to be known as YHVH–the God who created everything, and who exists outside of His creation. God, of course, had always been the Creator, but this had never been demonstrated unambiguously to humanity. Now it would be. The Exodus would be the vehicle for that.

Why was it not enough for God to be known as El Shaddai, a very powerful deity? Why was it so important for Him to be known instead as YHVH, the Creator-God? Was it just a numbers game? *One god or many? Quick: God wants to make sure you know the right answer!* It sounds frightful to ask this, but was God just on the celestial equivalent of an ego trip, wanting to make sure that humanity knew He had no competitors in the heavenly realm?

In reality, there was a much larger issue at stake than just numbers.

CHAPTER EIGHT

More than a Numbers Game

One of the big mistakes we make when thinking about monotheism is that we take its name too seriously. Monotheism, of course, means *belief in one God,* and it is therefore easy to succumb to the notion that the big difference between it and pagan systems of worship lies in the number of deities you believe in. Monotheists believe in one, polytheists, in many.

In reality, though, numbers are just the veneer. The really significant differences between monotheism and polytheism are not quantitative, but qualitative. For, as it turns out, whether a belief system contains one deity or many, directly affects how that belief system will answer some of the most important and deepest questions about the meaning of spirituality itself.

To see how that's so, let's contrast monotheism with polytheism, in very broad brushstrokes. Each system has a certain logic at the heart of it, and I'd like to try and trace that logical flow with you. Let's start with polytheism, or paganism; it was the dominant system in the ancient world, and was the theological backdrop against which the events of the Exodus unfolded.

The Logic of Paganism

Paganism begins at the dawn of history. Its logic is the none-too-subtle calculus of fear.

Man finds himself alone in the universe, at the mercy of powerful elemental forces. Punishing rainstorms threaten to erase his carefully constructed thatched-roof huts. The unrelenting heat of the sun threatens to bake the earth that he seeks to cultivate, leaving him vulnerable to the slow torture of famine. Every once in a while, the earth quakes beneath his feet. Nature is powerful, but radically unpredictable. In the shadow of that truth, man, aware of his fragility, seeks at least a truce with his environment; at most, he seeks to master it.

But how?

In our day and age, technological advancement has been our psychic salve. But before technological change was a staple of daily life, back in the days when the wheel or the chariot counted as major advances, when there were no weather satellites, no instant telecommunication—back in those days, what solace could be found? What truce could be wrung from nature's powerful clutches? What mastery over nature could we possibly pretend to?

Paganism had an answer to that question.

In the pagan mind, there was no single Creator of All; instead, the heavens were populated by a range of powers. When it came to interacting with humans, these powers were occasionally capricious, but usually indifferent. They might take pleasure, now and then, in tormenting the poor mortals with a devastating typhoon or something like that, but typically, man was not of great concern to these forces.

Nevertheless, man could at least *try* and win their favor. The key was that these forces, as powerful as they might be, were not all-powerful. No one force controlled everything. The power in charge of rain certainly had a mighty force at its disposal, but it had no similar control over the sun. Indeed, the sun was this god's enemy. The chaotic weather patterns man experienced—one day clouds, the next day bright sun—were evidence of the back-and-forth battles between these elemental forces. It was a constant ebb and flow.

The bottom line is that every god had its realm of power. Conversely, every deity had its own area of vulnerability: pagan deities had *needs*, and if you were clever enough, you could use those needs to get a god's attention.

The first thing to do, then, was to survey your environment and decide which of the many gods you wished to align yourself with. This wasn't too hard; it was mainly a question of self-interest: *Who does it pay to worship around here?* If I live on the coast and my economy is based on fishing, I will worship Dagon, the god of fish, as did the Philistines, a seafaring people that occupied the coastline (see 1 Samuel, chapter 5). If I live in Egypt, I might choose to worship the sun-god. Since my civilization relies on the predictable inundations of the Nile for regular irrigation of crops, I have no need to throw my lot in with the rain-god; I might as well ally with the opposing force of the sun instead.

So that's step one: *pick your god.* Step two? *Try your best to appease it.* As I mentioned before, gods in the polytheistic pantheon are powerful, but they are not all-powerful—which means they have needs. And if they have needs, they can be bribed; or, to put it more charitably, they can be bartered with. *I can give the god something of value. And maybe if I do that, the god will not be so oblivious to my quickly-wilting crops.* Hence, the rationale for sacrifice comes into being.

The more painful the sacrifice, the better: the god will see that I am serious about serving it. The more outrageous the sacrifice, the better. How better to get the attention of a temperamental but somewhat distracted, and possibly even bored, deity than through some sensational act like child sacrifice?

The Torah would ultimately outlaw these kinds of outrageous rituals, of which child sacrifice is emblematic, for in the Torah's world, offerings have an entirely different rationale. They have nothing to do with barter at all.

Let's explore why.

The Rationale of Monotheism

Let's consider the alternative logic of monotheism. Monotheism rejects the idea of a pantheon of gods reigning over a preexisting universe. It insists that there is instead one God, and that this One God is the Creator of all.

What implications follow from this?

Let's go back to our fragile mortal, contemplating the possibility of sacrifice. Imagine we could interview this human standing beside his newly-made altar. He or she is convinced of the truth that there is one God. So why worship that God? Is this person trying to barter with the deity?

With whom, exactly, would this person be bartering? There is no pantheon of gods. That's all a lie. If someone is going to go knocking on heaven's door, the only one upstairs to answer it is the all-powerful Master of the Universe—the One God, who designed and brought into being the totality of Creation. Are you going to barter with *that* God?

What needs does He have? What could you possibly give Him? Does Parker need your Monopoly money? What do you give for Chanukah to the One who has everything? It is easy to see that, in the monotheistic system, the pagan rationale for sacrifice falls apart.

But what replaces it? What *is* the rationale for worship in this system?

Knock-Knock-Knocking on Heaven's Door

There would have to be another reason entirely for this human to go knocking on heaven's door. And, indeed, once you accept the reality of a Creator-God, other rationales for worship *do* open up. Consider this: if the universe as we know it just happened, if it was always there, if it was the product of a crazy collision of chance factors, a random roll of the cosmic dice—if any of these possibilities were true, well, then, no one up there consciously authored all this.

That means nothing around me is the product of anyone's intention–pitiful little *me* least of all. My job, then, as a human, is to make my way in this cold universe as best I can. I am not thrust into a relationship with any transcendent force who can claim responsibility for my existence.

If, on the other hand, the universe is *not* the product of blind chance, but was created by a sentient being, well, that means there *is* intention behind existence. The universe is here because that being wanted it to be here, and willed it into existence. And guess what? I am part of that grand tapestry of existence, too. I find myself in possession of this marvelous gift called life–and I have the Creator to thank for that. I quite literally owe the world to this Being.

That changes everything. Sure, you might still fear the power of this Creator or be concerned about your own self interest, but now there are all sorts of other reasons why a human would want to reach out to the Divine. Most obvious might be the feeling of gratitude. A gift of gratitude makes sense, even if the recipient has no "needs" in the conventional sense of the word.[20] If a child buys flowers for Mom on Mother's Day, that gift is meaningful even if Mom has no "need" for the flowers, even if she could have easily bought them herself. A gift of gratitude is not about barter or fulfilling needs. It's about finding a way to express genuine recognition to someone for their kindness. Whether "needed" or not, the gift builds and nurtures the underlying relationship between giver and recipient.

A relationship between giver and recipient. Think about those words. The notion that a relationship is possible–and indeed desirable–between the human and the divine makes little sense

---

20. Cf. *Chovot Halevavot, Sha'ar Avodat Elokim.*

in the pagan system. A polytheistic god, a power such as the sun or the sea, is indifferent to the plight of mortals. Such forces have no inherent connection to humanity, and it is laughable for a person to try and establish a relationship with them. But in monotheism, the God that humanity seeks out is the Creator, the Parent of all living things. All of a sudden, a relationship between a human and this Deity doesn't sound so crazy anymore. Parents deeply wish for connection with their children. A child wants that connection too, for reasons that go well beyond self-interest or hope of material gain. To nurture a loving and lasting relationship with a parent is one of life's great triumphs.

The Advent of Love

Being in a relationship with your Creator involves a good number of things. It may, at times, involve expressions of gratitude. It may also involve talking through your needs and desires with the Creator by means of something we call prayer. It may involve abiding by certain rules set by the Creator. If Little Hat and Little Shoe believe in Parker, part of that is accepting that Parker makes the rules. Yes, Little Shoe might *want* to be awarded $3,000 for having landed on FREE PARKING, but, much to the relief of the other players, he doesn't get to just make up a rule that mandates this right in the middle of the game. The right and responsibility to make rules lies in the more objective hands of the system's Creator. If there is a Creator, we, as creatures, are obliged to rise to His expectations, and abide by His rules. But perhaps more than all of this, being in a relationship with our Creator implies something else. It implies the possibility of actually *feeling* something. Something that we humans call love.

Love. The idea that a human being ought to actually feel love toward the divine is perhaps *the* great innovation of monotheism. Take a look at the Shema—the basic credo of the faith of Israel. First come the words: "Hear O Israel, the Lord is our

God, the Lord is One." That sentence appeals to the mind; it expresses acceptance of an idea–belief in the One God. Now look at the very next words, and you will find that they address not the mind but the heart: "And you shall love the Lord your God, with all your heart, with all your might, and with all your soul." The Torah is clear about this. The most direct corollary of monotheism is love.[21]

And rightfully so: *If I really have a Creator, then my life is not just the byproduct of cold, blind chance. Someone wants me to be here, brought me into this world, and gave me the wherewithal to make something of myself here on earth.* Love seems an entirely fitting response to that.

God and the Heavenly Cookie Jar

Let us return, then, to the question I left you with at the close of the last chapter: why would it be important for God to reveal to the world that He was not merely El Shaddai, *a very powerful force*–but YHVH, the one Creator-God? The answer should now be evident. It wasn't just a matter of divine ego, or dispensing with false competition from imaginary gods. It was about changing the very meaning of spirituality. It was a matter of introducing the ideas of gratitude, morality, and love into the vocabulary of human interaction with the divine. It was a matter of revealing to mankind that there was a Parent up there in the heavens, a parent who cared about what went on with His children.

---

21. In a way, then, the governing principle of the texts that make it into the tefillin scrolls is love. I will argue later in the book that the "firstborn" ideas that are the final element included in these scrolls, are really about love as well. They evince a gift of love that a child can give back to a parent, by way of the commitments the child undertakes to serve the parents' agenda in the family. See chapter 18, *Birth Night*.

Imagine a household where children were somehow deluded about the identity of the grownups in charge of the family. They thought the grownups were just "powers" who, for some unexplained reason, controlled all the goodies in the house. The children knew that these folks controlled access to the cookie jar, or, when they were older, the keys to the car. And throughout their lives, the children would try to barter with the grownups for access—or try to appease them. What's wrong with this picture?

If we were to eavesdrop on such a home for a day or two, things might seem vaguely normal, but gradually, it might dawn on you that something dysfunctional is happening here. *These kids don't understand that the grownups are their parents.* Their relationship with these grownups, to the extent it could even be called a relationship, is entirely off-kilter. Missing from these kids is the warmth and connection that most children feel toward parents, not to mention the sense that, as a child, I am duty bound to my parents in some way, and, out of gratitude (if nothing else), I really *should* abide by the rules of the house.

As a matter of fact, if you were to observe this home, day after day and week after week, you might eventually conclude that the parents themselves are remiss. They would have an obligation, at some point, to make clear to the children who they really are, so that the relationship between parent and child could more closely align with reality.

We can begin to understand, then, why the Creator wished to reveal, at some point, the true nature of who He was to humanity. As a Heavenly Parent, it was important to make this known to the children in an unambiguous way. It was through the events of the Exodus that the Great Parent in Heaven, YHVH, would demonstrate His true identity.

But how?

CHAPTER NINE

The Hidden Agenda

If you were God, and you wanted to create some sort of historical demonstration of the truth of monotheism, how would you do it?

You'd want something that could stand the test of time, an event that people could look back upon generations later, and understand through it that the world really does have a Creator. Could such an event be engineered? What would it look like?

Maybe you would start with the people who are the hardest to convince. Not just one or two of them, but a whole nation. What if you took an entire civilization that was absolutely committed to the polytheistic world view, a civilization that regarded its own king as a god within a pantheon of gods, and managed to convince it that polytheism was a lie, that there was one supreme being that was the Creator, and that they and their king were subjects of that Creator?

That would be pretty impressive.

Maybe God was trying to engineer something like this. Maybe that was the hidden agenda we alluded to before, that stands at the heart of the Exodus.[22]

---

22. The idea that the Exodus had a dual purpose—freeing the Israelites, and establishing the knowledge that YHVH is the Creator, is suggested as well by R. Shlomo Gantzfried in *Apiryon, Parshat Beshalach* 15:2.

The biblical text seems to say as much. Just before the extended story of the Ten Plagues begins, God tells Moses the reason He is going through all this trouble:

וְיָדְעוּ מִצְרַיִם כִּי־אֲנִי יְקֹוָה בִּנְטֹתִי אֶת־יָדִי עַל־מִצְרָיִם
וְהוֹצֵאתִי אֶת־בְּנֵי־יִשְׂרָאֵל מִתּוֹכָם׃

And Egypt will know that I am YHVH, as I stretch
My hand out over Egypt, and deliver the Children
of Israel from their midst (Exodus 7:5)

There is an educational process going on here, God says, and Pharaoh and Egypt seem to be a key part of the target population.

Why Egypt?

Why Egypt and Pharaoh?

Well, for one, it would certainly be an effective way to broadcast the message of monotheism. If Egypt and Pharaoh ever came to recognize God, that would be an unprecedented event. Egypt was the most dominant civilization the ancient world had ever known. By the time the Exodus took place, the pyramids had already stood for a thousand years. The society was stable. They had a time-tested system of dynastic governance. And along with all this, the Egyptians were steeped in paganism; they subscribed to a vast pantheon of gods. So if you could somehow convince the king of that very powerful, very stable nation—a man who actually regarded himself as a god—that he was *not* a god; that there was no pantheon of gods; that he, like everybody else in the world, was a subject of a single Creator of All... well, that would undoubtedly stand as a great historical testament to the truth of monotheism. Future generations would be able to look back at this event, and see in it evidence of the existence of a Creator of All.

But perhaps there was a second reason, too. Maybe it wasn't only about getting word to travel, or making a historical example of Egypt. Maybe it was also about what Egypt's recognition of God would accomplish in the here and now. Maybe this could be the most direct way to effectuate Israel's freedom from Egyptian bondage. Let me explain.

The Demise of Might Makes Right

I've been suggesting to you here that perhaps the events of the Exodus had a dual purpose. They were designed to set Israel free from Egyptian bondage, but they were also meant, somehow, to demonstrate that the God behind it all was the Creator of All. But why would these two aims go together? Was God just looking to kill two birds with one stone? *The Hebrews need redeeming, and humanity needs to know it has a Creator—might as well save some effort and try and achieve both at the same time!* Was that what it was about?

A moment's reflection will reveal, I think, that these two aims are not unrelated, but two sides of the same coin. What was it, after all, that made it possible for Pharaoh to subjugate the Israelites? By "possible," I don't mean: *How did Pharaoh get the raw capacity to enslave the people?* Certainly, as a host nation to this minority immigrant population, the Egyptians possessed the physical power to overwhelm and enslave the Hebrews. By "possible," I mean: *What belief or idea did Pharaoh subscribe to that made it possible for him to justify what he was doing?*

The Israelites were minding their own business. They were good citizens. All of a sudden, Pharaoh gets it in his head that these people are numerous and might, in the future, arm themselves against the locals and take over Egypt. And so he decides to subjugate them, press them all into abject slavery, and ultimately, murder their male offspring by casting them into the Nile. In his own mind, how could he justify such manifest injustice?

The answer is: he didn't have to. He was the king. He had a national interest to protect. The rights of the minority were not of particular interest to him. And the rest is history. In short, *he had the power to do it, so he did it.* He wouldn't even have to worry that history would judge him harshly. History is written by the victors. If Egypt was victorious over these Hebrews, who would be around to say that it was all wrong?

Bottom line: might makes right.

As in Heaven, So on Earth

In adopting such a stance, Pharaoh would have been taking a page right out of the playbook of the pagan gods. In the polytheistic worldview, the gods don't command *moral* authority; their reign is based upon raw power. They clash with one another and the more powerful one wins. In the pagan pantheon, might really *does* make right.

For a pagan, the realm of the gods provides an example for the earthly realm. If power is the absolute basis of authority on high, why should it be any different down here? Pharaoh's subjugation of the Hebrews is no different than any god getting what it wants through the unrestrained use of power. Who is anyone else to dictate to me what I ought or ought not do?

Now let's return to a question we entertained at the beginning of this book. If you are the Master of the Universe, and you want to effectuate the release of the Hebrews from Egyptian bondage, what is the best way to achieve that aim?

Well, magic carpets and force fields would certainly be convenient and expeditious means to achieve your goal. So if "best" means "convenient," then yes, force fields and magic carpets might be the best way to set the Hebrews free. But it's not the cleanest, most elegant, or even the fastest way to set them free. For that, your goal might be to defeat the *idea* that keeps the Hebrews enslaved. If you could change the oppressor's allegiance to that idea, then servitude and oppression would fall away of their own accord.

If Pharaoh and his people became convinced, somehow, that there indeed exists a Creator-God, certain consequences follow. All of a sudden, there's a Parker that made the board, the tokens, the hotels, and everything else in the game, including the rules. Or, to switch metaphors: if the world is a great big house, well, there are rules of the house to which all children are expected to adhere, as long as they live there—rules set by the Great Parent in the Sky. If the Creator makes clear that He does not approve of the subjugation, intimidation, and slaughter of a weak minority population simply because their forced labor serves the needs of the strong—well, all of a sudden, there is a moral obligation to stop exploiting the weak. The expressed wish of the Creator Himself cannot simply be waved off as irrelevant.

If, somehow, Pharaoh could be convinced of the truth of the Creator-God's existence, and come to see himself as a subject in that Creator's kingdom—well, there could be no more elegant, nor speedier, way to cause the evil of Egyptian slavery to simply melt away, as if on its own.

Not as Easy as it Looks

We've talked about why God might wish to reveal Himself to humanity as YHVH, the Creator-God, and we've talked about how convenient and elegant it would be to achieve this through Pharaoh's own recognition of the truth of monotheism. Not only would that recognition stand, through the ages, as a testament to the truth of One God, but it might actually secure the release of the Hebrews in the quickest and most direct way: through the free-willed consent of the Egyptian monarch.

It's a great plan. The only question is: *Is it actually achievable?*

If you are the Master of the Universe, what are you going to do that will convincingly demonstrate your identity as Creator to all onlookers? It's not so easy. Remember, the Egyptians weren't atheists; they believed in heavenly powers. They just believed that there happened to be *many* of those powers. How do you convince a society of polytheists, led by a king who thinks he's a god, that the force he and his countrymen are facing is not one of the polytheistic powers, but is in fact the One Creator-God?

Let's try some possibilities on for size. Say you give Moses some divinely-powered magic tricks to perform? It's not convincing; Egypt has plenty of magicians. What about something more dramatic? Let's say Pharaoh arrogantly denies your request to free the Hebrews and you initiate a tidal wave that would level an Egyptian city. Would *that* prove to everyone in a polytheistic society that you are the Creator?

That wouldn't do the trick either. *The sea god has struck us. He must be angry at us for neglecting him. We had better offer sacrifices to the sea god to appease him.*

Maybe a really big earthquake. Would *that* convince Pharaoh that his heavenly opponent is the Creator?

That wouldn't work, either. *Looks like the earth god is mad at us, too.* Do you see the problem here? Any particular plague can be chalked up to the action of a particular, annoyed, provincial god. No matter what force you decide to muster, the polytheist can fit the catastrophic events into his narrative. Imagine a conversation between Pharaoh and his pagan sorcerers after any of the strikes described above: *Yes, that plague was awful, Sire, but no theological problem here; we've got a god in the pantheon for that!*

So, if you're the Master of the Universe, how exactly might you get your point across? How could you arrange the events of the Exodus to demonstrate that you are the Creator?

Plan A

There are a couple things you might try. You might, perhaps, try the direct route: have your leader on the ground, Moses, declare to Pharaoh that there is, in fact, a Creator and that he, Moses, is a messenger of that Creator. If Pharaoh is skeptical, as he might well be, then give Moses some way of proving his words, some sort of sign by which he could demonstrate the authenticity of his message. Not a magic trick, but a sign, a nonviolent but impressive symbolic demonstration, so overwhelmingly convincing it would be like skywriting *I am the Creator* into the clear blue sky above Egypt. You'd have to come up with an unimpeachable sign that would clearly and directly point to the existence of a single force that subjugates all other forces. If such a sign could somehow be dreamed up, that alone could carry the day. Pharaoh and Egypt would, of course, have to be open and honest enough to accept the evidence offered by the sign–but it would at least be worth a try.

As we'll see later on, it appears God tried to do exactly this. Pharaoh and Egypt, in the end, weren't up to the task of honestly accepting the declaration and the accompanying sign. But the good-faith attempt was made. We might call it Plan A–the optimal way of achieving the release of the Hebrews.

The Demise of the Alliance Theory

OK, but if Plan A doesn't end up working, what of Plan B? If Pharaoh and Egypt reject the nonviolent declaration and the substantiating sign, what then? Could Egypt still be educated in the idea of the One God, and be convinced, on its basis, to release their slaves?

Well, maybe plagues could work. Any one plague might not accomplish the goal. But *ten* plagues just might. The accumulated evidence of plague after plague, each displaying control over an entirely different force in the natural world–*that might just do the trick*. Play it out and you can see why.

First, the Nile turns to blood. If you're a good, upstanding polytheist, how do you react? You don't think the Creator has struck you. You might instead say, as we've suggested: *The river god seems to be angry with us*, and leave it at that... until the next plague strikes. Now the frogs are here, in the beds, the oven, the living room; you can't walk without stepping on frogs—and you conclude that the river god has teamed up with the amphibian god to strike your country. Most unfortunate. But then the third plague strikes, and the alliance against you has evidently grown. It seems that the insect god has somehow gotten into the act. What other way to explain the tens of millions of lice that are suddenly infesting every Egyptian home?

Do you get the picture? At what point does the elaborate intellectual edifice you are putting together collapse under its own weight? As plague upon plague hits, evincing a breathtaking array of natural forces, the slow accumulation of evidence starts to poke holes in the "alliance theory" of the plagues. Remember, in a polytheistic system, gods have rivalries; because they are looking out for their own well-being, alliances between gods are few and far between.[23] At some point, you have to sit back and ask yourself: *How many gods, exactly, are angry at us here?* And at some point, the simplest explanation is: *Wait a minute—there's no alliance here at all. There must be one force in charge of all of this.*[24]

---

23. Dimitri Meeks and Christine Favard-Meeks. *Daily life of the Egyptian gods* (Ithaca: Cornell University Press, 1996).

24. In his groundbreaking book *The Structure of Scientific Revolutions,* Thomas Kuhn documents patterns in the ways that various sea changes in scientific thinking—what we call scientific revolutions—have taken hold over time. All the great scientific revolutions, from Copernicus to Einstein, he argues, were brought about through the slow accumulation of evidence, creating problems with the reigning paradigm. Eventually, a tipping point was reached, where people moved to a new way of seeing things—an approach that seemed simpler and less convoluted than the old way. The Ten Plagues would have worked in a similar fashion. Each plague alone was another nail in the coffin of polytheism. Eventually, the cumulative evidence brought to bear by the plagues, collectively, would be unimpeachable.

But There's More

It wasn't just the *number* of plagues or their diversity that was remarkable. There was also something about *how* the plagues were manifested that indicated the hand of a Creator. We've laid the groundwork to finally understand something that puzzled us a good while back about the interaction between Moses and Pharaoh as the plagues unfolded. It had to do with power and precision. Let's revisit that issue now, and see what new light we can shed on it.

CHAPTER TEN

The Case for Monotheism

Power vs. Precision

Earlier, we noticed a pattern in Pharaoh's reaction to the various plagues that descended upon Egypt. For some reason, he seemed more impressed with the precision of a given plague than with the raw power evinced by that plague. This seems rather counterintuitive. If you were a king whose land and population were being battered by a series of harsh blows, wouldn't you care most of all about how devastating those blows were, the degree to which they degraded your land or imposed hardship upon your people? Why would the precision with which a plague came and went—whether Moses could turn off the frogs at precisely the moment you picked, or whether a given plague distinguished precisely between Israelites and Egyptians—matter so much to you?

We are now on the cusp of an answer to that question. As it turns out, the issue of power versus precision is one of the overlooked crossroads where the paths of paganism and monotheism diverge.

Consider paganism, a system in which competing gods constantly vie for power. The forces of nature are powerful, but which of them will hold sway at any given moment is anyone's guess. Sometimes the rain waters the crops; other times, the sun parches them mercilessly. The polytheist will tell you that this unpredictability comes from competition between the gods. Looking at nature through a polytheistic lens is like watching an eighteen-wheeler barreling down the highway at 85 miles per hour with seven strong men struggling for control of the steering wheel. There's plenty of power there, but precious little control or precision. The truck zigzags down the highway with frightening unpredictability.

In a polytheistic universe, you would see lots of power, but very little control. No one could predict with precision which force would hold sway at 4:30 PM next Tuesday. It is control, therefore–the precise, pinpointed application of power–that really gets Pharaoh's attention. Precise control over the plagues, even more than their power, calls into question the intellectual foundations of paganism. The emissary of a pagan god can't turn off its particular force at precisely the moment of your choosing. That Moses *can* do this suggests a hitherto unheard-of entity. It suggests a Creator whose control over the forces of nature is complete and absolute. It suggests a Force that does not share power with any true competitors.

Fire, Ice, and the Polytheist on the Fence

To summarize, then: if you were the Creator, how might you make that fact known to a king and a civilization steeped in polytheism, who were unjustly enslaving a people you wanted to set free? A first indication might come through the onset of ten accumulating plagues, each displaying control over an entirely different facet of the natural world. A second indication might come from *how* those plagues are wielded: strikes displaying consummate precision, predicted in advance as to when and where they begin and end, would point to a Creator-God as the originator of these strikes. And finally, we might suggest one more way a Creator's signature could be left on the plagues: *by causing diametrically opposed natural forces to work in harmony toward a common end.*

Picture a fine, upstanding polytheist attempting to explain away a slew of mysterious plagues afflicting his nation. The plagues clearly display a mastery of different forces of nature; their onset, culmination, and target area have been foretold with uncanny precision by a certain prophet who claims they are all the work of YHVH, the Creator of All. Our friend the polytheist has struggled against credulity to convince his friends and neighbors—and himself—that a grand alliance of pagan gods has been responsible for these misfortunes, but frankly, he's not quite sure he believes his own explanation anymore. He's on the fence. Now, could we dream up an event that might sway our friend the fence-sitting polytheist to discard his bogus alliance-of-the-gods theory once and for all?

I think we can: the seventh plague, the plague of hail. This plague, as we shall see, was unique. Indeed, the text tells us remarkable things about the hailstones that descended upon Egypt. They weren't like the hailstones you and I have seen before:

וַיְהִי בָרָד וְאֵשׁ מִתְלַקַּחַת בְּתוֹךְ הַבָּרָד

And there was hail—and fire encased inside the hail (Exodus 9:24)[25]

Fire and ice together in one hailstone...

Now, to some extent, *all* the plagues were unique occurrences. It wasn't like the Nile turned to blood every day. Cattle and livestock didn't suddenly drop dead every other Tuesday in ancient Egypt. Nevertheless, something about what was happening here, in the plague of hail, was *dramatically* unexpected, even by the high standards of the plagues themselves: fire and ice, coexisting in hailstones!

Let's go back to our imaginary friend on the fence, no longer sure about his theory that the plagues striking Egypt are the work

---

25. Translation here follows Saadiah Ga'on; see also Exodus Rabbah 12:4.

of an alliance of gods. How is he going to explain *this* plague? Fire is frozen inside the ice. If there were ever two gods that could be counted upon to *never* join forces, it would have to be the ice and fire gods. They are sworn enemies: mere contact between them leads to their mutual extinction.

When it comes to explaining the plague of hail, the polytheistic worldview draws a blank. This plague makes sense only in a world where fire and ice are servants of a single Being, the One who created them both. Only the Creator might prevail upon fire and ice to work together, harmoniously, in furtherance of a common goal.

Can the Divine Plan Be Foiled?

Fine; so there *were* ways, embedded within the Ten Plagues themselves, through which a Creator could make His identity known. Let's pull back the zoom lens, then, and return to our developing theory: the Exodus had a dual goal—free the Hebrews from slavery, but do so in a way that educates Pharaoh in the nature of the force he is opposing. That power is not a mere god in a pantheon of divine beings, but the one and only Creator. If the most established civilization of the ancient world, entirely devoted to paganism, were to embrace the idea of monotheism, if its leader were to accept the truth that the world contains a Creator to whom he is subject—that would certainly be a historical testament to the truth of monotheism.

It sounds like a great plan. There's only one problem with it: it all depends upon Pharaoh's will.

Which means that Pharaoh could ruin everything.

CHAPTER ELEVEN

Stubbornness and Courage

We are now in a position to come back to two conundrums that puzzled us toward the beginning of this book: what moral justification might there be for God to deprive Pharaoh of free will? And: why would God, who is evidently so interested in getting Pharaoh to say yes to freedom for the Israelites, suddenly harden Pharaoh's heart, and make him say no once the Egyptian monarch finally does say yes?

The answer to these questions is bound up in the ways Pharaoh could potentially "ruin" God's plan.

God's Plan Demands Pharaoh's Free Choice

Consider this:

If Pharaoh and Egypt's recognition of God as Creator, through the Exodus, is going to stand as a historical demonstration of the truth of monotheism, then this recognition of God they ultimately come to cannot be a sham; it cannot be coerced. Pharaoh's recognition of the Creator, in order to be meaningful, must be something Pharaoh *genuinely* comes to. Making Pharaoh *appear* to recognize God through some kind of divine sleight of hand—like depriving him of free will—would be cheating, and, frankly, pointless.

But what is to guarantee Pharaoh will ever make this free-willed recognition of a Creator? If Pharaoh really has free and unfettered choice throughout this whole Exodus affair, who knows what he might do? It's all very nice for God to carefully craft a brilliant demonstration of His being Creator through mastery over all the forces of nature–but what if Pharaoh doesn't play along?

There are at least two ways that Pharaoh could ruin everything through an unpredictable exercise of free will. The first is what we might call the problem of weakness.

The Problem of Weakness

Consider the following scenario: The first plague strikes. Pharaoh is overwhelmed by the devastation. He has not yet seen enough to convince him that this god of the Hebrews is the Creator. He still imagines an "ordinary" power is opposing him, but nevertheless, he surrenders, simply out of fear of what might yet come. In other words, what happens if Pharaoh wants to give in not for moral or theological reasons, but simply due to panic, anxiety or despair? What if the plagues are simply too powerful for him to withstand?

If this is how the Exodus story were to end, instead of demonstrating the truth of the Creator's existence, the one or two plagues that actually occur would end up demonstrating little more than the limited tenacity of Egypt's king. All that would have been achieved, in the end, is that Pharaoh, beaten, would add the god of the Hebrews to his vast pantheon of pagan powers. Not much of a victory at all.

Was there a way God might somehow neutralize this difficulty? I believe there was.

Consider this: if Pharaoh wants to give in because he thinks he's beaten, not because he thinks he's wrong, we might say that Pharaoh suffers from a lack of courage to pursue his vision. He's in this fight to hold onto his slaves–and ultimately, to his conception of himself as a god. But he lacks the courage to see that vision through to the end. So if Pharaoh were to suffer from that failure of vision, God might perhaps choose to lend Pharaoh the courage necessary to continue the fight.

This, indeed, is the approach adopted by the classic commentator known as Seforno.[26]

What Counts as Deprivation of Free Will?

Now let me ask you a question: if God, over the course of the Ten Plagues, "strengthens Pharaoh's heart," giving him courage to continue–do you think that counts as a deprivation of Pharaoh's free will?

I want to argue (and I think Seforno is on my side here): decidedly not. Lending Pharaoh the strength of heart to persevere isn't depriving Pharaoh of free will; if anything, it is *enhancing* his free will. If someone is discouraged, fearful, and ready to give in, and you give them a pep talk, encouraging them to pursue their goals–you've bolstered them. You haven't taken away anything from them. We all want the strength to forge onward to try and realize our visions.

In effect, God's stance toward Pharaoh, in strengthening his heart, would be something like this:

Let's not let expediency decide this conflict between you and Me. Let's decide this on principle.

If, throughout this struggle, you ever want to give in on principle, if you ever lose confidence in the justness of your position, if you ever come to the conclusion that I am in fact the Creator, and that you are duty bound to release My people that you have enslaved–I will gladly accept your surrender, and we will call an end to the conflict.

If, on the other hand, you have not changed your mind about any of this and you wish to continue to battle Me–but would give in merely

---

26. See *Seforno* to Exodus 7:3.

because your fear overcomes you, don't worry: I will give you the
courage to persevere, and see your vision through to the end.
    You be the one to decide.

How Would We See This All in the Biblical Text?

Later, we will come back to Seforno's approach and show how
it wends its way through the plagues. But in the meantime, let
me give you the gist of how we might see his ideas playing out
in the biblical text. Here's how we might identify points in the
biblical text where God "lends courage" to Pharaoh.

As it turns out, Pharaoh has many changes of heart over the
course of the plagues, but the Torah doesn't always use the same
verb to characterize a change of heart. It switches off between
two different verbs. One comes from the Hebrew root כבד (*k-b-d*),
and the other, from the Hebrew root חזק (*ch-z-k*).[27]

---

27. This is the kind of thing, by the way, that is hard to pick up if you are
reading a translation rather than the original Hebrew. For example, the 1917
JPS translation of the Bible uses *harden*—"Pharaoh's heart was *hardened*"—in
each line cited above, despite the fact that the original Hebrew employs
two different roots. This is not because the translator is trying to mislead
you. When rendering a text into another language, it is only natural to,
even unconsciously, smooth out some of the rough spots in the original
text. You are just trying to make the text more readable. But when it comes
to the Bible, that is a particularly perilous thing to do. In the Torah, the
"rough spots" are often where the clues to deeper layers of meaning lie. If
you smooth these out, you deprive your reader of needed clues, and render
them unable to see the full picture the Bible is trying to paint.

    What, then, are you to do, if you want to perceive some of the sophisti-
cation and elegance of the Bible, but your knowledge of Biblical Hebrew is
rusty or nonexistent? A good place to start, I think, is to consult more than
one translation. If you are willing to invest the effort in reading through two
or three English renderings of a given text, you'll spot the major discrep-

STUBBORNNESS AND COURAGE 87

Clearly, these are two terms, each with different meanings. We'll come back to *kibbud halev*, but let's talk for a moment about *chizuk halev*. The most literal way to translate those words is "strength of heart." What is strength of heart? It seems like a good thing to have. Those who have strength of heart are valorous and heroic. Such people, we might say, have vision, and they are willing to see things through to the end, despite difficulties along the way. They are, in a word, *courageous*.

Chizuk halev would thus denote the strengthening of one's heart, the gaining of courage. So for now, we can say this: if, in reading through the plagues, you ever find that God is the one to change Pharaoh's mind, and the phrase used to describe that change of mind is *chizuk halev*—then that, right there, is an instance of God lending courage to the embattled Egyptian leader, enabling him to continue the fight he still believes in, deep down.

The Problem of Stubbornness

In short order, we will read through the actual progression of the Ten Plagues and see where and when God strengthens Pharaoh's heart.[28] In the meantime, we need to consider a second problem

---

ancies between the different translations. It's a good bet that underneath those discrepancies are ambiguities in the original text that the various translators are struggling with. Each confronts the ambiguity differently, giving rise to the differences between their respective translations. By consulting these different translations, then, you'll be able to take a pretty good guess as to where the textual problems lie. (Best advice, though: enroll in a class in Biblical Hebrew. It's not as hard to learn as you think!)

28. A consequence of distinguishing between *chizuk halev* and *kibbud halev*, as we have done, is that it may change our thinking about whether God ever deprived Pharaoh of free will at all. To know for sure, we'd have to trace our way through the Ten Plagues, and for each instance in which

that could interfere with God's plan to reveal Himself through Pharaoh's free-willed recognition of a Creator-God. It is, in a way, the inverse of the problem we considered above. What if, instead of giving in too soon, Pharaoh never gives in and recognizes the Creator, even when the evidence is absolutely overwhelming? We might call this the problem of stubbornness.

As it happens, Pharaoh *does* occasionally act with something akin to blind stubbornness. The Hebrew word for that is the other verb we discussed above, which the Torah occasionally uses to characterize Pharaoh's change of mind. That, you will recall, is *kibbud halev*, which literally translates to "hardness of heart," or more colloquially, "stubbornness" (*kaved* in Hebrew means "heavy" or "hard").[29] The question I am raising now is: what happens if Pharaoh's stubbornness becomes so great that it reaches a point of no return? What if Pharaoh is finally so stubborn that, no matter how clear the evidence placed before him, he simply refuses to ever budge and acknowledge the truth?

Pharaoh changed his mind, ask two crucial questions:

What, exactly, is happening to Pharaoh's heart? Is the text describing Pharaoh as becoming more "courageous" or more "stubborn"? To find out, we need to look at the verbs the Torah is using: Is it talking about *chizuk halev* or *kibbud halev*?

Who, exactly, is doing it? Is Pharaoh the one acting upon his heart, or is God acting upon his heart? Whether Pharaoh's heart is becoming "stronger" or "harder," *who* is the one doing this to Pharaoh's heart?

29. Cf. *Da'at Torah*, by R. Yerucham Levovitz, *Sefer Vayikra*, page 117 (regarding *koved rosh*). When you think about it, *chizuk halev* and *kibbud halev* are opposites. Strength of heart is a good thing: an actual, biological heart is a muscle, and when it's strong, it's flexible. A hard heart is a bad thing: it suggests calcification, inability to change. Courage is the vision to pursue my goal; stubbornness is a doom-inducing blindness to the fact that my goal is not achievable.

One could well imagine him reaching such a point of no re-turn. After all, Pharaoh would certainly have reason to avoid acknowledgment of a Supreme Creator. He has a lot invested in the status quo. It's rather nice being ensconced at the top of the totem pole, and treated as a god by a fawning population of millions. He might not want to give that up.

Pharaoh's struggle to hold onto his slaves is not just an eco-nomic battle. It is also a struggle to hold onto his conception of *himself*. Were he to concede that the force opposing him is actually his Creator—well, that comes with a shattering and humbling duty to reappraise who he really is. People don't give up delu-sions about themselves very easily. Will this whole divine plan collapse if Pharaoh is too stubborn to see the truth, even when that truth is made clear to him?

It seems inconceivable that God's plan for revealing himself to the world as YHVH would rest entirely on so shaky a foundation, and could be so easily foiled. Yes, perhaps God will choose to win Pharaoh and Egypt's assent to the idea of a Creator, if it can be won. Perhaps there is a Plan A, a nonviolent sign of some sort that overwhelmingly indicates the existence of a Creator. Perhaps there is a Plan B, an effort to educate Pharaoh, over time, as to the existence of a Creator. But if these efforts fail, there has to be a Plan C.

Was there a Plan C? And did it ever have to be implemented? These are questions we will look to answer as we read through the story of the Ten Plagues together. We've developed some the-ories about Plans A, B, and C—what they might have been, and how they might be executed. But the ultimate litmus test is the text. As we return to the biblical text and actually read through the Exodus story, it will be time to see how theory translates into reality.

PART III

Putting the Exodus Story Back Together Again

CHAPTER TWELVE

The Path Not Taken

Having prepared the groundwork, it is time to reread the original text of the Exodus story. We have taken the story apart, analyzing each of its elements, but now it's time to gather all those pieces and put the narrative back together again. It's time to see how the tentative conclusions we've reached come to life in the biblical text itself.

The story of the plagues is, to some extent, the story of a protracted negotiation between Moses and Pharaoh, a process marked by constant changes of mind on the part of the Egyptian king. As we noted, those changes of mind are characterized by two different Hebrew phrases, *chizuk halev* and *kibbud halev*, which we have rendered as "strengthening of heart" and "hardening of heart," respectively. As we go through the story of the Ten Plagues, we will note the particular moments each phrase is used. We will find that paying attention to these alternating turns of phrase will help us discern the outlines of an otherwise-hidden drama.

Finding the Beginning

וְיָדְעוּ מִצְרַיִם כִּי־אֲנִי יְקוָה בִּנְטֹתִי אֶת־יָדִי עַל־מִצְרָיִם
וְהוֹצֵאתִי אֶת־בְּנֵי־יִשְׂרָאֵל מִתּוֹכָם:

*And Egypt shall come to know that I am YHVH, when
I stretch out my hand upon Egypt (Exodus 7:5)*

93

If the Exodus was designed, at least in part, as a process through which Egypt and Pharaoh would come to know YHVH–where exactly did that educational process begin?

It starts, I think, when Moses delivers his initial two speeches, the first time Moses has an audience with Pharaoh, just after he is chosen by God, at the Burning Bush, to lead the people. We were puzzled when we first considered these speeches a few chapters ago. Let's revisit them now.

SPEECH 1	SPEECH 2
Exodus 5:1	Exodus 5:3

כֹּה־אָמַר יְקוָה אֱלֹקֵי יִשְׂרָאֵל שַׁלַּח אֶת־עַמִּי וְיָחֹגּוּ לִי בַּמִּדְבָּר:	אֱלֹקֵי הָעִבְרִים נִקְרָא עָלֵינוּ נֵלֲכָה נָּא דֶּרֶךְ שְׁלֹשֶׁת יָמִים בַּמִּדְבָּר וְנִזְבְּחָה לַיקוָה אֱלֹקֵינוּ פֶּן־יִפְגָּעֵנוּ בַּדֶּבֶר אוֹ בֶחָרֶב:

Thus says YHVH, God of Israel: Send out My people, and let them rejoice before Me in the desert.

The God of the Hebrews happened upon us. Let us go, please, for three days in the desert and sacrifice to our God; otherwise, he might hurt us with pestilence or with the sword.

A Tale of Two Speeches

Let's remind ourselves about what happened here. How did the dialogue between Moses and Pharaoh proceed?

In Moses's first speech, he conveys a message from God to Pharaoh: *Let My people go so they can 'celebrate before Me in the desert.*' Pharaoh rejects that demand in no uncertain terms. The Egyptian king declares that he has no idea who this deity is, and in any case, he's not letting the slaves go. What struck us as strange was what happened next.

After Pharaoh's rejection of Moses's first speech, Moses did not choose to up the ante and threaten Pharaoh with great devastation should he continue to defy God. And Moses did not choose to return to God with Pharaoh's reply–*Pharaoh said no, and now I, your loyal servant, await Your next instruction.* Instead, Moses chose a strange middle ground:

וַיֹּאמְרוּ אֱלֹקֵי הָעִבְרִים נִקְרָא עָלֵינוּ נֵלְכָה נָּא דֶּרֶךְ שְׁלֹשֶׁת יָמִים
בַּמִּדְבָּר וְנִזְבְּחָה לַיקֹוָה אֱלֹקֵינוּ פֶּן־יִפְגָּעֵנוּ בַּדֶּבֶר אוֹ בֶחָרֶב:

And he said: The God of the Hebrews happened upon us. Let us go, please, for three days in the desert and sacrifice to our God; otherwise, He might hurt us with pestilence or with the sword. (Exodus 5:3)

In this second speech, Moses tries once more to convince Pharaoh to release his slaves, at least for a three-day holiday–but he uses timid language in a plea that seemed almost destined to fail. And fail it does. Pharaoh angrily imposes extra work upon the "lazy" slaves that have dared to ask for time off. What was Moses thinking? If Pharaoh rejected the first speech, wouldn't he clearly reject the second?

Two Visions of God

Earlier, we remarked that the two speeches of Moses seem to present two radically different visions of God. When we first noticed this, we hadn't yet drawn the contrasts between monotheism and polytheism that would allow us to place each of these competing visions of God in context. But looking at the speeches now, it seems evident that the God of Moses's first speech is God-as-He-truly-is, whereas the god that Moses presents in the second speech seems to portray the Almighty in terms we might use to describe a mere "power" within a larger pantheon of powers.

And maybe that's the whole point. A process of education is beginning here, a process in which Pharaoh and Egypt will learn of YHVH. As the first step in that process, Moses is putting the truth on the table, whether or not Pharaoh is prepared to hear it. In a sense, God and Moses owe it to Pharaoh to be honest with him–to make clear the facts of the matter, and let the Egyptian king respond as he will. So Moses sets it all out in his first speech: *There is a Creator-God, YHVH, and He is addressing you directly with a demand to let His people go, for He wishes to celebrate with them.*

YHVH is God's Creator-name. The Creator has an expectation of Egypt and a hope for Israel: he expects Egypt to let go these people it regards as slaves, and He wishes to celebrate with these people in the desert. The notion of celebration implies a deity that values a relationship with people. It implies that joy can be part of a relationship with the deity. This is all very foreign to Pharaoh, and he dismisses it out of hand:

מִי יְקֹוָה אֲשֶׁר אֶשְׁמַע בְּקֹלוֹ לְשַׁלַּח אֶת־יִשְׂרָאֵל לֹא
יָדַעְתִּי אֶת־יְקֹוָה וְגַם אֶת־יִשְׂרָאֵל לֹא אֲשַׁלֵּחַ:

Who is YHVH that I should listen to his voice to let Israel go? I do not know YHVH, and what's more, I will not let Israel go! (Exodus 5:2)

That there is a Being up there who truly desires a "personal" connection with people, a YHVH Creator-Being–this makes no sense to Pharaoh. Nobody celebrates with a god. They might appease a god, sacrifice to it–but celebrate? Pharaoh has never heard of a god like this. The Sages of the Midrash (cited by Rashi) suggest that Pharaoh looked down his list of known deities trying to find the one Moses named, only to conclude that, no, as suspected, this god was not on the list. Pharaoh dismisses Moses's words as theological nonsense, and wants to be done with the whole thing.

So did that first speech of Moses fail? Well, on the one hand, Pharaoh says no, and doesn't release his slaves. But in at least one respect, the speech succeeds. Pharaoh may have rejected what Moses has said, but he has heard it. The process of education has begun. Moses has set forth an end point for that process, a goal. One day, Pharaoh may yet come to recognize the kind of God Moses has introduced here. But until then, Moses and God will take small, incremental steps toward showing that this vision of the Creator is real.

The first of these incremental steps comes in the form of Moses's second speech. In it, Moses addresses Pharaoh in terms the Egyptian king can understand, to see if he can win his consent:

אֱלֹקֵי הָעִבְרִים נִקְרָא עָלֵינוּ נֵלֲכָה נָּא דֶּרֶךְ שְׁלֹשֶׁת יָמִים
בַּמִּדְבָּר וְנִזְבְּחָה לַיקוָה אֱלֹקֵינוּ פֶּן־יִפְגָּעֵנוּ בַּדֶּבֶר אוֹ בֶחָרֶב:

The power ['el'] of the Hebrews happened upon us. Let us go, please, for three days in the desert and sacrifice to our God; otherwise, he might hurt us with pestilence or with the sword. (Exodus 5:3)

In his second speech, Moses is, in effect, saying to Pharaoh:

Let me make things a little easier for you. Forget about that YHVH name that you found so confusing. Let's at least agree that this god who sent me is no less than an 'el,' a power. You know about powers. And forget, at least for the moment, the idea that there's some sort of precious relationship between this deity and a people He knows by a special name, Israel. Let's just call them Hebrews. And forget about that whole celebration thing. Let's just say we're really worried that our 'el,' our power, might get angry with us if we don't go into the desert to sacrifice to it. You can understand that, can't you? Arbitrary and capricious deities we must appease with sacrifices, who might strike us down if we don't obey? You know, sort of like your sun god? All we're asking for, Pharaoh, is a little religious freedom; a three-day break to appease our god, the same way you would appease yours.

Moses's second speech makes sense to Pharaoh. This god doesn't sound as crazy to him as the last one, which explains why his response to it is so different from his response to the first speech:

וַיֹּאמֶר אֲלֵהֶם מֶלֶךְ מִצְרַיִם לָמָּה מֹשֶׁה וְאַהֲרֹן תַּפְרִיעוּ
אֶת־הָעָם מִמַּעֲשָׂיו לְכוּ לְסִבְלֹתֵיכֶם: וַיֹּאמֶר פַּרְעֹה
הֵן־רַבִּים עַתָּה עַם הָאָרֶץ וְהִשְׁבַּתֶּם אֹתָם מִסִּבְלֹתָם:

*And the King of Egypt said to them: Why do you, Moses
and Aaron, disturb the people from their work? And
Pharaoh said: The people are many, and you are
distracting them from their burdens! (Exodus 5:4–5)*

Interestingly, Pharaoh does *not* reject Speech 2 out of hand the way he dismisses Speech 1. He understands exactly what Moses is telling him. Everyone in Egypt serves a god, it's just a question of which god they choose to serve. The Hebrews have their god; they are afraid of him and want to appease him. Makes perfect sense. Pharaoh dismisses Moses's second speech not because it is ridiculous, but because Moses and Aaron are riling up the masses. Pharaoh's gross domestic product is going to take a hit if the slaves start thinking about vacation time for religious worship. Which explains the very next thing Pharaoh decides to do: make the slaves work even harder because he considers them lazy.[30] Pharaoh's command is cold and heartless, but there is a certain

---

30. See Exodus 5:6–9: "And Pharaoh commanded, that very day, the taskmasters over the people, saying: Don't give straw to the people anymore to make bricks, as you did yesterday and the day before. They will go themselves to gather straw for themselves. Meanwhile, the quota for bricks that they had yesterday and the day before—keep it in place. Don't detract anything from it. Because they are lazy—that's why they are screaming, saying 'let us sacrifice to our god'! Make the work harder on the men..."

malicious logic in the king's reaction: *If you Hebrews are serving your god out of abject fear, the way we all serve our deities around here—that means you must fear this god more than you fear me. And that means I must be doing something wrong. I am the ultimate master here. My slaves' fear of me should dwarf all other fears. If these Hebrews have time to think about serving their god, they're evidently not working hard enough!*

Consequently, Pharaoh issues orders to make the slaves work harder. It's a perfectly logical, if evil, response. Pharaoh is just trying to make sure his slaves understand who their "true" master really is.

The Path Not Taken

We wondered earlier why Moses only asked for a three-day break for the Hebrews to worship their god in the desert. Why stoop to lying to the Egyptian king? But maybe Moses was not lying at all...

One of the hardest things to do when contemplating the past is playing "what if?" What if the United States had not intercepted a coded Japanese message indicating the precise location of the Japanese fleet in the Pacific just before the Battle of Midway? What if Lee Harvey Oswald had missed his target that fateful day in Dallas? How would our world look today if those events had played out differently? The truth is, we will never know. We can only speculate.

And so it is in the Torah. We will never know what would have happened had Pharaoh *not* reacted as he did to Moses's second speech. What if, instead of callously accusing his slaves of laziness, he had assented to Moses's small, baby-step request for a three-day holiday to allow the Hebrews to worship their god? It is an interesting question, so let's speculate for a moment.

Had Pharaoh initially responded cooperatively, in good faith, isn't it at least conceivable that the Israelites would have actually *returned* to Egypt after the three-day holiday he granted them?[31] Had events actually transpired this way, we might say that the first baby step would have succeeded. Pharaoh would have recognized God—not for what He truly was, to be sure, but at least as an *el,* a legitimate, if limited, power—and then it would be time to take a second baby step, to move the education process forward one step further. If Pharaoh continued to prove himself amenable to thoughtful consideration and reason, there might be no need for harsher measures like plagues. Slowly, step by step, Pharaoh could have been brought to understand the truth about this deity the Hebrews worshipped. The next step might be: *Pharaoh, we need to share with you something about this power we worship. He's a little, well... different from the polytheistic powers you worship*—and proof could then have been adduced to substantiate that truth.[32]

---

31. Cf. *Emet L'Yaakov*, 256. R. Yaakov Kaminetsky suggests precisely this: had Pharaoh agreed to the three-day holiday, the Israelites would certainly have returned, and Egyptian slavery would have ended in an entirely different manner than it did. R. Kaminetsky argues that the three-day offer was made in good faith, as it is inconceivable that God would have commanded Moses to lie to the Egyptian king.

32. How might the process of education have worked? Was there really a nonviolent educational option, short of the plagues as we would come to know them?

An answer might come from the signs. At the Burning Bush, Moses had worried that people might doubt that he had experienced a genuine encounter with YHVH (Exodus 4:1), so God gave Moses three signs. Later, God told Moses that, if Pharaoh should ask Moses for some kind of sign—presumably to establish the nature of the god he claimed to represent—Moses should perform a version of one of those signs in Pharaoh's presence. And, shortly thereafter, God directs Moses to perform that one sign in the presence of Pharaoh. One wonders if that particular sign, alone, contained all Pharaoh

At the end of these incremental steps, Pharaoh might come to realize that he, no less than Israel, is a subject of this One Power, this Master of the Universe, and consequently, he must abide by the Creator's wishes and set Israel free. History *could* have taken this path, if only Pharaoh had allowed himself to walk it. There would have been no plagues. No violence. Only gradual understanding of an overwhelming truth.

---

would ever need to understand the truth about YHVH–if only Pharaoh had genuinely opened himself to what the sign had to teach.

What *did* that sign teach? For the sign, Moses is instructed to tell Aaron to cast down his staff, at which point the staff would be transformed into a serpent (Exodus 7:9). When Moses and Aaron actually perform this sign (Exodus 7:10-12), something unexpected happens: Pharaoh's sorcerers mimic the sign. They cast down their staffs, which become serpents as well. Seemingly, Pharaoh has the last laugh. But why would God tell Moses to perform a sign so easily mimicked? Why would a God who clearly has the power to perform shattering plagues, to marshal all the forces of nature at His whim, choose to give Moses a single tool, easily foiled by nothing more than cheap magic tricks?

Unless the answer is: *The sign isn't over yet.* We will address this later, but it would seem that what happens *next* to Aaron's staff is part and parcel of the intended sign; indeed, it is its climax. After the sorcerers cast down their staffs to become serpents, the staff of Aaron swallows each and every one of those serpents.

Now, if *that* was the sign–what does it convey? Its message seems clear: *There may be many powers out there, but there is* one Power to rule them all. There is a Creator whose might dwarfs and subsumes every other force in the universe that He created.

Had Pharaoh been open to learning the truth about this Creator-God, it was there for him, on a silver platter. It was there in the only sign God ever instructed Moses to perform for Pharaoh, and it predated the plagues. The process of education did not *necessitate* the eventual violence of the plagues.

Alas, this path was not taken. Pharaoh instead responded with callous disregard to Moses's second speech, his plea for at least *some* understanding of the needs and desires of the enslaved Israelites—a brief respite from labor and a chance to relate to their god. He instead accused the Israelites of laziness, dismissed their allegiance to their deity, and doubled the intensity of their already punishing workload.

It is at that moment that Exodus Plan A was, so to speak, lost. The possibility of an Exodus coming through the nonviolent education of Pharaoh and Egypt would require Pharaoh's good-faith participation. It would require from Pharaoh an openness to Moses's words and to the signs and evidence that would back up the truth of those words. But good faith on Pharaoh's part was not forthcoming. And so, Exodus Plan B would have to be put into action. That is, the process of education would continue, but it would continue the hard way.

Pharaoh had, in effect, declared war against an opponent he considered imaginary, but he would soon come to learn that the Creator was not imaginary at all. Pharaoh would be shown the truth about this God of the Hebrews, but that revelation would come at a dear price. The wealth of Egypt, built, at least in part, through the backbreaking labor of hundreds of thousands of slaves—would fade. Egypt would taste something of the harshness it inflicted on its "lazy" slaves. Pharaoh would be shown over-powering evidence that the world has a Creator, a Parent who cares about the welfare of His oppressed children. The question is: would he ever choose to recognize it?

CHAPTER THIRTEEN

The Journey to Tomorrowland

With Pharaoh's rejection of Moses's two pleas, the stage is set for the plagues to begin. We are going to read through the Torah's recounting of the plagues, and as we do, we will pay special attention to some of the nuances we talked about earlier–the "power" and "precision" of the plagues, as well as the words the Torah uses to characterize Pharaoh's response to them: *chizuk halev* and *kibbud halev*, the "strengthening" and the "hardening" of Pharaoh's heart. We will regard "strength of heart" as a synonym for courage, and "hardness of heart" as a synonym for stubbornness.[33]

Taking stock of these various nuances will help us piece together a story hidden just under the surface of the biblical text. Let's jump in and see if we can unpack that story.

Of Staffs and Serpents

We'll begin just before the onset of the first plague. It is the first time we encounter either the "hardening" or the "strengthening" of Pharaoh's heart. Moses and Aaron meet with Pharaoh and deliver a sign to the Egyptian monarch: Aaron casts down his staff, and it instantly transforms into a serpent. Without missing a beat, the court astrologers and magicians in the company of

---

33. As we discussed in Chapter 11, *Stubbornness and Courage*.

Pharaoh cast down their own staffs. They are able to replicate the sign, through magic or sleight of hand; all their staffs turn into serpents, as well.

What is Pharaoh's response to this scene playing out in his palace? The words of the text here are instructive:

וַיֶּחֱזַק לֵב פַּרְעֹה וְלֹא שָׁמַע אֲלֵהֶם

And the heart of Pharaoh was strengthened, and he did not listen to [Moses and Aaron] (Exodus 7:13)

In the wake of his own magicians' successful replication of Moses and Aaron's sign, Pharaoh "strengthens his heart" and chooses to hold onto his slaves. The use of that term, *chizuk halev*, suggests that he fortified his resolve–he gave himself courage, as it were–which might strike us as a reasonable response, at least from Pharaoh's point of view. In light of what he's seen thus far, Pharaoh might regard Moses and Aaron as skilled magicians–but the capable response of his own magicians gives him heart, and reason to believe that they can counter whatever Moses and Aaron throw his way. Pharaoh thus "takes courage." He understands that he must steel himself for further battle against these Hebrew magicians, and increases his resolve.[34]

At this point, however, something unexpected happens. If you read the text carefully, you will notice that, in the very next line, the Torah seems to change its characterization of Pharaoh's response:

וַיֹּאמֶר יְקֹוָה אֶל־מֹשֶׁה כָּבֵד לֵב פַּרְעֹה מֵאֵן לְשַׁלַּח הָעָם:

And YHVH said to Moses: The heart of Pharaoh is hardened. He's refused to send out the People (Exodus 7:14)

---

34. It is clear in the text that Pharaoh is the one who is "strengthening" his own heart in this case. God is not involved in that decision.

God seems to misrepresent to Moses what has just happened. The text just told us that Pharaoh had strengthened his heart (*chizuk halev*), but then God Himself employs the term *kibbud halev*, suggesting that Pharaoh had *hardened* his heart, made himself stubborn. Which is it, then?

A Matter of Perspective

This little switch in language conveys something quite subtle. Whether Pharaoh's response is one of courage or stubbornness is a matter of perspective. Pharaoh thinks of himself as courageous, but God Himself sees things differently. As God expresses it to Moses, כָּבֵד לֵב פַּרְעֹה–he's made himself stubborn.

Why does God see things this way? If Pharaoh had looked at the matter carefully, he would, even at this early stage of the narrative, have seen an indication that Moses and Aaron were not mere magicians, but representatives of the one true God, the Master of all.

Right after Pharaoh's men replicate this supposed magic, something wondrous happens–and its import is unmistakable. The text doesn't make a big deal of it, so it's easy to miss the significance of what happens here. Yes, the astrologers *do* throw down their staffs and transform them into serpents, but there is a final act to that little magic show in the palace:

וַיִּבְלַע מַטֵּה־אַהֲרֹן אֶת־מַטֹּתָם:

And the staff of Aaron swallowed all the other staffs (Exodus 7:12)

You can almost picture the scene. When the king's astrologers cast down their own staffs in response to Moses and Aaron, it was a moment of high drama. The Sages of the Midrash (Exodus Rabbah 9:7) heightened that drama by suggesting that the astrologers jeered at Moses and Aaron when their staffs all turned to serpents; in the astrologers' eyes, bringing magic to Egypt was the ancient equivalent of bringing coals to Newcastle.[35] Pharaoh, at that moment, is flush with victory. He has shown these amateur magicians a thing or two. *If you've come to oppose me with magic, you're going to have to do better than that. You're playing in the big leagues here in Egypt; are you sure you have the right stuff?*

At that point, the little game of palace intrigue seems to be over. The staffs of Aaron and the astrologers revert to their original form. Everyone starts getting their coats on to go home. And then something wondrous happens. Aaron's staff, quietly and unobtrusively, swallows all the other staffs.

If one staff swallows many, what is that really saying?

Right there, at that moment, Pharaoh could have seen an indication of the bankruptcy of his polytheistic line of thought. If the one staff swallows the many, what does that say? It says that one rules over the many. All the powers of nature are ultimately answerable to one higher power, qualitatively above them all. They all answer to the Creator.

This is the incontrovertible sign we spoke about briefly earlier. It is the one and only sign God ever directed Moses to display before Pharaoh, and the reason is clear: the sign says *God is the Creator* as clearly as skywriting it into the deep blue Egyptian sky. So the message here is not hard to figure out. Pharaoh can't miss it if he's being objective. But he's *not* being objective. And that's God's point to Moses:

וַיֹּאמֶר יְקוָה אֶל־מֹשֶׁה כָּבֵד לֵב פַּרְעֹה מֵאֵן לְשַׁלַּח הָעָם:

And YHVH said to Moses: The heart of Pharaoh is hardened. He's refused to send out the people (Exodus 7:14)

---

35. In the words of the Midrash: "You're bringing straw to sell in Ephraym?" Ephraym was a city renowned for its abundant wheat harvest. Straw was so common there that it was all but valueless (*HaMedrash HaMevu'ar*).

Yes, Pharaoh might obstinately choose to see this fight as nothing more than a match of dueling magicians. He might believe that hardening his position counts as nothing more than "strengthening his resolve." But in fact, he is being stubborn. He is blinding himself to a truth he does not want to see. He is hardening his heart, not strengthening it.

Blood in the Water

Let's continue to chart the instances of *chizuk halev* (strength of heart) and *kibbud halev* (hardness of heart) as these phrases wend their way through the plagues–for indeed, the next thing that happens in the biblical narrative is the onset of the first plague. The Nile turns to blood, and the Egyptians are forced to dig wells to find drinkable water. And what is the response of the palace to this miracle? Before Pharaoh can even respond, the astrologers seize the moment. Once again, they are able to replicate the eerie phenomenon: using the magical arts or sleight of hand, they too turn water into blood. And only then does Pharaoh react:

וַיֶּחֱזַק לֵב־פַּרְעֹה וְלֹא־שָׁמַע אֲלֵהֶם

And Pharaoh's heart was strengthened, and he did not listen to [Moses and Aaron] (Exodus 7:22)

Pharaoh's heart was again "strengthened"; he sought the courage and resolve within himself to stay in the fight. Yes, on the one hand, Moses and Aaron had demonstrated something impressive–an ability to strike at the core of Egyptian infrastructure, the Nile. But on the other hand, his magicians were able to replicate that trick. *They're still magicians, those two–and no one outdoes Egypt when it comes to magic. I just need to outlast them...*

The Frogs of Tomorrowland

The next plague to strike Egypt is the plague of frogs. We talked about this plague before; Moses got into that strange dance with Pharaoh over precisely when the Egyptian king would like Moses to turn off the frogs. Moses had challenged Pharaoh:

וַיֹּאמֶר מֹשֶׁה לְפַרְעֹה הִתְפָּאֵר עָלַי לְמָתַי אַעְתִּיר לְךָ
וְלַעֲבָדֶיךָ וּלְעַמְּךָ לְהַכְרִית הַצֲפַרְדְּעִים מִמְּךָ וּמִבָּתֶּיךָ

*Glorify yourself over me: exactly when should I beseech
God, on behalf of your servants and your people, to
rid you and your houses of frogs?* (Exodus 8:5)

Moses is playing "pick a time, any time" with Pharaoh. And Pharaoh is going along with the challenge, saying "tomorrow." He opts to endure another twenty-four hours of frogs, just to see if Moses can halt the plague precisely on Pharaoh's timetable. Moses obliges, saying that it will indeed happen tomorrow, but then curiously adds:

כִּדְבָרְךָ לְמַעַן תֵּדַע כִּי־אֵין כַּיקֹוָה אֱלֹקֵינוּ:

*As you wish! So that you should know, that there is
none like YHVH, our God!* (Exodus 8:6)

We had asked earlier: why is Moses's ability to turn off the plague on cue so terribly important? Why does it become *the* most important indicator of who God is? It is as if the turning off of the plague is somehow more impressive than its miraculous onset!

As I've previously indicated, Moses is making an issue of precision. He is suggesting that God's control over the forces striking Egypt is absolute. This God of the Hebrews that Moses calls YHVH can start or stop these plagues at a moment's notice, entirely at will.

This is Pharaoh's first indication that he might be up against something more than garden-variety pagan magic. *There is a force in the world that can predict exactly when this thing is going to turn off?* That's something you don't find in the polytheistic universe. And after this plague, when Pharaoh reneges on his commitment to let his slaves go, look at the language the Torah uses to express this turn of events:

וְהַכְבֵּד אֶת־לִבּוֹ

And Pharaoh hardened his heart... (Exodus 8:11)

It's the first time the text uses that language. All of a sudden, the Torah characterizes Pharaoh's decision to hold on to his slaves as an act of stubbornness. What earlier was seen as courage is now deemed blind obstinacy. What changed?

Pharaoh has seen for the first time, in the plague of frogs, an indication that this YHVH is more than some polytheistic force. This deity is not just powerful, but completely and utterly in control, able to calibrate the cessation of the plague precisely to Pharaoh's whims. Had Pharaoh allowed the implications of this to enter his heart, he would have had to abandon the struggle; he would have had to recognize YHVH's true identity as the Heavenly Power that has no competition. But Pharaoh does not do this. He "hardens his heart," keeping the threatening evidence at arm's length. He blinds himself to the implications of what he's just seen, and continues his struggle against the God of the Hebrews. All of a sudden, Pharaoh has a new enemy. It is no longer just Moses, or even Moses's God, that Pharaoh opposes. He is now at war against the ancient and timeless enemy of all stubborn men: reality itself.

But reality is the most tenacious of foes; it has a way of piercing even the most stalwart of defenses. If Pharaoh's brush with the frogs of Tomorrowland is his first skirmish against this implacable adversary, the rest of the plagues narrative is the story of Pharaoh's last stand. We shall soon see who will be the victor.

CHAPTER FOURTEEN

Escalation

In the next plague, Pharaoh's astrologers are back—but this time they have bad news for the king. Lice is the current un-pleasantness facing Egypt: swarms are infesting both man and beast. And the astrologers, seeking to replicate the plague, find that this time they can't do it. They had managed to copy every seemingly supernatural occurrence wrought by Moses and Aaron thus far—the staff-to-serpent trick, water into blood, and even the sudden appearance of frogs—but this time, they are at a loss. Unhappily they report this news to Pharaoh, and their language in doing so is intriguing:

וַיֹּאמְרוּ הַחַרְטֻמִּם אֶל־פַּרְעֹה אֶצְבַּע אֱלֹהִים הִוא

*And the astrologers told Pharaoh: It is the
finger of 'elohim'* (Exodus 8:15)

The astrologers have concluded that it's not magic, this time. What has just happened to Egypt, they declare, is the work of heaven. But remember, in a polytheistic society such as Egypt, saying something is a manifestation of the divine is not the same thing as saying it is the work of God, as you and I know that term. Indeed, when talking to Pharaoh, the astrologers used the word *elohim*, the generic name for a divine power. They are not ratifying Moses's outrageous vision of a Creator-God. Rather, *a mere god has struck us.*

What the astrologers tell Pharaoh, then, is alarming in one sense, but comforting in another. On the one hand, this plague is more serious business than the last one. *What we've seen here, clearly, is not magic but the work of a genuine divine power.* On the other hand, it's not unmanageable. Pharaoh himself is supposedly divine as well, so this is not necessarily anything Egypt can't handle. *Let's not panic here, Sire. No reason to upset the whole theological applecart over a few supernaturally-conjured lice.*

And Pharaoh's response to the whole affair fits with that tone:

$$\text{וַיֶּחֱזַק לֵב־פַּרְעֹה וְלֹא־שָׁמַע אֲלֵהֶם}$$

And Pharaoh's heart was strengthened, and he did
not listen to [Moses and Aaron] (Exodus 8:15)

Once again, we are back to the language of *chizuk halev,* "strength of heart." Pharaoh has been told that the force he is struggling against is more powerful than he had anticipated. So he responds the way anyone confronting great power would: he grits his teeth and increases his resolve. Pharaoh strengthens his heart.

Animal Farm

A pattern seems to be developing in these plagues. They are intensifying along alternate lines: power and precision.[36] The last plague we discussed, the plague of lice, was more *powerful* in the sense that mere human sorcery was insufficient to replicate the effects of the plague. The blow was clearly the work of some force

---

36. This dual intensification creates a case for the idea that the force behind all of this is the Creator of all. Only the Creator is able to marshal perfect precision in the application of power, and only the Creator possesses the ability to marshal the nth degree of raw power. The plagues are gradually building toward these two parallel endpoints.

more powerful than mere human artifice. So that plague, lice, was an intensification along the axis of *power*. The next plague that strikes is the plague of wild animals, and it represents an intensification along the axis of *precision*:

וְהִפְלֵיתִי בַיּוֹם הַהוּא אֶת־אֶרֶץ גֹּשֶׁן אֲשֶׁר עַמִּי עֹמֵד עָלֶיהָ
לְבִלְתִּי הֱיוֹת־שָׁם עָרֹב לְמַעַן תֵּדַע כִּי אֲנִי יְקֹוָה בְּקֶרֶב הָאָרֶץ:
וְשַׂמְתִּי פְדֻת בֵּין עַמִּי וּבֵין עַמֶּךָ לְמָחָר יִהְיֶה הָאֹת הַזֶּה:

And I shall wondrously distinguish the Land of Goshen, on which My people stand, in that there will be no wild animals invading it—so that you know that I am YHVH in the midst of the land. I shall put a division between My people and your people; tomorrow, shall this sign be (Exodus 8:18–19)

To be sure, the plague of frogs had already evinced a kind of precision, in the realm of time. Pharaoh chose the time, and God shut off the plague precisely at the moment of his choosing. But this new plague, the plague of wild animals, goes beyond that: It adds into the mix precision in a new realm, the realm of space. Not only will the plague strike at a specified time—tomorrow—it will strike only in a particular place. Goshen will be spared the plague's untoward effects.

What is this increased precision intended to demonstrate? The verse doesn't leave that to your imagination. God will "wondrously distinguish" the geographical areas affected by the plague "so that you shall know that I am YHVH in the midst of the land." Precision, in time and space, is the unmistakable signature of the Master of both these realms, YHVH Himself; this plague will demonstrate that the Creator is behind what is happening.

Again, though, Pharaoh blinds himself to the implications of the plague. He is not prepared to relinquish his inflated view of himself as a god on par with the "god" against whom he struggles:

וַיַּכְבֵּד פַּרְעֹה אֶת־לִבּוֹ גַּם בַּפַּעַם הַזֹּאת וְלֹא שִׁלַּח אֶת־הָעָם:

And Pharaoh hardened his heart this time too, and
did not send out the people (Exodus 8:28)

Again, Pharaoh shields himself from the facts, continuing his
brazen battle against reality itself.

Dever: When Precision Becomes Fine-Tuned

The next plague to befall Egypt is *dever*, the death of Egyptian
livestock. But it entails something else: an escalation in the level
of precision built into the plague.

Like the last plague, the new plague of *dever* is forecast by God
to strike at a particular time:

וַיָּשֶׂם יְקֹוָה מוֹעֵד לֵאמֹר מָחָר יַעֲשֶׂה יְקֹוָה הַדָּבָר הַזֶּה בָּאָרֶץ:

God set a particular, appointed time for the plague, saying:
Tomorrow, this thing will happen (Exodus 9:5)

And, as with the last plague, the new plague of *dever* displays
precision in the realm of space—but *dever* takes spatial precision
to a previously-unseen level:

וְהִפְלָה יְקֹוָה בֵּין מִקְנֵה יִשְׂרָאֵל וּבֵין מִקְנֵה מִצְרָיִם
וְלֹא יָמוּת מִכָּל־לִבְנֵי יִשְׂרָאֵל דָּבָר:

God shall wondrously distinguish between the cattle of Israel
and the cattle of Egypt; not one [head of cattle] belonging
to the Children of Israel shall die (Exodus 9:4)

Not only will the plague distinguish between Israel and Egypt on
the macro level, affecting all geographical areas in Egypt but the
Land of Goshen. It will discriminate, sharply, at even the most
minute level. Not a single head of cattle belonging to Israel will
be affected.

As we noted earlier, this increased level of precision catches
Pharaoh's eye. More than anything else about this plague, his
attention is captured by its uncanny, knife-edged accuracy:

וַיִּשְׁלַח פַּרְעֹה וְהִנֵּה לֹא־מֵת מִמִּקְנֵה יִשְׂרָאֵל עַד־אֶחָד

And Pharaoh sent—and, behold! Not one of
Israel's animals had died! (Exodus 9:7)

It was predicted that not a single head of cattle belonging to
Israel would die, and so it was; the actual damage to Egypt paled
in comparison to this one fact. No polytheist's gods are capable
of wielding this kind of precision. Is he, Pharaoh, really doing
battle with just another god in the pantheon?

How much longer can Pharaoh insist that it is business as
usual in the freewheeling, amoral world of paganism to which
the Egyptian mind has grown accustomed? How much longer
can he insist that might makes right, that he can hold onto
his slaves if he wants to? How much longer can he continue to
pursue a policy of limited genocide against male infants, and
disregard the appeal of the god who wants this people set free?
How much longer can Pharaoh steel himself against the evidence
that is mounting against his position?

If Pharaoh is to continue to battle against this force that opposes him, his only chance is to make himself even more impervious to the facts that threaten his besieged worldview. And
indeed, this is exactly what we find in the biblical text, in the
immediate aftermath of *dever:*

וַיִּכְבַּד לֵב פַּרְעֹה וְלֹא שִׁלַּח אֶת־הָעָם:

And Pharaoh's heart was hardened, and he did
not send out the people (Exodus 9:7)

Kibbud halev, the hardening of Pharaoh's heart, takes a further,
poisonous step forward with the king's reaction to *dever.* Pharaoh

further walls himself off from reality after this fifth plague. His stubbornness becomes even more desperately entrenched.

Shechin: When Power Overwhelms

If *dever* represented an escalation in the realm of precision, the next plague constitutes an escalation in the realm of power. The sixth plague comes in the form of *shechin*, boils, which blight the skin of all Egyptians. And with this plague, the court astrologers are back. When we first met these astrologers, they coolly took the sting out of the early plagues by showing Pharaoh that they could replicate their effects. *Nothing to worry about, Sire, we've got this under control.* Later, they were the ones to dispassionately survey the effects of a plague and announce to the king that something more powerful than magic was at play. *Looks like one of the gods is angry at you, Sire.* But now, control and dispassion couldn't be further from these astrologers' minds:

וְלֹא־יָכְלוּ הַחַרְטֻמִּים לַעֲמֹד לִפְנֵי מֹשֶׁה מִפְּנֵי הַשְּׁחִין
כִּי־הָיָה הַשְּׁחִין בַּחַרְטֻמִּם וּבְכָל־מִצְרָיִם:

And the magicians could not even stand before Moses
because of the boils; for the boils were upon the magicians,
and upon all the Egyptians (Exodus 9:11)

This time, not only can't the astrologers replicate the effects of the plague, they are so overwhelmed by the boils that they can't even stand upright and pontificate about the meaning of the plagues anymore. They are reduced to simple victims of the plague, like any other Egyptian untrained in the magical arts.

Throughout the plagues, the astrologers have functioned as a barometer of a plague's raw power. The first plagues could be replicated—*no need to sweat this, Pharaoh.* The first time the astrologers could not replicate a plague, they made it known to Pharaoh that the plague was the work of a qualitatively more powerful force: *This is beyond magic; it is the purview of the gods.* And now, the effects of the sixth plague are so intense that the astrologers are no longer even able to function as astrologers.

With the power of the plagues at its apex, God enters the picture for the first time. Until now, the biblical text is very clear that Pharaoh had been the one to strengthen or harden his own heart; God had not involved Himself in the affairs of Pharaoh's heart.

Now, for the first time, that will change.

CHAPTER FIFTEEN

Hail to the King

וַיְחַזֵּק יְקֹוָה אֶת־לֵב פַּרְעֹה

And God strengthened the heart of Pharaoh (Exodus 9:12)

For the first time, during the sixth plague, God is on record as having interfered, so to speak, in the affairs of Pharaoh's heart.

Why?

Seforno's Theory in Action

Ironically, there was always a danger that the plagues would defeat their own purpose.

We mentioned this danger earlier. As the sheer force of the plagues increased, it was always possible that a given plague would simply prove to be too much for the Egyptian king. The plague's force might compel Pharaoh to throw in the towel not out of conviction but out of mere expediency. That is, Pharaoh might still hold fast to his convictions, to his right as a god to make his own rules, and to oppress and enslave Israel should he choose to. Nevertheless, he might give in simply because he was beaten down, and lacked the mental toughness and resolve to continue the struggle.

Earlier, I cited the theory of the classical commentator Seforno, who argued that if this had ever occurred over the course of the plagues, God would have intervened and lent Pharaoh the courage to persevere. And that seems to be exactly what happens in the sixth plague:

וַיְחַזֵּק יְקֹוָה אֶת־לֵב פַּרְעֹה

And God strengthened the heart of Pharaoh (Exodus 9:12)

As we saw at the close of the last chapter, the plague of boils was a new high-water mark in terms of the sheer power displayed. Evidently, that power finally broke Pharaoh. Left to his own devices, Pharaoh would have given in simply because his reservoir of courage had finally run dry.

God, however, did not wish the Egyptian king to capitulate out of mere expediency. If it was courage that Pharaoh was lacking—well, God would supply him with the courage to pursue his vision. Should Pharaoh ever actually give in on his vision, should he ever acknowledge his subservience to his Creator—that would be another matter entirely. God would surely accept a surrender on grounds of principle. But failing that, God would ensure that Pharaoh was equipped with the mental resolve to press his case to the very end. The issues at stake were too important to be decided in any other way.

His Heart Is the Battlefield

The great turning point in the plagues was the seventh plague, hail. To the casual reader, the plague of hail might seem like just the next in a series. But the Torah itself regards the plague of hail as unique among the plagues. How else are we to understand these words, which Moses is instructed to deliver to Pharaoh:

כֹּה־אָמַר יְקֹוָה אֱלֹקֵי הָעִבְרִים שַׁלַּח אֶת־עַמִּי וְיַעַבְדֻנִי: כִּי
בַּפַּעַם הַזֹּאת אֲנִי שֹׁלֵחַ אֶת־כָּל־מַגֵּפֹתַי אֶל־לִבְּךָ וּבַעֲבָדֶיךָ
וּבְעַמֶּךָ בַּעֲבוּר תֵּדַע כִּי אֵין כָּמֹנִי בְּכָל־הָאָרֶץ:

*Thus says YHVH, God of the Hebrews: Send forth My
people, that they may serve Me. For this time, I will send
all My plagues into your heart... so that you shall know
there is none like Me in all the world* (Exodus 9:13-14)

What does that mean, "I will send all My plagues into your
heart"? Evidently, this one plague is viewed as tantamount, on
its own, to all the other plagues at once.[37] Somehow, this is a
unique plague, designed to demonstrate that its architect, the
God of the Hebrews, is unique, too. For bear in mind the end
of the verse:

בַּעֲבוּר תֵּדַע כִּי אֵין כָּמֹנִי בְּכָל־הָאָרֶץ:

*...so that you shall know there is none like Me
in all the earth* (Exodus 9:14)

The text suggests that this one plague carries a message about
the oneness of God that is so overt, so utterly convincing, that
it can be seen as equivalent to all the other plagues combined.
Finally, look at how this same verse characterizes the target of
the plague, as it were. Even more than the *land* that the plague
will strike, it is designed to strike upon a more personal battlefield:

בַּפַּעַם הַזֹּאת אֲנִי שֹׁלֵחַ אֶת־כָּל־מַגֵּפֹתַי אֶל־לִבְּךָ

This time, I will send all My plagues into your heart (Exodus 9:14)

The ground to be conquered in this plague is nothing less than
Pharaoh's heart itself. For some reason, this will be the plague in
which the battle for Pharaoh's conscience is finally won or lost.

---

37. This, indeed, is Rashi's interpretation of the language here (see also
Chizkuni and *Mizrachi*, ad. loc.)

A Veiled Warning

The sense that something climactic is about to happen, that things cannot just remain the same after the coming plague, is further buttressed by an ominous warning delivered to Pharaoh just before the onset of the hail:

וְאוּלָם בַּעֲבוּר זֹאת הֶעֱמַדְתִּיךָ בַּעֲבוּר הַרְאֹתְךָ
אֶת־כֹּחִי וּלְמַעַן סַפֵּר שְׁמִי בְּכָל־הָאָרֶץ:

*And now, take pause; for it was only for this reason that I have
allowed you to stand: it was to show you My strength, so that
My name will be told of, all over the world* (Exodus 9:16)

It's as if God is addressing an unspoken question troubling the careful reader. Why has God bothered to prop Pharaoh up, to allow him to continue to oppose Him? Moreover, this is where God gives Pharaoh insight into what has really been going on. Remember, this comes right after God had propped up Pharaoh, giving him the tenacity and the strength, after the last plague, to continue to pursue his vision. Why would God do that? In a way, this is God's answer to the questions we raised at the beginning of this book: why bother with all this? Why does Pharaoh play such an important role here? Why not simply shunt him aside and deliver Israel, with or without the Egyptian king's consent?

Now, just before the plagues reach a decisive crescendo, the Almighty Himself seems to pause, and in a brief moment of stillness before the storm, addresses this very question to Pharaoh: *Let's get real, Pharaoh. Haven't you been wondering about this? Why do you think you're still alive?*

And then God gives Pharaoh the answer:

וְאוּלָם בַּעֲבוּר זֹאת הֶעֱמַדְתִּיךָ בַּעֲבוּר הַרְאֹתְךָ
אֶת־כֹּחִי וּלְמַעַן סַפֵּר שְׁמִי בְּכָל־הָאָרֶץ:

It was only for this that I've allowed you to stand: it
was to show you My strength, so that My name will
be told of, all over the world (Exodus 9:16)

God is telling the Egyptian king that there is a reason he is still
here, a reason larger than Pharaoh himself. He is part of a momentous drama—the revelation of the Creator to humankind.
And because the drama that is unfolding is in fact so much
larger than him—because, in truth, he is not really the center of
the action—there is an ominous undercurrent in God's words
to him. *Despite your evil oppression of the Israelites, you can still play*
a constructive role here. But if you choose not to play it, there are other
ways My ends can be achieved...

We had wondered earlier if there was ever a Plan C. What if, in
the end, Pharaoh never gave in? It seemed inconceivable to us that
something as important as the revelation of the Creator-God to
mankind would depend, in the final analysis, on the free-willed
recognition of one monarch and the nation he led. Yes, it would
certainly be nice if Pharaoh and Egypt would oblige, given their
sociopolitical position in the ancient world. It would be nice
if Pharaoh came to understand *why* he must release his slaves.
But what if, in the end, Pharaoh and Egypt refused to go along?

God seems to be suggesting that there is, indeed, a Plan C. If
Pharaoh and Egypt will not be willing participants in the revelation of the Creator, then they will be unwilling participants in that
drama. God would prefer that this revelation come about through
Egypt's free-willed recognition—either all at once, through a sign,
or over time, with the plagues. But if not, it will come about
through their destruction. One way or the other, the slaves will
be freed and the world will learn that there is a Creator. And one
way or the other, Pharaoh and Egypt will be the vehicles. The
only question is: will they be actors, or mere pawns? Let's read
through the events surrounding the plague of hail, and see how
this all plays out:

The Uniqueness of the Seventh Plague

The Torah seems to regard the plague of hail as utterly unique. How is that so?

Like other plagues, the plague of hail is designated to arrive at a precise time–tomorrow. By this point in the plagues, that is not unusual. But other aspects of the plague do make it unusual: first, it is the only plague that comes with a warning from God as to how the Egyptians can avoid, or at least soften, the effects of the plague:

וְעַתָּה שְׁלַח הָעֵז אֶת־מִקְנְךָ וְאֵת כָּל־אֲשֶׁר לְךָ בַּשָּׂדֶה
כָּל־הָאָדָם וְהַבְּהֵמָה אֲשֶׁר־יִמָּצֵא בַשָּׂדֶה וְלֹא יֵאָסֵף
הַבַּיְתָה וְיָרַד עֲלֵהֶם הַבָּרָד וָמֵתוּ:

Now therefore send, quickly bring in your cattle and all that
you have in the field; for every man and beast that shall be
found in the field, and shall not be brought inside a house–the
hail shall fall upon them, and they shall die (Exodus 9:19)

A second characteristic of this plague also distinguishes it from any previous plague. As we noted earlier, fire was actually frozen into the hailstones:

וַיְהִי בָרָד וְאֵשׁ מִתְלַקַּחַת בְּתוֹךְ הַבָּרָד

And there was hail–and fire encased inside the hail (Exodus 9:24)[38]

When we get down to the granular level, it seems that this plague's uniqueness is expressed by these two special qualities: the warning, and the fire and ice living side by side in the same hailstones.

Let's talk about the warning first. Doesn't it seem a bit odd that God would warn His adversary about how to escape the

---

38. Translation here follows Saadiah Ga'on; see also Exodus Rabbah 12:4.

effects of the strike about to come his way? If I am truly at war with you, why would I reveal to you, my enemy, how you could save yourself from the blow I am about to deliver?

The very issuance of that warning sends a message.

When in modern warfare do you find nations warning their foes before striking? You might warn them when you possess overwhelming force, when your power so vastly outstrips your enemy's that it simply doesn't matter anymore. Or you might warn them when you are possessed of a sense of compassion for your foe even as you fight them; when you sense the tragedy of the useless loss of human life that will be brought about if your enemy blindly and stubbornly insists on further resistance. In the face of such an unequal battle, a refined sense of compassion dictates that I reveal to you, my enemy, how to avoid the worst of what is about to befall you.

God warned Egypt before the hail. God told them how to survive it. The message was clear: *You may have made yourselves into My enemy, but this not a battle of equals. Here's what you can do to survive...* A power so assured of victory that it can afford to warn its enemy? A divine power that has compassion for its foe? If you are Pharaoh listening to this warning, this doesn't sound at all like a pagan god addressing its enemy. A Creator-God might have compassion for a rebellious child, but not a polytheistic divinity. Not a mere force of nature.

And now let's talk about fire and ice in the same hailstone. As we mentioned earlier, that, too, makes absolutely no sense in a polytheistic universe. The fire and ice gods are mortal enemies. They extinguish one another; an alliance between them is impossible. Only one Being would conceivably have the authority to force cooperation between fire and ice: the God who created both of them.

Fire, Ice, and the Genesis of Morality

What is Pharaoh's response to these unprecedented qualities of the plague of hail? Here is the language of the verse:

וַיִּשְׁלַח פַּרְעֹה וַיִּקְרָא לְמֹשֶׁה וּלְאַהֲרֹן וַיֹּאמֶר אֲלֵהֶם
חָטָאתִי הַפָּעַם יְקֹוָה הַצַּדִּיק וַאֲנִי וְעַמִּי הָרְשָׁעִים:

*And Pharaoh sent and called to Moses and Aaron and said
to them: I have sinned this time. YHVH is the righteous One,
and my people and I are the wicked ones* (Exodus 9:27)

This talk of sin, of who is righteous and who is wicked–this is *moral* language. It is the first time Pharaoh has used language like this. Pharaoh is convinced here, for the very first time, that he's been in the wrong all along. This is the first time Pharaoh has ever seen his conflict with God in these terms, and we are now in a position to understand why.

You don't "sin" against a pagan power. You don't owe anything to such a power; your reason for appeasing it is blind self-interest. You only sin against your Creator, your Parent in Heaven, against whom you've rebelled. Finally, all the hardness of heart, all his desperate efforts to avoid recognizing that he, Pharaoh, is subject to his Creator–are all washed away. Pharaoh finally gets it. *YHVH, the Creator-God, has been in the right this whole time–and my people and I, who have been enslaving the Hebrews in defiance of our Creator's will–we have been the wicked ones.*

At long last, Pharaoh has recognized his Creator, and has accepted the implications that follow from this. Pharaoh has pulled himself back from the brink of the abyss. The hope of having Pharaoh recognize his Creator and respond to His wishes has finally been fulfilled.

Or has it?

Why Isn't the Story Over?

If it's all over at this point, everyone should live happily ever after. Israel should be packing their suitcases for an exciting and long-awaited trip into the desert, and Egypt should be standing by, helping the former slaves carry their bags to the nearest waiting camel. But that's not how the story ends. No Egyptians provide valet services. No Israelites pack their bags. Indeed, we have reached only the seventh plague; three more plagues are yet to come.

Why? Why doesn't this fairy tale have a happy ending?

That's what we must figure out next.

CHAPTER SIXTEEN

The Desecration of Remorse

Immediately after the plague of hail, Pharaoh does something that seems altogether ordinary and unremarkable. He changes his mind:

וַיַּרְא פַּרְעֹה כִּי־חָדַל הַמָּטָר וְהַבָּרָד וְהַקֹּלֹת
וַיֹּסֶף לַחֲטֹא וַיַּכְבֵּד לִבּוֹ הוּא וַעֲבָדָיו:

*When Pharaoh saw that the rain, the hail and the thunders
had ceased—he continued to sin, and he hardened
his heart, he and his servants* (Exodus 9:34)

Now, Pharaoh is *always* changing his mind; that's nothing new. By now, the cycle has become almost tiresome: a plague descends upon Egypt, Pharaoh summons Moses and promises to let his slaves go—and when the plague is lifted, Pharaoh reneges on his promise. That's how it always goes. And yet, after the plague of hail, when Pharaoh hardens his heart *this* time, it's completely different. It is a tipping point in the whole Exodus story. Things will never be the same.

The biblical text itself makes this evident. The verse above not only tells us that Pharaoh reneges after the hail, it also editorializes a bit; it calls Pharaoh's reversal a *sin*. Although Pharaoh has said earlier that he sinned, the text has never before characterized Pharaoh's change of mind that way. Why, all of a sudden, does the Bible view Pharaoh's actions as "sinful"? What's changed?

Pharaoh had never yet *consciously* recognized a moral force to which he was subject; he had never consciously recognized the existence of a Creator. Whenever he had previously hardened his heart, he was dogmatically reaffirming his polytheistic view of the world and his own place in it. In essence, he was ignoring all evidence that militated against his beliefs. But ignoring evidence is a *subconscious* act of resistance. Humans can do this without really being aware of it—and thus, it can't really be called a sin. It is not an overt act of evil.

All that changes after the plague of hail. In the seventh plague, the facts finally break through Pharaoh's copious defenses. He is no longer able to ignore the evidence. He finally acknowledges, fully and consciously, the existence of YHVH, and the notion that he is duty bound to rise to this Creator's expectations. He understands that continuing to enslave the Hebrews against the will of the Creator is morally wrong.

Having made this acknowledgment, there is no going back for Pharaoh. There is no way for him to unsee what he has seen. So when Pharaoh hardens his heart this time, after he has already accepted the reality of this Creator-God—he is doing something very different than before. He is engaging in a conscious act of rebellion against the Creator. He is saying, in effect: *I know there is a Creator, that I am duty bound to listen to Him, and I know what He wants from me. But I just don't care. I'm keeping my slaves anyway.* When Pharaoh reneges now, after the hail, he is not keeping the facts at bay; he is taking things he knows to be true and throwing them out, as it were, onto the sidewalk.

This is nothing less than a defilement of the truth. It is a free-willed and conscious act of evil. It is a true sin.[39]

---

39. It is not coincidental, I think, that the biblical narrator calls Pharaoh's change of mind a *sin* (Exodus 9:34) just after Pharaoh uses this very word to express his remorse for having kept hold of his slaves (it was during the plague of hail that Pharaoh first called his own actions sinful; see

Courage in the Service of Blindness

When Pharaoh hardens his heart after the plague of hail, Pharaoh does something else; according to the text, he also strengthens his heart. This is the first time that the text has used both key phrases at once—*kibbud halev* and *chizuk halev*—to describe Pharaoh's state of mind:

וַיַּרְא פַּרְעֹה כִּי־חָדַל הַמָּטָר וְהַבָּרָד וְהַקֹּלֹת וַיֹּסֶף לַחֲטֹא וַיַּכְבֵּד
לִבּוֹ הוּא וַעֲבָדָיו: וַיֶּחֱזַק לֵב פַּרְעֹה וְלֹא שִׁלַּח אֶת־בְּנֵי יִשְׂרָאֵל

When Pharaoh saw that the rain, the hail and the thunders had ceased—he continued to sin, and he hardened his heart, he and his servants. And Pharaoh's heart became strengthened, and he did not send out the Children of Israel (Exodus 9:34–35)

Having made the fateful decision to rebel outright against the wishes of his Creator, Pharaoh strengthens his mental resolve for the coming battle. Gathering whatever reserves of courage he can summon, he pursues a path of willful, self-imposed blindness to the truth. Pharaoh does all of this entirely of his own choosing, and these choices dash to pieces any hope that Pharaoh will, on his own, release the Hebrews in conscious submission to the Creator's will.

Pharaoh has now shown himself to be incorrigible. Having fleetingly recognized things as they truly are, he has now spitefully backtracked on that recognition. Having briefly expressed genuine remorse for his defiance of God and oppression of the

---

Exodus 9:27). It makes perfect sense, really: only after Pharaoh himself is willing to use the word *sin* to characterize his own actions, is the biblical narrator willing to use that word. Only after the king himself views himself as morally subject to God's will is it a moral failure for Pharaoh to renege and continue to defy God.

Hebrews, he has now desecrated that remorse. And remorse, once desecrated, does not bear the indignity kindly.

Pharaoh will again, later in the plagues, confess his sin, but that confession will ring hollow. Remorse is a noble and sublime product of the free and unfettered human will. Once you cynically mock it, it doesn't come easily anymore. And so it is with Pharaoh. He will never again see the truth of things as clearly as he does now. His actions in the wake of the seventh plague are fateful: he has started down a path that will be difficult, if not impossible, to depart from. In the great drama of the Exodus, he has chosen, in effect, no longer to be an actor, but a pawn.

Plan C

Thus, it is here, at this moment, that what we earlier called Plan C begins. It starts with the very next words of the biblical text:

וַיֹּאמֶר יְקוָה אֶל־מֹשֶׁה בֹּא אֶל־פַּרְעֹה כִּי־אֲנִי הִכְבַּדְתִּי אֶת־לִבּוֹ וְאֶת־לֵב עֲבָדָיו לְמַעַן שִׁתִי אֹתֹתַי אֵלֶּה בְּקִרְבּוֹ: וּלְמַעַן תְּסַפֵּר בְּאָזְנֵי בִנְךָ וּבֶן־בִּנְךָ אֵת אֲשֶׁר הִתְעַלַּלְתִּי בְּמִצְרַיִם וְאֶת־אֹתֹתַי אֲשֶׁר־שַׂמְתִּי בָם וִידַעְתֶּם כִּי־אֲנִי יְקוָה:

And YHVH said to Moses: Go to Pharaoh—for I have hardened his heart, and the heart of his servants, that I might establish My signs in the midst of them. And so that you will be able to tell your children, and your children's children, how I played with Egypt, and My signs which I have done among them. [I have done this] so that you will know that I am YHVH. (Exodus 10:1–2)

We have never before seen language like this. The entire divine plan has evidently changed course. No longer do we hear the idea, so ubiquitous until this point, that the coming plagues will arrive so that *Egypt* will know that YHVH is God. No, the object is different now. The plagues will continue, to be sure, and they will continue to demonstrate the truth of the Creator-God.

But Egypt and Pharaoh are no longer their intended audience. Instead, all this will happen…

וִידַעְתֶּם כִּי־אֲנִי יְקוָה:

*…so that **you** will know that I am YHVH* (Exodus 10:2)

Israel is the intended audience now. Pharaoh and Egypt may never recognize God, but Israel will. The Israelite slaves who are the beneficiaries of the Exodus process will see in that process unmistakable evidence of the Master's complete dominion.

Not only will they see evidence of God's dominion over nature, they will also see God's dominion over the world of human affairs. In the final plagues, and at the climactic battle at the Sea of Reeds, Israel will witness God's complete and total domination of the greatest, most powerful empire known to mankind. Egypt will still be a vehicle for knowledge of the Almighty to come into the world—but now that knowledge will come not through Egypt's free-willed actions, but its utter destruction. Pharaoh will now be a pawn in the process, not an actor. He will be used for the Almighty's own ends.

The military defeat of the Egyptians on behalf of a band of defenseless slaves shall stand as eternal testimony to the existence of the Creator. What Israel will witness, in the assault that brings them their freedom, is not a battle of equals, where one side squeezes out a victory over the other. No. God tells Moses that they will see something else entirely:

תְּסַפֵּר בְּאָזְנֵי בִנְךָ וּבֶן־בִּנְךָ אֵת אֲשֶׁר הִתְעַלַּלְתִּי בְּמִצְרַיִם

*You will be able to tell your children, and your children's children, **how I played with Egypt*** (Exodus 10:2)

In the final three plagues, Israel will see God toy with Egypt. The greatest military power in the world will seem as if it were a mere plaything in the hands of its Heavenly Foe. Egypt will crumble without its human adversary, Israel, lifting so much as a finger against it. The forces of nature, at the behest of their Creator, shall conspire to shatter the oppressor.

Toying with Pharaoh

But how will this take place? How will God ensure that Pharaoh stays in the game until the bitter end, until his own forces are demolished?

One easy way would be simply to deprive Pharaoh of choice. God could tamper with Pharaoh's free will and compel the Egyptian leader to remain recalcitrant in the face of plague after plague, until his final destruction is complete.

That, however, would be rather unfair, wouldn't it? In any case, it would be far from elegant. No, the Master of the Universe is capable of better than that. Pharaoh's days of foiling God's designs for the Exodus, of forcing detours in the divine plan, are over. This time, the Almighty will be able to count on Pharaoh to comply perfectly with His wishes. Pharaoh will have full and unconstrained free will until the very end–and yet God will see to it that Pharaoh endlessly pursues his lost cause. Indeed, of all the ways in which God "plays" with Pharaoh in the final plagues, this is perhaps the most exquisite.

CHAPTER SEVENTEEN

Pharaoh's Last Refuge

How did Pharaoh look himself in the mirror in the morning, after having turned his back on his clear-eyed realization that God was, in fact, the Creator? After the plague of hail, Pharaoh took refuge in his own stubbornness.

It was, in a way, his last bastion, the last tool with which he could resist the Almighty. If the evidence for the Creator's existence was too powerful to argue against, it could still be ignored outright by a sheer act of will. To do this was irrational, to be sure, but since when is that an insurmountable problem? Pharaoh could simply declare to himself that the facts no longer mattered, that they were a mere distraction. If you doubt people's ability to do this, just look at politicians who declare, in the face of a sure loss, that they don't believe the polls. Reality becomes just another enemy to be managed, and what better weapon to combat it than bullheadedness?

In his own mind, then, Pharaoh would now enthrone stubbornness as a virtue. What you and I would see as blindness to reality, Pharaoh embraced as a damn-the-torpedoes kind of bravery. Stubbornness in the face of all comers, even the facts, would be his final refuge. His own hardened heart would become his fortress.

When a Fortress Becomes a Prison

Stubbornness, though, is a fickle friend. It can swiftly be turned
against you, as Pharaoh will soon learn. In the final three plagues,
the Almighty transforms Pharaoh's fortress into a prison.

God declares His intention to do this in a verse we cited at the
end of the last chapter, one that lays out the transition to what
we've been calling Plan C. Let's analyze it carefully.

וַיֹּאמֶר יְקוָה אֶל־מֹשֶׁה בֹּא אֶל־פַּרְעֹה כִּי־אֲנִי הִכְבַּדְתִּי אֶת־לִבּוֹ

And YHVH said to Moses: Go to Pharaoh—for I
have hardened his heart (Exodus 10:1)

The tricky part here is that the verse places responsibility upon
God for the hardening of Pharaoh's heart, which seems to flat-
out contradict what earlier verses told us. Remember, right before this, the text had been very clear that it was Pharaoh, not
God, who both "hardened" and "strengthened" his heart in the
aftermath of the plague of hail. So why would God now take
responsibility for doing that? Didn't Pharaoh adopt his attitude
of stubbornness all by himself? Which set of verses is accurate,
the first or the second?

The answer seems to be: both. They are each half of a composite picture. Pharaoh decided to adopt an attitude of stubbornness,
and God took advantage of that attitude, playing on it to further
increase Pharaoh's recalcitrance. And there was poetic justice in
this: Pharaoh thought his stubbornness a refuge, a last bastion
of strength. Pharaoh was wrong, though. Denial of reality is
never a strength; it is always a weakness. So God exploited that
vulnerability, carefully corralling Pharaoh's own bullheadedness
into the force that would bring about his ruin. To explain:

Natural, or Supernatural?

When the text says that God made Pharaoh's heart stubborn (Exodus 10:1), you and I tend to think of a supernatural occurrence. We think of God as using some sort of divine, supernatural power as a kind of underhanded weapon against Pharaoh's psyche, getting into his mind and changing it. But perhaps that's not the case. Maybe God was making use of an entirely *natural* process to influence Pharaoh. Maybe God was using Pharaoh's own stubbornness against him as a weapon that would force the Egyptian king deeper and deeper into a prison of his own making. How, exactly, did it work?

וַיָּבֹא מֹשֶׁה וְאַהֲרֹן אֶל־פַּרְעֹה וַיֹּאמְרוּ אֵלָיו כֹּה־אָמַר יְקֹוָה אֱלֹהֵי
הָעִבְרִים עַד־מָתַי מֵאַנְתָּ לֵעָנֹת מִפָּנָי שַׁלַּח עַמִּי וְיַעַבְדֻנִי׃

And Moses and Aaron came to Pharaoh and said to him: Thus says YHVH, the God of the Hebrews, 'How long will you withhold yourself from bowing in submission before Me? Send out my people that they may serve Me!' (Exodus 10:3)

How remarkable these words are. Moses and Aaron have never spoken to Pharaoh with this kind of audacity before. "How long will you withhold yourself from bowing in submission to Me?" Who talks that way to the King of Egypt? It is hard to convey in English just how provocative these words really are. I've translated the Hebrew word *le'anot* here as "bow in submission." But to put that in context, keep in mind that the verb here, *'-n-h* (ענה), appearing as it does in its *pi'el* form, is the classic Hebrew term for "enslavement" or "oppression." It is, in fact, the precise term the Torah used earlier to describe the Egyptian subjugation of Israel.[40] The use of the term again, now, is wryly ironic. The

---

40. See Exodus 1:11, וַיָּשִׂימוּ עָלָיו שָׂרֵי מִסִּים לְמַעַן עַנֹּתוֹ בְּסִבְלֹתָם, "they set over them taskmasters to oppress them with their burdens."

biblical text has the flavor of something like this: *Pharaoh, you have brutally subjugated My people, stripping them of their dignity—and now you will pay for that by subjugating yourself to Me, and being stripped of your own dignity.*

Talking like that to the most powerful sovereign in the ancient world is chutzpah in the extreme. What is Moses up to here? It would seem to be counterproductive. Why would you want to antagonize the Egyptian leader? You think Pharaoh is going to give in to you when you talk like that? Of course he won't!

But maybe that's the whole point.

God has declared that he would "harden Pharaoh's heart" (Exodus 10:1), and this is exactly how He is going about it. In Plan C, God has a secret weapon. It is nothing fancy, nothing supernatural; the secret weapon is Pharaoh's own pride, the root cause of his stubbornness.

Poetic Justice

Indeed, why *didn't* Pharaoh agree to release the slaves after the seventh plague? There seemed every reason to do so. Pharaoh had come to the difficult realization that he is the created and God the Creator. He admitted that he and his people had been wicked. So why, after those breathtaking admissions, did he move away from what he now understood to be true? Why lapse into a stubborn refusal to accept what you already know? The answer can be summarized in one word: pride.

Pharaoh was the absolute power in Egypt. For someone like him, a self-styled deity in the pantheon of gods, to concede that he is nothing of the sort, but a created being in service to his Creator—*that's a real step down.* So yes, Pharaoh had made that acknowledgment. But what keeps him from sticking to it is pride, his own hopelessly inflated sense of self.

From this point forward, this very pride will become God's primary target. God will find ways to play upon Pharaoh's arrogance, forcing him into one corner after another. From the seventh plague onward, Pharaoh will be deprived of the chance to give in, simply because his own sense of self will not let him do it. Stubbornness shall now yield even more stubbornness. Pride will keep Pharaoh in the fight, even as his imminent destruction looms. His ego will be his undoing.

Locusts: the Purveyors of Economic Doom

So let's pick up the trail. Moses and Aaron have just made this outrageous demand of Pharaoh: *Why don't you just get it over with and bow in abject submission before God, already? Why continue wasting everyone's time?* Now look at the rest of the verse. These are their very next words:

כִּי אִם־מָאֵן אַתָּה לְשַׁלֵּחַ אֶת־עַמִּי הִנְנִי מֵבִיא מָחָר
אַרְבֶּה בִּגְבֻלֶךָ: וְכִסָּה אֶת־עֵין הָאָרֶץ וְלֹא יוּכַל לִרְאֹת
אֶת־הָאָרֶץ וְאָכַל אֶת־יֶתֶר הַפְּלֵטָה הַנִּשְׁאֶרֶת לָכֶם מִן־הַבָּרָד
וְאָכַל אֶת־כָּל־הָעֵץ הַצֹּמֵחַ לָכֶם מִן־הַשָּׂדֶה:

If you indeed refuse to send out My people, I shall hereby bring locusts, tomorrow, into your realm. They shall utterly cover the earth, such that you won't even be able to see the ground. They will devour whatever has been left over for you that has survived the hail. They will eat all [the produce of] the trees, and that which the fields grow (Exodus 10:4–5)

The locusts will eat every shred of remaining produce, every last crop. The hail had wiped out much of the harvest, but the locusts would get the rest. Egypt was an agrarian society, the breadbasket of the ancient world. In the times of Joseph, they had sustained all the other nations with their abundance of grain. But locusts, swarming over the earth so that you couldn't even see the ground? Starvation would become a real possibility. Locusts are the economic nuclear option.

Immediately after delivering the news, the text tells us that Moses and Aaron simply turned around and left (Exodus 10:6). And what happens? As we might now expect, the threat of these locusts does not cause Pharaoh to back down. Moses had primed the Egyptian king to reject his ultimatum, and he walked right into the trap. Had Moses first told Pharaoh and his court about the locusts, and then given the king a chance to respond, saving any provocative talk for later, perhaps Pharaoh would have taken the opportunity to think things over rationally, and surrendered. But by the time Pharaoh hears about the locusts, his blood is boiling at being addressed so outlandishly by these representatives of his lowly slaves. He's not going to back down, now.

A Word from Pharaoh's Servants

It is at this point, according to the Torah, that Pharaoh's servants get into the act. This is the first time we hear them speak up and address their king:

וַיֹּאמְרוּ עַבְדֵי פַרְעֹה אֵלָיו עַד־מָתַי יִהְיֶה זֶה לָנוּ
לְמוֹקֵשׁ שַׁלַּח אֶת־הָאֲנָשִׁים וְיַעַבְדוּ אֶת־יְקֹוָה
אֱלֹקֵיהֶם הֲטֶרֶם תֵּדַע כִּי אָבְדָה מִצְרָיִם:

And Pharaoh's servants said to him: For how long shall this man be a snare for us? Let the men go, that they may serve YHVH their God. Do you not yet know that Egypt is destroyed? (Exodus 10:7)

Pharaoh's servants are quite able to see the truth of the matter. They understand that Egypt is on its last legs, that an attack of locusts would be devastating, and might well push the populace to its breaking point. But they understand something else, too: in describing Moses as a "snare" (or a "trap," depending on how you translate the Hebrew term *mokesh*), they seem to intuit that

Moses is laying an ambush for them.[41] And in this, of course, they are correct. It *is* a trap. But will they be able to persuade their master to resist taking the bait?

The servants are unable to effect a direct change in the policy of Pharaoh's administration. To listen to them outright would certainly be too humiliating for the monarch. Nevertheless, with the servants' willingness to raise their voices against their master, a milestone has been reached. The absolute political power that Pharaoh has enjoyed until now is slowly slipping from his grasp. His own servants are now at odds with him.

This new tension in the palace explains what happens next:

וַיּוּשַׁב אֶת־מֹשֶׁה וְאֶת־אַהֲרֹן אֶל־פַּרְעֹה וַיֹּאמֶר אֲלֵהֶם
לְכוּ עִבְדוּ אֶת־יְקֹוָה אֱלֹקֵיכֶם מִי וָמִי הַהֹלְכִים:

And Moses and Aaron were returned to Pharaoh, and
[the king] said to them: Go serve YHVH your God.
Exactly who will be the ones going? (Exodus 10:8)

The Hebrew *vayushav* (וַיּוּשַׁב) is an unusual passive conjugation of the verb "to bring back." It suggests that Moses and Aaron were "brought back" to the palace court, but it doesn't say who brought them. Who *are* these anonymous people who return Moses and Aaron to the royal court? It almost seems as if they are intent on hiding their identities, and the text obliges them by not revealing to us, the readers, who they are.

Seemingly, it was the servants. After being rebuffed by Pharaoh, it seems that some anonymous servants quietly set off in search of Moses and Aaron. Evidently, they caught up with Moses and Aaron, and hastily returned them to Pharaoh. The servants are desperately trying to broker a deal; they do have *some* power, if only covert power. Pharaoh may have resisted their advice, but

---

41. See *Targum Yonatan* and *Kli Yakar*; cf. *Bechor Shor* and *Abravanel*.

he can't shut them out of the process completely; they are a force he must, in some way, contend with. And so, with Moses and Aaron once again before him, and his disgruntled servants standing off in the shadows, it seems that Pharaoh is finally ready for a concession—a grudging one, to be sure, but a concession nonetheless: *You can go serve your God. But tell me, who exactly do you want to go?*

The Fig Leaf

Pharaoh's question implicitly offers a way out of the impasse. All Moses has to do is tell Pharaoh what he wants to hear, and this can all be over. Pharaoh is looking for a face-saving solution to this slavery crisis, a fig leaf of sorts. And Moses can give it to him, right here, right now.

At this point, if you're Moses, what do you say? Two hundred and ten years of slavery can come to an end immediately, if you give the right answer. All you have to do is say is something like this: *I don't know, Pharaoh, exactly who is going. Maybe we can leave behind some cattle or something. Would that work for you?* If Moses says that, we have a deal on our hands. Pharaoh can save face, Moses and the people can leave, and everyone can go home happy.

So what, in fact, happens? Here is Moses's *actual* reply:

וַיֹּאמֶר מֹשֶׁה בִּנְעָרֵינוּ וּבִזְקֵנֵינוּ נֵלֵךְ בְּבָנֵינוּ וּבִבְנוֹתֵנוּ
בְּצֹאנֵנוּ וּבִבְקָרֵנוּ נֵלֵךְ כִּי חַג־יְקֹוָה לָנוּ:

And Moses said: With our young and our old we will go. With our sons and with our daughters, with our flocks and our cattle, we will go. After all, it is a holiday to YHVH for us! (Exodus 10:9)

Moses's reply seems tone-deaf. *We're taking everybody, Pharaoh—even Sally's pet sheep, and Bobby's lizard. How could we leave anyone behind? What kind of celebration would it be without every last person—even the pets?*

No fig leaf, there.

Of course, Moses is anything but tone-deaf. It is all part of a coherent strategy: Pharaoh will not be getting any olive branches. God will not let him off the hook with any face-saving measures. Pharaoh can give in if he wants, but he is not going to be able to salvage his pride.

Pharaoh dismisses Moses's demand, and has Moses expelled from the palace (Exodus 10:11). And the locusts come.

No Hoof Left Behind

By the time the next plague—darkness—arrives, Pharaoh is ready to negotiate again. He summons Moses back to the palace with a new proposal:

לְכוּ עִבְדוּ אֶת־יְקוָה רַק צֹאנְכֶם וּבְקַרְכֶם יֻצָּג גַּם־טַפְּכֶם יֵלֵךְ עִמָּכֶם:

Go and serve YHVH. Just leave behind your flocks and your cattle. Your children can also go with you (Exodus 10:24)

Pharaoh offers new ground here: Everyone can go—just leave some cattle behind. In saying this, Pharaoh's desperation is evident. Last time around, he had merely hinted that he was looking for a face-saving concession; this time, he is overt about it. *Just give me something here—leave some cattle behind, and we can call it a day...*

Pharaoh's new offer is the scantest of fig leaves for the Egyptian monarch. And what is Moses's response to it? Not only does he refuse the offer, he ratchets up his demands. Here's the language of the text:

וַיֹּאמֶר מֹשֶׁה גַּם־אַתָּה תִּתֵּן בְּיָדֵנוּ זְבָחִים וְעֹלוֹת וְעָשִׂינוּ לַיקוָה אֱלֹהֵינוּ:
וְגַם־מִקְנֵנוּ יֵלֵךְ עִמָּנוּ לֹא תִשָּׁאֵר פַּרְסָה כִּי מִמֶּנּוּ נִקַּח לַעֲבֹד אֶת־יְקוָה
אֱלֹקֵינוּ וַאֲנַחְנוּ לֹא־נֵדַע מַה־נַּעֲבֹד אֶת־יְקוָה עַד־בֹּאֵנוּ שָׁמָּה:

You, too, [Pharaoh], will give us animals for offerings, that
we will offer to YHVH our God. And our cattle will go with
us. We will not leave a hoof behind! For we will take from that
cattle offerings to serve YHVH our God. And we don't know
what we will offer until we get there! (Exodus 10:25–26)

Moses's response seems purposely provocative. *Actually, Pharaoh,*
thanks for bringing up the cattle. We're going to be taking all of it. And
speaking of cattle, you need to provide us with even more—because we
may not have enough on our own. Moses's tone-deafness is not
accidental. If Pharaoh is going to avoid destruction, at this point,
he will have to sacrifice his pride. This, however, is not something
he will do. Having made a fortress of his own hardened heart,
Pharaoh is not likely to abandon it, even in the face of certain
destruction.

All in all, we might say this about God's involvement in
Pharaoh's recalcitrance: in the end, it appears that God really
did harden Pharaoh's heart. But there was nothing supernatural
about the process. Pharaoh had free will to the bitter end. His
pride just didn't let him use it.

Pharaoh and Moses at the Brink

Let us return to Moses and Pharaoh at the palace. Moses, in demanding that Egypt contribute cattle to facilitate the offerings
of the departing Israelites, seems to make a mockery of Pharaoh's
position, and the Egyptian king is not amused. Pharaoh, in anger,
calls an end to negotiations, and demands that Moses exit his
presence—permanently. "Watch yourself," he tells Moses, "Don't
see my face ever again; for on the day you see my face, you will
die" (Exodus 10:28).

Moses accepts the king's demand. He turns to tell him:

כֵּן דִּבַּרְתָּ לֹא־אֹסִף עוֹד רְאוֹת פָּנֶיךָ:

You have spoken well; I will see your face
again no more (Exodus 10:29)

Just then, as Moses starts to walk away, God appears to Moses, and has him deliver one last message to Pharaoh. Moses turns to the Egyptian tyrant and explains what God has told him. There will be yet one last plague. It will happen this very night, at midnight: all firstborn in Egypt shall die.

Strangely, though, this plague will be different than all the rest.

In all the prior plagues, the Children of Israel were automatically shielded from the effects of the plague. For example, when the Egyptian livestock were struck, animals belonging to Israelites were automatically unaffected (Exodus 9:4). The same with darkness—the plague attacked only the Egyptians, not the Israelites (Exodus 10:23). Until now, the Israelites have had diplomatic immunity from the plagues, as if they are driving around with United Nations license plates and couldn't be ticketed. But suddenly, when the tenth plague rolls around, the Children of Israel are no longer granted this automatic immunity. We are led to believe that Israelite firstborn will perish along with Egyptian firstborn unless the Israelites *do something*. They need to bring a special offering known as *Korban Pesach,* the "Pesach offering," and place blood from this offering on the doorposts of their homes.

But why would that be necessary?

The Pesach Offering

The answer to the question of why the Israelite firstborn were vulnerable that night is bound up with some issues we raised at the very beginning of this book. Having seen the progression of Plans A, B, and C throughout the development of the plagues, we are now, at last, in a position to revisit those themes. We had noticed that the *bechor* motif is strangely prominent; it shows up in the way the Torah memorializes the Exodus, in the name we give to our holiday of freedom (Passover), and even in the way we think of chosenness itself.

Why?

CHAPTER EIGHTEEN

Birth Night

Early in the Exodus narrative, God gives a strange appellation to the People of Israel. He refers to them as His *bechor*, His firstborn child. Specifically, God informs Pharaoh, even before the first of the plagues strike, that he must release God's *bechor*, and if he fails to do so, God will ultimately strike Pharaoh's firstborn in retaliation. Back in the introduction to this book, we posed some questions about the logic behind that comparison: in what sense is Israel to be regarded as God's bechor? Why, how—and when, for that matter—did they receive such a designation?

I'd like to suggest a theory to you. This peculiar *bechor* status of Israel that God mentioned before the plagues even began—maybe it was not something preexisting, but a hope for Israel's destiny; maybe, in the end, it would be something Israel had to earn. When? At the culminating moment of the Exodus—at the other moment God had spoken about, when he spoke of Israel this way. God had said: "Israel is My firstborn child... and if you [Pharaoh] fail to set him free, I will strike your firstborn." Maybe it was the moment all firstborn were threatened—the tenth plague—that God "took possession" of Israel as His own "firstborn."

What God was really telling Pharaoh was this: there would come a time when God would kill all *bechorot* in Egypt except His own. If you made the choice, that night, to become God's *bechor*, the *bechor* of the Transcendent Parent, you would survive. If you were the *bechor* only of an earthly parent, you would perish.

If Israel achieved that designation the night they went free, it would seem that they achieved it through the *Korban Pesach,* the Pesach Offering. Somehow, that offering was transformative. After all, God didn't need blood on the doorposts to distinguish Egyptian houses from Israelite ones. God wasn't missing a good GPS device. No, the *Korban Pesach* actually *did* something: it transformed the people from a band of slaves into an independent nation committed to God in a certain, special way–a way that could best be described through the designation *bechor.*

What exactly are we to make of that designation? What does it mean to be the bechor of the Almighty, and how would *Korban Pesach* be a key to effecting this transformation?

Transition Point

Let's pull back the zoom lens for a moment for some perspective on these questions.

Looking back at the miraculous events of the Exodus as a whole, we can now see that these events were designed to achieve two purposes: they would free Israel, and demonstrate the existence of a Creator. Now, ask yourself this: if your national existence was birthed through events of such magnitude and moment, would you be able to separate your own, national freedom from the meaning of the miraculous events that gifted that freedom to you? Would it even be right to separate the two?

If God demonstrated Himself as Creator by bringing you out of bondage and making you free, you would want to dedicate that gift of freedom back to the Creator in some way. But how could you do that? What could you possibly do for the Creator that He couldn't do for Himself? The *Korban Pesach* was the beginning of Israel's attempt to answer that question. It suggested a willingness on the part of Israel to do something deeply personal for the Creator, to play a special role within God's "family"–a role that helps bind the family together. It suggested their willingness to be God's *bechor,* his "firstborn child."

The Family Dynamics of Monotheism

We don't often think of humanity as comprising God's family, but if God is Creator and we are His children, then a family is exactly what we are—but what good is a family if the children don't know they are a part of it? We talked earlier about the tragedy of a child who relates to his parent as a mere power. The adult in the house is, in the child's mind, someone who restricts his access to the cookie jar, but whose concern for the welfare of the child doesn't go beyond that. That child's situation is tragic because not only does he fail to understand his connection to his parent, he fails to understand that he is part of a family. He estranges himself not just from his parent, but from his brothers and sisters, too.

The audacious idea of monotheism is that we humans have a Heavenly Parent, and consequently, we are all brothers and sisters: members, as it were, of a grand "divine family." The so-called brotherhood of mankind is real to the extent that we humans—men and women—are here not just through an accident of fate, but through the love of a Creator. The Exodus was the event that made clear to humanity that it had a transcendent Parent. But it was also the event in which one member of that divine family of nations, a just-born member, took a first, momentous, step and declared itself part of the family. Israel was the first nation to burst onto the world scene wholly devoted to the idea of being a child in the family of the One God, the Creator of All.

From the very beginning, there was a hope—a hope that this understanding would spread.[42] And in time, it would. Over centuries and millennia, other "children"—other peoples and nations—would understand themselves to be part of the family,

---

42. For an expression of that hope, see, for example, the second half of the prayer *Aleinu*, traditionally said at the end of every major prayer service in synagogues worldwide.

too. The idea of monotheism would catch on and be adopted by others. They, too, would in time discard the lie of polytheism, and come to understand that they are children of this Parent in Heaven. So, over time, the family would grow. But as it grew, the family needed something that the Parent, for all His power and omniscience, would not be able to provide.

It needed the services of a *bechor*.

Generation Gap

Parents who wish to pass their values down to their children are beset by the challenge of the generation gap. Every family, by definition, has one. Children, by their nature, want to emulate their parents. They want to be like Mommy and Daddy. But how can they? Their parents live in a different world. Parents go to board meetings. They make budgets for the family. They drive other family members to doctor's appointments. If I'm seven years old, how do I emulate any of that?

That's where the idea of a *bechor* comes in. A *bechor*—an actual firstborn, or any child, really, who adopts this role[43]—can serve as a bridge between the generations.[44] A *bechor* can take the values

---

43. Interestingly, being a *bechor* is not simply a matter of birth order. While according to Jewish law (Deuteronomy 21:15–17), a parent cannot subvert the right of a firstborn, various stories in the book of Genesis suggest that any child in a family can emerge as a child-leader, regardless of birth order. Being a *bechor*, ultimately, is less about biology than it is about the role you play in the family. And so it is on the national level: Israel may be regarded as a *bechor* in the family of nations, but membership in Israel is open to all. Any individual who wishes to adopt its principles, live by its ways, and join the nation, is welcome to do so, regardless of bloodline.

44. The actual structure of the Hebrew word *bechor* suggests this. By tradition, Hebrew letters are associated with various numerical values, in

of the parents and live them, tangibly, in a child's world. When a child-leader does that successfully, he or she takes a noble idea and breathes life into it, transforming that ideal into behavior that makes sense in a child's world. That kind of behavior then becomes a real, living possibility for the other children, too.

For example:

Mommy is CFO at a large hospital and sensitively negotiates a fair and equitable labor agreement between management and hospital staff. The agreement especially protects the non-unionized sanitation workers, the most vulnerable employees, from exploitation by their managers.

She discusses the situation with her family at the dinner table. The details are beyond the grasp of her grade-school children. But one night when Mommy is working late, Bobby, one of her children, creates a fair and equitable rotation among the siblings for who clears the table and when. As part of this, he provides special protection to Sally, the youngest, who used to get browbeaten by Billy into doing his share of the work as well as her own.

---

a system commonly called *gematria*. For example, the Hebrew word for "father" is *av* (אב), comprised of an א and a ב, the first two letters of the Hebrew alphabet. The numerical value of א is 1, ב is 2. And now look at the Hebrew word for "firstborn." It is *bechor* (בכר). The numerical value of these three letters are 2, 20, and 200, respectively. The numerical progression of the letters indicates a kind of conceptual relationship among them: a man starts as just one person, but when he becomes a father, now there are two. Hence, the Hebrew for "father" is *1 as a bridge toward 2*. Similarly, the first of the children is a *bechor*, who is meant to be a transition figure that bridges the gulf between parent and child. The *bechor* starts with the 2 [ב] that is the tail end of "father," and becomes a bridge toward all the other 2's in this numerical system—namely, 20 [כ] and 200 [ר] (See R. Yitzchak Hutner, *Pachad Yitzchak, Sukkot*, chapter 54, sections 12 and 14).

If the kids wanted to know what Mommy was up to at work, if they wanted to know how to emulate her, they just got a first-hand look at how her values play out in their world. Bobby just became the bridge.

The Generation Gap Writ Large

If the generation gap is an issue of concern for any family, imagine the challenge it poses for the divine family—for the relationship between God, the Great Parent in the Sky, and His own children.

Humans are possessed with the desire to emulate God, just as they have the desire to emulate their own human parents. It's a fine sentiment, to want to emulate God; but how is a human to make good on it? At least with a flesh-and-blood parent, you have *some* intuition of how to translate their values into your world. The parent is a rung above you, but you're at least the same species. God, however, is the ultimate extraterrestrial being; He is, quite literally, not of this world. You can't touch, feel, or see God; His immensity dwarfs the human mind. If you were God, how could you transmit your values to your children?

It comes as no surprise, then, that at the moment God revealed to humankind His existence as Creator and Parent, He was also on the hunt for something. He was in the market for a *bechor*.

כֹּה אָמַר יְקֹוָה בְּנִי בְכֹרִי יִשְׂרָאֵל: וָאֹמַר אֵלֶיךָ שַׁלַּח אֶת־בְּנִי וַיְעַבְדֵנִי וַתְּמָאֵן לְשַׁלְּחוֹ הִנֵּה אָנֹכִי הֹרֵג אֶת־בִּנְךָ בְּכֹרֶךָ:

Thus says YHVH: My firstborn child is Israel. I say to you: Send out my child that he may serve Me... (Exodus 4:22–23)

Moses said these words to Pharaoh at his very first audience with him. He did so because it truly *was* God's agenda in the Exodus that His child be released to serve Him—and thereby begin to translate divine values into human actions on the world stage. Israel would be given a Torah and taken to a land of her own.

There she could build a society, and mold this society according to the Torah's precepts. In so doing, she would be a living example of what it means to live the Parent's agenda in the world of the child, in the world of people and nations.

Looking back on it, there was a certain justice in the ultimatum Moses delivered to the Egyptian king before the plagues: *Allow my bechor to serve Me, or lose your own bechorot, Pharaoh.* God had an overarching vision: He wished to transmit His values to humankind, to all His children—but to bring about that vision, God required the service of a *bechor*. If Pharaoh denied the Almighty this, then God would deprive Egypt of the very same benefit: *How will you transmit the values of Egypt from generation to generation without the benefit of your child-leaders?*

Birth Night

When did Israel first begin to act out this destiny as a *bechor*? It happened when they took their first step toward making the monotheistic idea tangible and concrete in the world, on the night they were born as a nation. That night, God would ask something of Israel: *Would you be My bechor? If so, here's what I need you to do...* The people were asked to make a bold and brazen choice; they would be forced to choose between freedom and slavery. This would also be their first act of service to the divine Parent, the first time they could demonstrate what it means, in real life, to live as committed monotheists.

They were asked to take a sheep or a goat, deities the Egyptians worshipped, and to tie the animal up beside their beds for three days, in full view of their Egyptian neighbors. Then, in defiance of the Pharaoh that subjugated them, they were asked to slaughter this Egyptian god, and to paint their doorposts with the animal's blood.[45] It was a harrowing act of rebellion for a slave population

---

45. This interpretation follows *Ramban* to Exodus 12:3, citing Exodus Rabbah 16:2.

to undertake. With the blood on their doors, they were, in effect, saying to their masters, to Pharaoh, and to themselves: *Egypt stops at this door. Within this house, monotheism reigns.*

That brazen act made them free. The Children of Israel were choosing allegiance to their Heavenly Father, and disavowed the right of Pharaoh to demand their subservience. That night, they would begin to translate the idea of monotheism into concrete deeds. And so that night, through the medium of *Korban Pesach*, Israel *became* the *bechor* of the Almighty. It was, in a way, Israel's "oneness offering"–for it proclaimed the oneness of God.[46]

For the Israelites, this would be the first step on a long journey. The nation would leave Egypt this night, and begin a journey to their land. Once there, they would try to faithfully observe the Torah they had been given, and to build a society worthy of their

---

46. The classical commentator known as Maharal suggests precisely this: everything about the Pesach Offering seems to bespeak *oneness*. The animal slaughtered for the Pesach offering must be *one* year old (Exodus 12:5). Those who eat its meat must count themselves as a *single group* to be eligible to eat that particular offering's meat (Exodus 12:4, with *Rashi*). The meat must be roasted over an open flame, not boiled–because, Maharal suggests, when you boil meat in a liquid, it falls apart, but when you roast it, it remains whole. The animal must be roasted over a fire with its carcass bunched up together, head over knees, compacted into a *single mass*. Moreover, no bones of the Pesach offering may be broken (Exodus 12:46): the *unity* of every bone must be preserved. Even the time during which the offering is eaten, Maharal suggests, points to oneness. According to the verse, we are to eat the offering *bechipazon*, "in haste" (Exodus 12:11); that is, in as narrow a time period as practical, as close as possible to a single point in time (*Gevurot HaShem*, chapter 35). The *Korban Pesach* was truly a "oneness offering." Through it, an individual attested symbolically to his or her faith in monotheism, and rejected the alternative–the Egyptian worship of a pantheon of gods.

Parent's vision. Their concrete example would become something other "children," other peoples and nations, could find ways to emulate. Israel would thus facilitate connection between Parent and children within the grand family. In so doing, she would achieve a reason to be.

All in the Family

What, then, is the best name for the holiday that celebrates the events of the Exodus? We have seen that, for God, the Exodus revealed His identity as Creator. But for Israel, it was up to them to *respond* to God's revelation as Creator. They did so by committing to serve the Heavenly Parent as a *bechor*, so for them, the holiday was Passover. The name commemorates the day they committed to serving the Creator as the *bechor* of His family. Hence, it is only fitting that Israel would mark the deliverance of the Exodus with ceremonies involving *bechorot*. And it is only fitting that discussion of these ceremonies would make it into the "little black boxes," because these ceremonies touch on the very mission statement of Israel.

Passover looks at the events of the Exodus as significant not in terms of history but in terms of destiny. When you think about becoming free, you think about where you are now, in relation to an awful past. When you think about becoming a *bechor*, you think about where you are now, in relation to the future you must help bring into being. The name Passover embodies Israel's response to the events that gifted her a national existence. The nation would exist, now and henceforth, in service of the larger family—the greatest family there ever was. They would exist to nurture the bond between Parent and children in the great divine family comprising God and humanity, or, as a later verse puts it, to be "a kingdom of priests and a holy nation" (Exodus 19:6).

One thing stands out about being a "priest" or a *bechor*: your life is essentially selfless; your mission is one great act of service.

The minute it starts becoming about you—*I have this special relationship with the Parent, and that makes me the greatest thing since sliced bread*—that's when you know you've failed. A good parent, heavenly or earthly, loves *all* his children, and a *bechor* is meant to serve the purposes of that love, helping parents and children connect more effectively. A *bechor* who ignores the existence of those other children, basking in his own perceived exclusive relationship with the Parent—subverts his mission and becomes a failure. The mission of Israel only makes sense because God is intensely interested in a relationship with all humanity, and it is up to Israel never to betray its mission by losing sight of that.

The Sea of Reeds

The story of the Exodus is not over, though, with the Smiting of the Firstborn and the exit of Israel from the Land of Egypt. The Exodus saga has one great, last act: Egypt's pursuit of Israel into the desert, and the destruction of Pharaoh's army in the waves of the Sea of Reeds.

If our theory about the Exodus is correct, we might expect to see the underlying themes we have been talking about continue to resonate, even come to a crescendo, in the last, climactic story of the Splitting of the Sea. If the Exodus was about the revelation of a Creator in the world, then it stands to reason that this idea should somehow echo in the last great act of the story, at the Sea.

Let's get our feet wet.

CHAPTER NINETEEN

Creation and Uncreation

The Mystery of the Fruit Trees

In the wake of the devastating tenth plague, Pharaoh sends the Children of Israel out of Egypt and into the desert—and yet, three days later, he has a change of heart. He chases down the Israelites with an army of infantry, six hundred chariots, horsemen, and expert archers. With their backs to the Sea of Reeds, the Children of Israel watch in terror as Pharaoh's forces approach. And just as doom seems imminent, the most spectacular miracle of the Exodus occurs. The sea splits.

With walls of water forming sheer cliffs on either side of them, the Israelites walk through on dry land. The Egyptian army chases after them in hot pursuit. When they do, the walls of water collapse upon them, and the pursuers are utterly destroyed. With this, the Egyptian threat to Israel is finally neutralized. Victory is complete.

That's the story the text tells us, more or less. It is a very fine story. It has drama, miracles, and a winning underdog. But for some reason, rather than leave this story well enough alone, the Sages of the Midrash felt compelled to add some commentary to it—commentary that, at face value, seems outrageous.

When the Children of Israel walked through the sea on dry land, the Sages tell us, if you glanced to the right or left you wouldn't just see walls of water. No, there was landscaping, too. There were fruit trees, they tell us, on the sides of the path. Apples and pomegranates, the Midrash says, were available for the taking (Exodus Rabbah 21:10).

The question, of course, is why the Sages felt a need to tell us this. Fruit trees? Were the miracles recorded in the biblical text itself not impressive enough, that the Midrash thought it necessary to add these extra flourishes? What were they doing there, anyway? Was it like a roadside concession stand—*apples, 50 cents a basket*—the kind of thing you'd find on old country roads when you are out for a Sunday drive? The whole thing seems outlandish.

The Pattern the Sages Saw

I don't think the Sages were being outlandish at all. They saw a subtle pattern in the biblical text, and, with a wink and a nod, they were trying to point it out to you and me, so that we could see it too. To discern what the Rabbis perceived, let's play a favorite little game of mine. I call it Where Have We Heard All of This Before? We will briefly review the story of the Splitting of the Sea, and as we do, we will find ourselves reminded of an earlier story. As we continue to read and accumulate details, the resemblance between the stories becomes ever sharper. Let me show you what I mean:

Just before the Sea of Reeds miraculously split, Israel and Egypt spent a night facing off against each other, each ensconced in separate camps. According to the text (Exodus 14:21), on that night, God caused a "great east wind" to blow over the waters "all night long." Now, hold that image in your mind. It is dark, water is everywhere, and there is a wind, from God, blowing over the waters. Now, where in the Torah have we met an image like that before? It happened at the very beginning. The beginning of everything:

וְחֹשֶׁךְ עַל־פְּנֵי תְהוֹם וְרוּחַ אֱלֹקִים מְרַחֶפֶת עַל־פְּנֵי הַמָּיִם:

*Darkness was upon the face of the deep, and a wind [lit.] of
God was blowing over the face of the water...* [47] (Genesis 1:2)

This is the second verse of the Torah. It describes the world before God had created even the very first thing, light. It describes
a world that was dark, in which water was everywhere; a wind of
God was blowing over the waters. It describes a world that just
happens to possess the very three elements that later appear just
before the Splitting of the Sea of Reeds: darkness, wind, and
water everywhere.

Is There More?

Now, it may be that the apparent correspondence between these
two stories is a mere coincidence. How would we know whether
the connection we just saw is real, and intended by the Torah, or
just the product of our overactive imagination?

To know that it's real, you'd have to see more. You'd have to
see other points of connection emerge between the two stories.

Let's see if more exist.

The Advent of Separation

Follow me, then, as we go back to the beginning of Genesis. Right
after the text tells us of the dark water-world of pre-Creation,
with a wind of God hovering over the waters, God brings forth

---

47. The end of the Torah's description of pre-Creation is often translated
as "a spirit of God was hovering over the waters." But the word rendered
as "spirit" is *ruach* (רוּחַ), a Hebrew word that can mean "wind" or "spirit."
That same word, *ruach*, describes the wind that blew that night over the
waters of the Sea of Reeds.

the very first element of a new universe: light. And immediately after creating light, the Almighty "separates between the light and the darkness" (Genesis 1:3–4). Now let's fast-forward to the scene we've been discussing at the Sea of Reeds. Anything there that reminds us of this?

Something suspiciously similar *did* happen at the sea.

The Torah records that, as the Israelites traveled toward the Sea of Reeds, the Divine Presence led them. That Presence, according to the text, manifested itself by day as a pillar of cloud that would show them the way forward, and by night as a pillar of fire that would provide light for the people (Exodus 13:21). So the pillar traveled in front of the people. However, the Torah also records that once the Egyptians converged on the Israelites at the shore of the Sea of Reeds, the pillar that had been traveling ahead of the people took a position behind them instead (Exodus 14:19), so as to provide a barrier between the Egyptian forces and the People of Israel (Exodus 14:20).

But the barrier put in place by the pillar didn't just separate between the two groups of people; fascinatingly, it also separated between darkness and light. The text states:

וַיָּבֹא בֵּין מַחֲנֵה מִצְרַיִם וּבֵין מַחֲנֵה יִשְׂרָאֵל וַיְהִי הֶעָנָן וְהַחֹשֶׁךְ
וַיָּאֶר אֶת־הַלָּיְלָה וְלֹא־קָרַב זֶה אֶל־זֶה כָּל־הַלָּיְלָה:

And [the pillar] came between the camp of Egypt
and the camp of Israel, and there was cloud and
darkness, and it lit up the night (Exodus 14:20)

Look carefully at that verse and you'll notice something puzzling about it. The verse first states that "there was cloud and darkness." That language seems to intimate that the divine pillar took the form of a cloud, and that the cloud further darkened the night–perhaps by obscuring whatever dim light had been present from the light of the moon and the stars. But now read the very next words: "...and it lit up the night."

Wait a minute, what kind of pillar was this? It sounds like it was a pillar of fire, lighting up the night. That was the usual function of the divine pillar when it took the form of fire. But how could that be? The preceding words led us to believe that the pillar took the form of a *cloud*—and, if anything, had the very opposite effect, creating a more profound darkness than had existed previously in the nighttime sky!

Rashi provides us what seems the only logical way out of the apparent contradiction. The pillar that separated Egypt from Israel took *both* forms: when the Egyptians gazed upon the pillar, all they saw was cloud—a cloud that utterly blackened the already dark night sky. But when the Israelites on the other side of the divine pillar gazed upon it, they saw its alternate form, fire—and that fire served its regular purpose of lighting up the night (*Rashi* to Exodus 14:20).

Thus, in a very real way, the Divine Presence had separated between light and darkness—just as it had once done so long ago, at Creation.

So we seem to have found another element that binds the Splitting of the Sea narrative back to the original Creation story. Are there others?

Another Degree of Separation

Let's return to Genesis, and trace what happens next in the Creation story.

After setting forth that first, primal division between light and darkness on Day One of Creation, the Torah tells of a second great division, one that takes place on Day Two:

וַיֹּאמֶר אֱלֹקִים יְהִי רָקִיעַ בְּתוֹךְ הַמָּיִם וִיהִי מַבְדִּיל בֵּין מַיִם לָמָיִם: וַיַּעַשׂ אֱלֹקִים אֶת־הָרָקִיעַ וַיַּבְדֵּל בֵּין הַמַּיִם אֲשֶׁר מִתַּחַת לָרָקִיעַ וּבֵין הַמַּיִם אֲשֶׁר מֵעַל לָרָקִיעַ וַיְהִי־כֵן:

*And God said: Let there be sky in the middle of the waters, and
let it divide between water and water. So God made the sky,
and it divided between the water that is above the sky, and the
water that is below the sky; and it was so* (Genesis 1:6–7)

So in Genesis, we hear of sky–atmosphere, air–dividing between
two great sources of water, one above and one below. The simplest
way to understand the verse might be to think of the "waters
below" as the seas, and the "waters above" as water vapor, taking
the form of clouds. In between the clouds and the seas is sky,
which is to say, air. Prior to Day Two, we seemingly had a world
where there was only water–but now the waters have parted, as it
were, and a vast air pocket is placed between the two great sources
of water in the world, terrestrial water and celestial water. Does
that sound like anything back at the Sea of Reeds? A division of
water with sky in between? That, of course, is the whole essence
of the drama: a great body of water splits in two, and between the
two walls of water is breathable air, through which the Israelites
can safely pass:

וַיָּבֹאוּ בְנֵי־יִשְׂרָאֵל בְּתוֹךְ הַיָּם בַּיַּבָּשָׁה וְהַמַּיִם
לָהֶם חֹמָה מִימִינָם וּמִשְּׂמֹאלָם:

*And Israel came into the middle of the water, on
dry land; and the water was for them a wall, to
their right and to their left* (Exodus 14:22)

The two stories of water-splitting are almost exactly the same. The
difference between them is just a matter of orientation: at Creation,
the waters split vertically (water above and water below), whereas
at the sea, the waters split horizontally (waters on two sides).

Land Ho!

The parallels continue. Back in Genesis, what was the next thing
that happened in the Creation story? After the darkness and the

wind hovering over the waters, after the division between light and darkness, and after the division between the two great bodies of water—what was the *next* episode in the Creation saga? The next thing the Torah tells us is this:

וַיֹּאמֶר אֱלֹקִים יִקָּווּ הַמַּיִם מִתַּחַת הַשָּׁמַיִם
אֶל־מָקוֹם אֶחָד וְתֵרָאֶה הַיַּבָּשָׁה וַיְהִי־כֵן:

And God said: Let the waters beneath the heavens be gathered into one place, and let the dry land appear. And it was so (Genesis 1:9)

Of course, at the Sea of Reeds we have a version of this event, too: right in the middle of the ocean, waters recede, and dry land is revealed. It is worth noting that this particular word for "dry land," *yabashah*, is an unusual word in Scripture. It appears nowhere else in the Five Books of Moses other than in the Creation story and the Exodus drama.[48]

---

48. The word appears at the Splitting of the Sea, at Creation—and at one other juncture in the Exodus story. Interestingly, it's back at the Burning Bush, when Moses is given a mysterious divine sign: God asks him to take water and pour it out onto *yabashah*, dry land, where it will take on the appearance of blood.

All in all, then, the word appears in connection with the very first set of miracles of the Exodus (the signs at the Burning Bush) and the very last set of miracles of the Exodus (the Splitting of the Sea). One wonders, given the rarity of the word, and its appearances bookending the Exodus, whether the two occurrences of the word within the Exodus story are related. Perhaps the sign at the Burning Bush involving the *yabashah* foreshadowed things yet to come at the Sea of Reeds. In other words, at the Burning Bush, before any plague had yet struck Egypt, God provided Moses with a vision of the final blow that would strike Egypt. What is the last sight that Israel would ever have of Egypt, their former tormentors? When would they know it was over? The last they would see of Egypt would be the sight of water turning into blood where the water meets dry land: blood washing up on the shore, after the destruction of the Egyptian army in the waves.

Moreover, the purpose of the dry land—its function in each story—is the same. In Creation, the dry land was a platform upon which animal life and human life would flourish. And at the sea, the sudden appearance of dry land in the midst of the waters serves the same purpose: it is a vehicle for the survival of human and animal life. The people of Israel, and their animals—the ones Moses had bargained for so assiduously, as he steadfastly refused to leave "even a hoof behind"—all these mammals had their existence threatened by the imposing waters of the sea, as the Israelites faced off against Egypt with their backs to the sea. But they would all survive, because of the dry land—they would successfully pass through the life-giving *yabashah* that had been revealed by the receding waters.

Déjà Vu All Over Again

It's all happening again.

The first four events of Creation have now transpired again, one after another, at the Sea of Reeds.

What, you may ask, is the fifth and next event in the Creation? Intriguingly, it doesn't seem to have a twin at the Sea of Reeds. Does that mean we've been fooled, that the pattern we've seen is imaginary? Well, what is that fifth event in Creation?

You may have guessed it. It's the appearance of vegetation, crowned by fruit trees:

וַיֹּאמֶר אֱלֹקים תַּדְשֵׁא הָאָרֶץ דֶּשֶׁא עֵשֶׂב
מַזְרִיעַ זֶרַע עֵץ פְּרִי עֹשֶׂה פְּרִי לְמִינוֹ

And God said: Let the earth bring forth grasses that
will multiply, and trees with fruits, that will produce
other fruits of its kind... (Genesis 1:11)

Along come the Sages of the Midrash, to fill in what they see as missing—almost as if to reassure the reader that the pattern they've seen is real. *If everything else from Creation has shown up at the sea, you mean to tell me the one thing that's missing was vegetation, that there were no fruit trees? There must have been fruit trees!*

Creation and Uncreation

Let's stand back and survey the picture the Torah paints for us. The connections between Creation and the battle between Egypt and God at the sea seem, indeed, to be real. But what do they mean? What does the Torah intend to convey to the reader by telling these stories in parallel?

I'd like to suggest a possible interpretation, one that emerges from the theory we've delineated over the course of this book, concerning the Exodus as a whole. The Exodus events, we've suggested, were a ratification of God's role as Creator. Both Israel and Egypt had a choice to make: would they confront those events and take to heart that the world has a Creator, that all the powers of nature derive from a single Transcendent Force? Would they understand that this Creator cares about the welfare of His children and responds to their oppression?

Israel made its choice in the affirmative when they offered the Pesach Offering, the oneness offering affirming their allegiance to the Creator. And when they did, a new "creation" came into being. Israel was birthed as a nation. But Pharaoh and Egypt made a choice in the negative. They chose to turn their backs on the existence of a Creator, and hold fast to a lie—to the fiction that the world is governed by chaotic powers at constant war with one another, that there is no Parent of All who cares about His children.

And so, in the very last act of the Exodus saga, each nation would have it the way they liked it. Those who acknowledged the existence of the Creator would have the benefits of creation, and those who denied the Creator would live in an uncreated world.

At the sea, Israel would experience a world in which the great divisions of Creation held fast, in miraculous new iterations. Theirs would be a world in which there would be light, safely shielded from utter darkness; theirs would be a world in which waters miraculously separated and breathable air, wondrously, allowed to persist in between, a world in which dry land, astonishingly, appeared in the face of receding waters. The One Force that created these awe-inspiring divisions in the first place would once again miraculously put them in place, now—as the astonishment that was Creation manifested itself in history once more.

But Egypt would not reap the benefit of these Creation "divisions." Instead, in a twist of divine justice, Pharaoh and his army would live in a world of their own making.

If you prefer to deny a Creator, then live in a world without one! At the sea, Pharaoh and his minions inhabit an uncreated world, a world that is an expression of the primal chaos of pre-Creation. This world has no divisions. It is a world in which light is suffocated by darkness, water encompasses all, and both breathable air and habitable land are invaded by the menace of unrestricted, chaotic water.[49]

The Curtain Closes on Plan C

In the destruction of Egypt's armies at the Sea of Reeds, Plan C comes to its conclusion. Egypt is a tool by which evidence of the Creator comes to the world, instead of a conscious, deliberate, truth-telling witness to that evidence. But in an ironic twist, just before the waves destroy the pursuing chariots, the Almighty tells Moses that, in the events about to transpire, "Egypt shall know that I am YHVH" (Exodus 14:4). The irony is that this was the realization that Pharaoh had done everything possible to insulate

---

49. It is the second verse of Genesis all over again: "chaos, darkness on the face of the deep, and a wind of God hovering over the waters" (Genesis 1:2).

himself against: that his nemesis was the Creator. But in the end, despite himself, Pharaoh would know the truth. As the walls of water collapsed around the Egyptian pursuers, as the chaos of uncreation engulfed them, they would, in those final moments, see that it was the Creator they had battled. Nothing less than the undoing of Creation unfolded before their eyes.

The Exodus that Might Have Been

Egypt's defeat at the sea is so complete that one is tempted to wonder whether there really ever *was* hope for a different ending. We had suggested earlier that there were other ways the Exodus could have unfolded. There had been a Plan A and a Plan B, each of which had entailed an attempt to draw Pharaoh and Egypt into a conscious and free-willed recognition of the Creator. Each of these plans would have ended with Egypt releasing the slaves of its own accord, a consequence of Egypt's submission to a Creator who claimed the Israelites as His own. But, having seen the Exodus as it actually came to pass—Egypt's armies routed at the Sea of Reeds by the most dramatic divine miracle that ever was—it seems only natural to wonder: Was either of those other plans ever *really* the way things were supposed to turn out?

Another way, perhaps, of asking the question: even if we were to accept that Plan A or B had originally been on the table, should we care that those plans never materialized? Was it not enough that the entire nation of Israel came to know YHVH? What, if anything, was lost when those plans failed to come to fruition? And if something terribly important *was* lost, is that loss permanent? Is there some sort of unrealized potential in the Exodus whose loss we should mourn, or perhaps seek to recapture?

These are the questions we shall turn to in Part IV, the final section of this book. In it, I will make the argument that hidden in the story of the Splitting of the Sea are whispers of another version of the Exodus saga. This "Phantom Exodus" story seems to exist almost in another realm entirely–perhaps, we might say, in the realm of the divine imagination, if not in the hard, cold world of reality. This parallel story has much to teach us about the real Exodus, which it throws into sharp relief, highlighting the triumphs of the Exodus, and the aching pathos of its missed opportunities. This "Phantom Exodus" tells us of an Exodus that Might Have Been–and an Exodus that Might Yet Be.

PART IV

Joseph and the Phantom Exodus

CHAPTER TWENTY

All the King's Horsemen

The story of the Splitting of the Sea is, of course, the great and glorious climax of the Exodus. But I want to share a problem that has always gnawed at me. It concerns something God says to Moses, when informing him that Pharaoh's armies will soon come chasing after the departing Hebrews.

God tells Moses that the Egyptian king will notice the somewhat erratic track of the Israelites through the desert (Exodus 14:3), and, sensing that they're vulnerable, will want to pursue them. He then goes on to say that He will lend Pharaoh the courage to do just that:

וְחִזַּקְתִּי אֶת־לֵב־פַּרְעֹה וְרָדַף אַחֲרֵיהֶם וְאִכָּבְדָה בְּפַרְעֹה וּבְכָל־חֵילוֹ

And I shall strengthen the heart of Pharaoh,[50] *and
he will chase after you...* (Exodus 14:4)

---

50. Here, as earlier, we understand the Hebrew phrase *chizuk halev,* or "strength of heart," as a synonym for courage. Pharaoh will regret having allowed Israel to leave, and will sense the people's vulnerability in the desert. Thus, he will perceive an opportunity to do them in, or recapture them. God will "strengthen his heart," or lend Pharaoh the courage to follow through on that desire. Thus, despite the losses Pharaoh earlier suffered during the plagues, he will dispatch the Egyptian army anyway, to pursue his escaping slaves.

So far, so good. But now read the next half of that verse. That's the part that always haunted me:

וְאִכָּבְדָה בְּפַרְעֹה וּבְכָל־חֵילוֹ

...and I shall be honored through Pharaoh and all his army... (Exodus 14:4)

You'll forgive me if this sounds too forward, but doesn't that sound like a mean thing to say? Here God is, about to destroy many hundreds of people—and He speaks of the honor that will come to Him through their deaths? It seems "unbecoming" of the Almighty to speak this way. Yes, the Egyptians are the enemies of the Israelites, and yes, it is better that they be destroyed than be allowed to recapture and reenslave Israel, but still, it's one thing to defend Israel by killing her enemies, and another to derive honor from all that killing. Why put it that way?

My Creations Are Drowning and You Sing about It?

Now, for a long time I kept quiet about this. I suppose it just felt like an uncomfortable thing to bring up. I could imagine the potential rejoinder: *The verse ever so slightly offends your sensibilities, Fohrman? Well, who cares about your sensitivities? That's what God said! No one is asking for your personal approval.*

But it's not just my own sensitivities that seem to run afoul of this verse. The Sages of the Talmud once suggested that the Almighty shares those very same sensitivities. Here's what the Sages say:

אֵין הַקָּדוֹשׁ בָּרוּךְ הוּא שָׂמֵחַ בְּמַפַּלְתָּן שֶׁל רְשָׁעִים דְּאָמַר רַבִּי
שְׁמוּאֵל בַּר נַחְמָן אָמַר רַבִּי יוֹנָתָן: מַאי דִּכְתִיב וְלֹא קָרַב זֶה
אֶל זֶה כָּל הַלָּיְלָה בְּאוֹתָהּ שָׁעָה בִּקְשׁוּ מַלְאֲכֵי הַשָּׁרֵת לוֹמַר
שִׁירָה לִפְנֵי הַקָּדוֹשׁ בָּרוּךְ הוּא אָמַר לָהֶן הַקָּדוֹשׁ בָּרוּךְ הוּא:
מַעֲשֵׂה יָדַי טוֹבְעִין בַּיָּם וְאַתֶּם אוֹמְרִים שִׁירָה לְפָנָי?

The Holy One, Blessed is He, does not rejoice in the downfall of the wicked. For R. Shmuel bar Nachman said in the name of R. Yonatan: In the moment [when Egypt was destroyed at the Sea], the ministering angels wished to sing in joy in the presence of the Holy One. But the Holy One said to them: My own creations [the Egyptians] are drowning in the Sea, and you want to sing before Me? (Megillah 10b)

It turns out that the Sages ascribe the same intuition to the Almighty himself: a victor doesn't rejoice at the downfall of his enemies, particularly if the victor is God. God is the creator; even His enemies are His creations. There is something bitter in the taste of victory over them.

This is all quite puzzling. If God feels it's wrong for the ministering angels to sing in joy at the death of His creations, why would God say that He is taking glory and honor for Himself in those deaths? Maybe the deaths have to happen, and maybe Israel, the direct beneficiaries of Egypt's downfall, can rejoice without their song appearing unseemly. But for the Creator of all to rejoice, for Him to want honor out of this? It doesn't seem to add up. It doesn't seem nice. The Sages themselves don't seem to think it's nice.

What's going on here?

Did the Sages Know Something We Don't?

But it gets even stranger.

This idea that the Almighty looks askance at rejoicing in His creations' suffering–where, in the Sages' view, does that idea come from? What biblical text do they adduce as its source? As we have just seen, the Sages used this very episode of the Egyptians' deaths at the Sea of Reeds as a proof-text! Now it all seems truly absurd. How could they have picked this one episode, out of the entire Torah, as an example of divine compassion, when the text itself seems to contravene the very idea they are suggesting? They were surely aware of the verse in which God states that He will take honor from the cavalry of Egypt and their armies. How could they ignore it?

I want to suggest to you that we have misinterpreted the verse, not they. When the Almighty spoke of taking honor from all the king's horses and all the king's men, he wasn't talking about taking glory from death at all.[51] What the verse really means is something else entirely.

That *something else* will be a key to helping us see another whole world of meaning in the story of Israel's confrontation with Egypt at the Sea of Reeds. It will be a window that will allow us to glimpse the Exodus that Might Have Been.

The Rest of the Picture

God's curious declaration about taking honor from Pharaoh's armies is like a jigsaw piece that just won't fit. Rather than try to force it, I propose we set the piece aside for a while and discover some other parts of the puzzle. The picture is larger than we might imagine.

So let's rewind a bit. We have been examining the Exodus story, all the way through to its culmination at the Sea of Reeds. That

---

51. Indeed, the words "death" and "destruction" never appear in the verse. The text speaks of God taking "honor" from Pharaoh's armies (Exodus 14:4) or from his horsemen and archers (Exodus 14:17)—but never does God mention the deaths of any of these people. The simple reading of the verse would indicate that the honor God draws is somehow from the armies, horsemen, and archers *themselves*, not their deaths. What exactly this would mean, though, is not immediately obvious—all these forces are tools of the enemy, not God. These are themes we will revisit toward the end of this book.

climactic episode is one bookend to the Exodus story. I would like to return to the other bookend of the Exodus story, all the way back in the book of Genesis, *before* Egyptian servitude begins: the story of the death and burial of the patriarch, Jacob. I believe that these two bookends match up in remarkable ways.

What we are going to do in the following pages with the story of Jacob's burial is something akin to what we've done until now with the Exodus story. We are going to delve into the story, and try to unearth its hidden nuance and drama. We shall find that this nearly-final episode of the book of Genesis is laden with meaning. All that we need to apprehend it is a willingness to approach the story with honesty, and a commitment to read it with open eyes.

CHAPTER TWENTY-ONE

A Moment of Truth

Babysitting Arrangements

The story of Jacob's death and burial seems, on its face, unremarkable. On his deathbed, Jacob had asked Joseph to bury him in the family tomb at Machpelah, back in the Land of Canaan. When he dies, the family, led by Joseph, buries him there, in compliance with his wishes. The whole thing seems pretty straightforward.

Given the outward placidity of these events, it is no wonder that the verses detailing Jacob's burial don't typically get much attention from the casual reader of the Torah. But I believe that this oft-overlooked story holds great tension and drama. If we fail to see the drama in this episode, it just means we haven't read closely enough.

A clue to its significance comes from a verse that appears to tell us something so trivial and ordinary that one wonders why it needed to be said at all:

וְכֹל בֵּית יוֹסֵף וְאֶחָיו וּבֵית אָבִיו רַק טַפָּם
וְצֹאנָם וּבְקָרָם עָזְבוּ בְּאֶרֶץ גֹּשֶׁן:

And the whole house of Joseph, his brothers, and his father's house [all went up to bury Jacob]; only their little children, their sheep and their cattle did they leave behind in the Land of Goshen (Genesis 50:8)

Imagine the Torah had *not* gone out of its way to tell you whether the people joining Jacob's funeral procession had brought their little kids along. Let's say we hadn't been told whether the sheep and cattle came, either. Imagine that none of this information had been given to us. Would you have read the story of Jacob's burial, closed your bible in astonishment, slapped your knee, and exclaimed: *But what happened with all those little children? Did they take them along, or leave them with babysitters? What were the daycare arrangements like?*

You probably wouldn't have said that.

The babysitting arrangements and animal-care logistics for the trip to Canaan are of very little interest to future generations. Why does the Bible bother to tell us about these things?

Converging Stories

I have now brought up with you two little oddities in the stories that bookend the Exodus. We wondered about the "honor" God takes from the death of the Egyptians, and about the discussion of babysitting logistics for Jacob's burial. These two oddities don't seem to fit in their respective stories. But perhaps they *do* fit, once we adjust our view of each story.

In the pages that follow, I want to suggest to you that these two narratives are not really separate stories; they converge in remarkable ways. Once we appreciate this, we'll not only understand how each wayward puzzle piece fits, but find ourselves in possession of a grander and richer perspective on the Exodus story itself. We will be able to see the Exodus that actually occurred through the prism of the Exodus that Might Have Been.

In order to achieve that new perspective, we must look more closely at the Burial of Jacob episode. Let's do that now.

Delicate Negotiations

The patriarch Jacob was eventually buried in the land of Canaan, but that didn't just *happen*. It was a delicately negotiated matter between Jacob and his son Joseph. The casual reader might gloss over the negotiations without a second thought, but curiously, the Torah finds those negotiations important enough that it devotes a number of verses to telling us about them. Evidently, these events are worthy of our consideration.

The Torah begins its account of this father-son negotiation by providing the reader some chronological context for the scene: we are told it takes place seventeen years after Jacob first came to live in the land of Egypt (Genesis 47:28). At that time, Jacob, by now approaching death, calls for his beloved son, Joseph, and tells his son that he wishes to be buried in the place where his fathers were buried. The Torah then gives us Joseph's response to his father's request:

וַיֹּאמַר אָנֹכִי אֶעֱשֶׂה כִדְבָרֶךָ:

He said: I shall do as you have asked (Genesis 47:30)

Ties that Bind

If the book of Genesis ended right here, and you had to guess what happened next, what would you imagine? If you were Jacob, lying there on your bed at that moment, and you had expressed this request to your loyal son, and he had answered in the affirmative—*Yes, Father, I will surely do what you've asked; you can count on me to bury you in the family tomb*—if you had heard those words from Joseph, what would you do next?

I don't know about you, but if I had been in Jacob's shoes at that moment, I might've said something like: *Thank you very much, son. I knew I could count on you.* Something in that general ballpark, at least. But that is not at all what Jacob says. Instead, he tells his son:

הִשָּׁבְעָה לִי

Swear to me [that you'll do it] (Genesis 47:31)

Is this for real? Here is your loyal son, assuring you that he'll do exactly what you asked of him, *and you ask him to swear that he'll really do it?* What a terribly awkward thing to ask of him! Is Jacob intimating that he doesn't trust his son?

Whatever Joseph might think of his father's demand, Joseph takes the oath. And then, again, Jacob does something strange. According to the verse, he "bows toward the head of the bed" (Genesis 47:31).

The Sages of the Midrash wondered why he would do that. What significance did that oblique act have? Here was the interpretation they gave to it:

עַל שֶׁהָיְתָה מִטָּתוֹ שְׁלֵמָה שֶׁאֵין בָּהּ רָשָׁע שֶׁהֲרֵי יוֹסֵף מֶלֶךְ
הוּא וְעוֹד שֶׁנִּשְׁבָּה לְבֵין הַגּוֹיִם וַהֲרֵי הוּא עוֹמֵד בְּצִדְקוֹ

*[He prostrated himself to God] because his legacy[52] was
whole, insofar as not one of [his children] was wicked—for
Joseph was [Egyptian] royalty, and furthermore, he
had been captured [and lived] among heathens, and
yet he remained steadfast in his righteousness* (Rashi,
from *Sifrei Va'etchanan* 31, *Sifrei Ha'azinu* 334)

---

52. The Hebrew word *mitah* (מִטָּה), which appears in the verse, can have more than one meaning. In the simple sense of the text, it means "bed," which is to say: *Jacob prostrated himself toward the head of the bed.* But the word can also have the connotation of "legacy," or "children" (the products of one's bed), and it is in this sense that the Sages expound the verse: Jacob bowed out of thanks, because his "bed," his *legacy*, was complete.

According to the Sages, when Joseph agreed to Jacob's request, He saw evidence in it of his son's abiding righteousness. Despite Joseph's many years in Egypt, he had not assimilated into the heathen culture. Jacob now felt his legacy was complete, and he bowed in gratitude.

Time to Take a Bow

Let's take a moment to ponder what the Sages are telling us here. They suggest that Jacob had a revelatory moment at the conclusion of this discussion with Joseph about burial arrangements. Seventeen years into his life in Egypt, he finally realized that his son had not assimilated into heathen culture. The problem is: should it really have taken Jacob seventeen years to realize this?

Put yourself in Jacob's shoes at this moment. Looking back over the course of your life, if you could identify any one moment—and *only* one moment—at which you came to realize that yes, your beloved son was still a loyal, God-fearing member of this budding family of Israel, when exactly would that moment have been?

It would probably have been seventeen years earlier, when you first set eyes on your long-lost son after two decades apart. Joseph had run to greet him, had embraced him and cried, had set the family up in Goshen and taken care of their every need. Power hasn't made him forget his roots. *That* seems like the moment Jacob should have realized what a good son Joseph is. Why, then, do the Sages say that it is only *now*, on his deathbed—seventeen years later—that Jacob understands this?

The Sages of the Midrash seem to be telling us that, despite the fact that Joseph had taken care of the entire family, there was some *other* area of concern Jacob had about Joseph, that, in his mind, somehow dwarfed all other considerations. He needed to know that Joseph would bury him in Canaan. He needed Joseph to *swear* to him that he would.

But what was so important about this burial request? Why, exactly, would this one request tell Jacob what he felt he needed to know about Joseph?

To discover the answers to these questions, we must review some of the history that has transpired between three men: Jacob, Joseph, and the Pharaoh that lived in Joseph's day.[53] An intriguing triangle takes shape in the relationships between these three men. And Jacob's deathbed request casts this uneasy triangle into a crisis—a crisis from which it may never recover.

---

53. This, of course, is a very different person than the Pharaoh who lived, generations later, in the days of Moses. In the coming chapters, I will refer to this person simply as Pharaoh, and the intent will be to refer to Joseph's Pharaoh.

CHAPTER TWENTY-TWO

The Triangle

Joseph spent many years in Egypt as a high Egyptian official, second only to Pharaoh. During all this time, why did he never write home?

It is one of the most perplexing questions of the Joseph saga. If Joseph really loved his father, and it seems that he did, why did he never inform his father that he was safe and sound? Just a postcard, at least: *Here I am, Dad, in Egypt. You'll never believe it, but I'm Pharaoh's right-hand man now. Weather is fantastic. Wishing you were here.* Anything. Why does Joseph maintain radio silence?

It is a question that has been discussed, over the ages, by many commentators. I want to call your attention to an interpretation advanced by R. Yoel Bin Nun, a contemporary thinker.[54] He suggests the possibility that Joseph may have been the victim of a terrible misunderstanding.

Let's recall how Joseph ended up in Egypt. One day, his brothers threw him in a pit and sold him as a slave. *We* know that Jacob was clueless about what really happened to Joseph; his child just disappeared. But what is less obvious, R. Bin Nun suggests, is that the cluelessness was mutual: Joseph had no idea what really happened with Jacob that day, either.

---

54. See *Megadim*, Volume 1, pages 20–31.

The Omniscient Reader

To see that this is true, go back and read the Sale of Joseph story, but erase any preconceptions you may have about it. Keep in mind that sometimes, when you read a biblical story, you, the reader, have an omniscient, bird's-eye view that none of the actual participants in the story had. In such cases, you can't let what *you* know bias your view of the story.

Coming back, then, to the Sale of Joseph, ask yourself: what crucial event are you aware of that Joseph himself is not?

The event I'm thinking of occurs immediately after Joseph is hauled out of the pit and into a caravan, to be taken down to Egypt and sold as a slave. The Torah tells us that the brothers took Joseph's special, striped coat, smeared it with blood, and brought it back to their father. Their anguished father saw what the brothers wanted him to: his beloved child had met his end somewhere in the desert.

טָרֹף טֹרַף יוֹסֵף:

Joseph has been torn to pieces! (Genesis 37:33)

Now, we know about the bloody coat; we know that Jacob has been deceived by his sons. But there's no way that *Joseph* knows this; he's off on a caravan when all this is taking place. So if you were Joseph, and you didn't know that your father had been tricked–how might that affect your interpretation of what happened that day? What terrible, tragic misunderstanding might you arrive at?

Let's replay the events leading up to the Sale of Joseph, as Joseph himself might have apprehended them:

There I was, seventeen years old, tending sheep with my brothers. There were some tensions in the family, sure. My brothers didn't seem to like me very much. And then I started having these dreams. The first

one involved me and my brothers, harvesting wheat out in the fields,
when all of a sudden the sheaves of wheat belonging to my brothers
started bowing to my sheaves. And then I had a second dream: the
sun and moon and eleven stars were all bowing to me. That dream
seemed to involve my father, too, so I told him about it. And then, for
the first time I can remember, my father became angry at me. He
publicly rebuked me:

'Shall your mother, your brothers, and I all come bowing to you?'
he said.

Suddenly, right after that, Father had a mission for me: Your
brothers are tending sheep in Shechem. I think I'll send you to them...

Why did Father ask me to do that? It was dangerous. He knew
my brothers were jealous of me. I was scared about going there to
meet them, but I complied.[55] *I hoped that things would go well... but*
they did not. I was jumped, thrown into a pit, and sold off as a slave.

And there was never any search party.

Now, not knowing that Jacob was in fact deceived into thinking Joseph was dead, not knowing he was horrified and in mourning over the apparent loss of his beloved son—what false suspicion
might Joseph entertain?

R. Yoel Bin Nun suggests that Joseph may have believed he
had just been thrown out of the family. Was his father in on it

---

55. In the text, Joseph says *hineini* (הִנֵּֽנִי), "here I am," when his father calls
upon him to meet his brothers in Shechem (Genesis 37:13). In the book
of Genesis, *hineini* has a chilling echo. It was how Abraham expressed his
readiness to go on a journey when God, his Father in Heaven, called upon
him to sacrifice his son. Here, Joseph uses the same phrase to express to his
earthly father his readiness to go on a journey that may involve sacrifice.
The use of *hineini* may be the Torah's way of conveying to us that Joseph
knew something of the dangers of the journey before he set out to meet
his brothers.

from the beginning? Maybe. Or maybe the brothers forced their father's hand; perhaps they told Jacob that it was either him or them, someone had to go. Maybe it even happened after the fact: maybe the brothers came home and told Father that Joseph was safely on his way to Egypt, that it might be unsavory, but it was the only way the family could remain intact. It doesn't matter. Either way, he's been thrown out of the family.

And it's not as if nothing like this had happened before.

When Sarah felt that Ishmael was a corrosive influence, soon enough, he was out of the family. In the next generation, Rebecca had favored Jacob, and before you knew it, Esau was out of the family. Had the same thing just happened to *him*?

In Egypt, Joseph would have had a long time to ponder the circumstances of his abrupt disappearance from the family. After a stint as a relatively privileged servant in the house of a nobleman, he found himself cast into prison for a crime that he did not commit, and there he languished for many years—until, at long last, someone new and wonderful came into his life.

It was Pharaoh.

Pharaoh

One day, Joseph found himself suddenly extricated from jail, and thrust into the presence of the king of Egypt. Evidently, Pharaoh had been having some dreams that troubled him, and he had heard that Joseph knew how to interpret such things. The king asked Joseph to listen to his dreams, and to tell him their meaning.

The verses that speak of these events hint at just how redemptive Pharaoh's presence in Joseph's life, at that moment, really was. The text tells us, for example, that Pharaoh sent for Joseph and had him pulled out of the *bor* (בּוֹר), "pit" (Genesis 41:14). This is an odd turn of phrase, since, technically,   Joseph was not in a *bor*; he was in a prison, described earlier (Genesis

39:20) as a *beit hasohar* (בֵּית הַסֹּהַר). In using the term *bor*, the text seems to blur the lines between the story happening now, and a story that happened many years ago. For indeed, there *was* a time when Joseph was in a pit. He was put there by his brothers thirteen years ago. The text seems to convey that, when Pharaoh pulled him out of jail all these years later, it felt like déjà vu for Joseph, like getting out of that pit at last.

After getting a haircut, Joseph was given a nice new change of clothes by Pharaoh. Here too, the verse seems to evoke memories from thirteen years ago. Right before his brothers threw him in the pit, they stripped him of his special clothes, the beautiful striped coat that his father had given him. Now, he would get beautiful new clothes—all courtesy of Pharaoh.

A pattern is taking shape in these verses. A version of the terrible events of thirteen years ago seems to be happening again, but *in reverse*. Thirteen years ago, Joseph was first stripped of his clothes and then thrown in a pit; now, he is first taken out of a "pit," and then given new clothes. And it is not just the *order* in which the events occur that is reversed; their *significance* is reversed, as well. Last time around, Joseph was thrown into a pit, and now he is pulled out of one. Last time around, Joseph was stripped of clothes; now he's getting new ones.

The pattern of reverses continues. The next thing Pharaoh does is the reverse of something that happened thirteen years ago, *before* Joseph was thrown in a pit, and *before* he was stripped of his new clothes. Here's how the text describes the event:

וַיִּשְׁלַח פַּרְעֹה וַיִּקְרָא אֶת־יוֹסֵף

And Pharaoh sent for Joseph (Genesis 41:14)

The opposite of being brought close to someone is being sent away from someone. And that's exactly what happened to Joseph before he was stripped of his clothes: *He was sent away* from *Jacob*. His father had sent him to go check on his brothers. That event—his father's decision to send him—was the first in a series of terrible dominoes that culminated in Joseph's sale into slavery. It was the initial step toward that first "pit." Now, that whole disastrous chain of events would be redeemed. Instead of a man sending him away toward a pit, another man would now bring him close, after pulling him *out* of a "pit." That man was Pharaoh.

Through this pattern, the Torah may well be telling us something about the relationship Pharaoh is beginning to create with Joseph. Pharaoh is acting out a precise inverse of Jacob's role in this story. Whatever disappointment Joseph might have felt toward his own father—*How could you have sent me away? Where were you when I was stripped, and begging to be taken out of the pit?*—it is all being redeemed by the actions of Pharaoh, who will be a father-in-exile for him. Thirteen years ago, his father sent him away. Now, a new father will bring him close.

Three Paternal Gifts

After bringing Joseph into his presence, Pharaoh tells him his dreams and asks Joseph what he makes of them. Here, again, if Joseph were to conjure a magical portrait of an ideal father out of thin air, he could not have done better. Back in Canaan, Joseph's real father had reacted caustically when Joseph asked him to hear his dream; but this new father, Pharaoh, will ask Joseph to hear *his* dream, and will eagerly await Joseph's interpretation.[56]

Joseph successfully interprets Pharaoh's dream. The dreams the king has been having about seven cows and seven ears of

---

56. Thus, the pattern of reverses continues. The reverses are suggested even by the syntax of the two verses. When Pharaoh tells Joseph of his dream, the Hebrew is חָלַמְתִּי חֲלוֹם, "a dream, I dreamt" (Genesis 41:15). Thirteen years earlier, when Joseph told his dream to his brothers and then to his father, the Hebrew is חֲלַמְתִּי חֲלוֹם, "I dreamt a dream" (Genesis 37:9). The verbs are reversed.

wheat signal seven years of plenty for Egypt, followed by seven years of ravaging famine. Joseph warns Pharaoh that it is time for Egypt to begin saving and rationing the life-giving wheat, and before Joseph knows it, he has a new job: Pharaoh wants *him* to administer the grain supplies of the entire kingdom. Suddenly Joseph becomes the second most powerful man in all of Egypt: only the king himself, Pharaoh says, shall outrank him (Genesis 41:40).

Not only does the king give Joseph a new job, he gives him a wife, and a new name: Zaphenath-Paneah. Now, what kind of person gives you a job in the family business, helps find you a wife, and gives you a name? That would be your father.

A Familiar Position in the Family

Not only does Pharaoh relate to Joseph as a father would, he places Joseph in a position, relative to him and to Egypt, virtually identical with the position that Joseph had been given years before, by his own father, in his own family. The first verses of Genesis 37 portray Joseph as the right-hand man of his father; now he becomes Pharaoh's right-hand man. Pharaoh will look to Joseph as a conduit, wielding the crown's influence within the larger system. You might say that Joseph has become Pharaoh's adopted *bechor*–his adopted firstborn.

Back in Canaan, Joseph's leadership role in the family had been something of a sore point for his brothers. Somehow, Father *did* seem to view him as his deputy–perhaps Jacob viewed him as *bechor*. Indeed, the Sages of the Midrash seem to view the special coat that Jacob gave his son not merely as a mark of paternal endearment, but as an emblem of Joseph's leadership position in the family, a token of his *bechor*-like status.[57]

---

57. See Genesis Rabbah 84:16. For a detailed elaboration of the symbolism of this coat as it pertains to the *bechor* idea, and some of its fascinating implications, see Appendix B, *One Coat, Two Coats*.

The notion that Joseph was regarded by Jacob as his first-born seems preposterous, on the face of it; many children had been born to Jacob before Joseph. But there was a sense in which Joseph *could* qualify as firstborn. He was the firstborn of Rachel—and Rachel, after all, was the wife Jacob had always *intended* to marry.

In Egypt, Joseph is second-in-command in a national system. Of course, a nation is not a family, but, almost as if to jog the reader's memory of Joseph's former position, the text gives us language that evokes the idea of family. This is Pharaoh's description of Joseph's new, far-reaching authority:

אַתָּה תִּהְיֶה עַל־בֵּיתִי

You shall be in charge of my house (Genesis 41:40)

And the overtones of Joseph's "national" *bechor* position come across in other ways, too. To exemplify Joseph's new status as second-in-command to the king, Pharaoh has him ride in a chariot, aptly called *mirkevet ha-mishneh* (מִרְכֶּבֶת הַמִּשְׁנֶה), literally "the chariot of the Second One" (Genesis 41:43). And the Hebrew verb for "ride"? With a wink and a nod, it just happens to be the word *bechor*, spelled backwards. "And he gave him to ride" (וַיַּרְכֵּב אֹתוֹ) "in the chariot of the Second One" (בְּמִרְכֶּבֶת הַמִּשְׁנֶה). *R-kh-b* (רכב) is *b-kh-r* (בכר) spelled backwards.

A New Life

So, as Joseph rises to power in Egypt, he becomes the son of two "fathers." The reader is left to wonder: is there a competition of sorts between the two men? In Egypt, Joseph seems to retain his devotion to the God of his ancestors (Joseph is quick to mention the name of the Almighty at almost every turn);[58] but what of

---

58. Genesis 41:16, 41:51 and elsewhere.

his emotional connection to his family? Where do his loyalties
lie? This is the challenge that now faces Joseph. Will the power,
love, and acceptance showered upon him by his adoptive father
loosen, and ultimately break, the bonds that tie him to his *actual*
father and brothers–especially given Joseph's uncertainty over
what happened back on that fateful day at the pit?

These questions are never more achingly evident than in the
name Joseph gives to his first child, born to him in Egypt, from
the wife Pharaoh provides for him:

וַיִּקְרָא יוֹסֵף אֶת־שֵׁם הַבְּכוֹר מְנַשֶּׁה כִּי־נַשַּׁנִי
אֱלֹקִים אֶת־כָּל־עֲמָלִי וְאֵת כָּל־בֵּית אָבִי:

And Joseph called the name of his firstborn Manasseh,
[in gratitude] 'that God has caused me to forget my
travails, and all my father's house' (Genesis 41:51)

If the name of Joseph's firstborn expresses his sense that God
has freed him from his tortured past, the name of his second
child expresses his grim determination to make the best of a
new future:

וְאֵת שֵׁם הַשֵּׁנִי קָרָא אֶפְרָיִם כִּי־הִפְרַנִי אֱלֹקִים בְּאֶרֶץ עָנְיִי:

And the name of the second he called Ephraim,
'because God has caused me to be fruitful in the
land of my oppression' (Genesis 41:52)

It is striking that even with all the glitz and power of his new
position, Joseph still regards Egypt as "the land of his oppression."
Why is that so? Perhaps it is because he first came to Egypt as
a slave–in which case, the land no longer seems quite so harsh.
Or perhaps, in Joseph's mind, Egypt is more *essentially* the land
of his oppression. Perhaps Joseph regards this land, as good as
it has been to him, even surrounded with all the trappings of
wealth and power–as a land of exile. Perhaps Joseph yet pines

for home. The reader doesn't know which it is. And perhaps that ambiguity in the biblical text is intentional; perhaps Joseph doesn't know which it is, either.

Future Shock

It is at this moment, after the birth of these two children, that suddenly and without warning, these questions stop being theoretical and become very practical indeed. For, as the famine Joseph predicted descends upon the civilized world, who should happen to show up at Joseph's door but his brothers, seeking grain to bring back to their family in Canaan.

Suddenly, the *bechor* of Pharaoh looks into the faces of his own brothers, the ones who could not stomach him as the child-leader in their family. In a flash, the past is not so safely buried anymore. Just as Joseph was starting to get comfortable in his new life and look toward the future, the past has rudely intruded upon his present. And in this mixed-up present into which fate has cast him, the triangle of love that binds him to both his fathers—to Pharaoh and to Jacob—shall be sorely tested.

CHAPTER TWENTY-THREE

The Land of Nearness

Initially, Joseph keeps his distance from his brothers. They do not recognize him, and he is not forthcoming about his true identity. In fact, it is unclear whether he *ever* intends to reveal it to them.

All that changes, though, when Judah makes an impassioned speech to Joseph—never suspecting that the high Egyptian official standing before him is really his long-lost brother.

In his speech, Judah pleads with Joseph for the release of one of the brothers Joseph is holding prisoner, having arrested him on trumped-up charges of theft. The brother being held is not just any brother; he is Joseph's only full brother, the only other child born to Rachel and Jacob. The first words the Torah uses to introduce Judah's speech are instructive:

וַיִּגַּשׁ אֵלָיו יְהוּדָה

And Judah drew near to him (Genesis 44:18)

Judah really is "drawing near" to Joseph. In the speech that follows, he will lay everything out for Joseph, all the personal details that heretofore had been concealed. Before, Judah had been negotiating with an impersonal Egyptian official. Now Judah speaks as one human being to another, appealing to whatever sense of goodness and compassion this man might possess.

Joseph will hear one theme resonate over and over again in Judah's speech: he will hear how deeply attached Jacob is, even after all these years, to the child of Rachel that so suddenly and mysteriously disappeared from his life, so long ago. He will hear how Jacob, who never recovered from that loss, will not be able to bear losing Benjamin, his only remaining link to his late beloved wife Rachel (Genesis 44:27–29).

In an instant, R. Bin Nun argues, Joseph's world is turned upside down. Suddenly, he learns the truth about his father. *This whole time, my father thought I was dead! For all these years, Father had somehow been deceived. He never threw me out of the family, no! Every moment I've been away, he has been mourning me...*

Sobbing, Joseph reveals himself to his brothers. At first, his words are so shocking and overwhelming that his brothers are simply numb:

וַיֹּאמֶר יוֹסֵף אֶל־אֶחָיו אֲנִי יוֹסֵף הַעוֹד אָבִי חָי
וְלֹא־יָכְלוּ אֶחָיו לַעֲנוֹת אֹתוֹ כִּי נִבְהֲלוּ מִפָּנָיו:

And Joseph said to his brothers: I am Joseph; Is my father still alive? But his brothers could not answer him, they were so shaken in his presence (Genesis 45:3)

So Joseph tries again. This time, he borrows a tactic, touchingly, that Judah himself has just used in his impassioned speech. He repeats his declaration about who he really is, but finds a way to make it warmer, to humanize his words and make them more personal:

וַיֹּאמֶר יוֹסֵף אֶל־אֶחָיו גְּשׁוּ־נָא אֵלַי וַיִּגָּשׁוּ וַיֹּאמֶר אֲנִי יוֹסֵף אֲחִיכֶם

And Joseph said to his brothers: Draw near to me, please. And they drew near. And he said: I am Joseph, your brother (Genesis 45:4)

He tells them not just that he is Joseph, but that he is Joseph, *their brother.*

Judah, just moments ago, had "drawn near" to Joseph. He had let his guard down and spoken personally. Now, Joseph will do the same. He asks his brothers to "draw near" to him, and speaks to them gently, personally. And then he brings up the delicate subject of the pit. *Yes, it is true that you sold me down to Egypt all those years ago*, he tells them; but then he adds, magnanimously:

וְעַתָּה אַל־תֵּעָצְבוּ וְאַל־יִחַר בְּעֵינֵיכֶם כִּי־מְכַרְתֶּם
אֹתִי הֵנָּה כִּי לְמִחְיָה שְׁלָחַנִי אֱלֹקִים לִפְנֵיכֶם:

But now, do not be sad or angry that you sold me
here. For it was [to provide you with] sustenance, that
God sent me here, before you... (Genesis 45:4)

A New Light on an Old Dream

With these words, a kind of reconciliation takes place between these long-separated brothers. Many years later, to be sure, the brothers will come to Joseph and seek a more lasting rapprochement. But in the meantime, Joseph's magnanimity seems to make a mark upon them. It changes their view of him. When the brothers return to Canaan, they report to Jacob the astounding news about Joseph:

עוֹד יוֹסֵף חַי וְכִי־הוּא מֹשֵׁל בְּכָל־אֶרֶץ מִצְרָיִם

Joseph is still alive, and he indeed rules over
all of Egypt! (Genesis 45:26)

Those words contain subtle echoes of the painful past. They parallel the brothers' indictment of Joseph, delivered in anger so many years before. Back then, the brothers used the same verb in their response to Joseph's dream. When Joseph told them about their sheaves of wheat bowing to his, they had said:

אִם־מָשׁוֹל תִּמְשֹׁל בָּנוּ

*Will you really **rule** over us?* (Genesis 37:8)

Now, years later, they finally come to understand that dream's real significance. The dream never meant, as they had suspected at the time, that Joseph would rule over them. Yes, when Joseph was just seventeen years old, it sure *sounded* like that: *Our sheaves will bow to your sheaves.* But with the passage of years, and with Joseph's demonstrated kindness to them, a different meaning of the dream had become clear to the brothers: *It is not over us that Joseph will rule, but over Egypt!* The dream was talking about the future, it was talking about now...

In retrospect, it was all perfectly obvious: why, after all, had the dream taken the form of bundles of wheat? The brothers were herdsmen, not wheat farmers! But the dream was talking not of present megalomania, but of future opportunity: in the future, the family of Jacob would be desperate for wheat–and Joseph would have the wheat they needed. Their sheaves would thus bow to his. The hidden message of the dream was that Joseph would have the opportunity to save the family, an opportunity that Joseph was now making good on.

The Land of Nearness

Joseph's goodwill, and his feelings for his family, become immediately evident in another way. He instructs his brothers to rush back to Canaan and bring their father back with them to Egypt. Once they return, he tells them, he will be in a position to provide for all of them:

וְיָשַׁבְתָּ בְאֶרֶץ־גֹּשֶׁן וְהָיִיתָ קָרוֹב אֵלַי אַתָּה
וּבָנֶיךָ וּבְנֵי בָנֶיךָ... וְכִלְכַּלְתִּי אֹתְךָ שָׁם

You will settle here in the Land of Goshen, and you shall be
close to me—you, your children and grandchildren... and
I will sustain you all there (Genesis 45:10-11)

Note that Joseph's desire to help goes beyond providing the utilitarian benefit of food at a time of crisis. That could have been accomplished without bringing everyone to Egypt and giving them homes in Goshen. He was the second most powerful man in all of Egypt. He could've easily provided for his family back in Canaan by sending a convoy of camels every three months, loaded with food and provisions. In asking them all to come to Goshen, Joseph has another agenda—one that he is perfectly up-front about: *he wants to be close to them.*

Reread Joseph's words to the brothers. Settle in Goshen so "you shall be close to me." And not just *you*, Joseph's brothers. No. "You, your children, and grandchildren." Joseph wants to watch his brothers' children and grandchildren grow up. He has been isolated from his real family for so long; now, it is closeness with them that he craves.

Even the name for the place where he will settle his family, Goshen, is redolent with the idea of "nearness." Was Goshen a pre-existing name—or simply the nickname Joseph gave to the region, right there, on the spot? We will never know, but *Goshen* does seem suspiciously close to *geshu na* (גְּשׁוּ־נָא), the first personal words Joseph said to his brothers, just a few lines previously (Genesis 45:4). *Geshu na* means "draw near, please." Could it be that, in Joseph's mind, the Land of Goshen is the Land of Nearness?

The Prison of Power

There is a poignant irony in Joseph's position. Usually, if you wants to be near one's family, either they can move to you, or you can move to them. In Joseph's case, the latter does not appear to be an option: Joseph can't leave Egypt. Egypt needs his steady hand to steer it through a crushing national crisis; he cannot simply abscond. He would not even be able to provide for his family if he left. Ironically, though Joseph escaped prison through Pharaoh's perception of his uncanny abilities, he is now, in a way, a prisoner of those very gifts.

Whether or not Joseph senses how potentially shackling his great power is, Jacob seems to have some inkling of it. On the way down to Egypt to visit Joseph for what he perhaps assumes will be an extended weekend with his long-lost son, Jacob stops at Beer-sheba for the night. There, he has a prophetic dream. God addresses him with this message:

אַל־תִּירָא מֵרְדָה מִצְרַיְמָה כִּי־לְגוֹי גָּדוֹל אֲשִׂימְךָ שָׁם:

Do not fear going down to Egypt, for I will make
you a great nation there (Genesis 46:3)

Why is God saying this? Who mentioned anything about fear? Jacob should have been full of joy; why would he be fearful? Evidently, though, there *is* something to fear about this journey—and Jacob, despite his outward happiness at the chance to see Joseph, senses it as he sets out on his way. He and his family are going down to Egypt; Joseph will provide for them there. *But how will they ever leave?*

Be Afraid. Be Very Afraid.

Decades earlier, Jacob had received a double promise from the Almighty: he would have many descendants, and these descendants would be given the Land of Canaan as their ancestral homeland (Genesis 28:13–14). Anyone listening to that promise, at the time, might well have assumed that these two gifts would come simultaneously. That is, Jacob's destiny was to settle in the Land of Canaan, have children, and build the nascent family of Israel in its homeland. And, as a matter of fact, this seems to have been precisely what Jacob aimed to do when he returned with his family to the Land of Canaan after a long sojourn in the house of his father-in-law, Laban. He was coming home, hopefully for good:

וַיֵּשֶׁב יַעֲקֹב בְּאֶרֶץ מְגוּרֵי אָבִיו בְּאֶרֶץ כְּנָעַן:

And Jacob settled in the land where his fathers had
sojourned, in the Land of Canaan (Genesis 37:1)

This would be Jacob's great triumph: His ancestors had all lived
in Canaan, but they had lived there as sojourners; they weren't
permanent residents. Jacob would be the first to really *settle* there,
he hoped. The verbs in the verse make that clear: Jacob *settled* in
Canaan, where his forefathers had only *sojourned*. Jacob, returning from Laban's household, thought that his life's mission was
nearly in reach: all he had to do was settle down, have kids, and
let them build a nation in their own land.[59] But that was before
the sale of Joseph. Now, years later, that dream was starting to
fade. Joseph was in Egypt, and slowly, inexorably, with the best
of intentions, Joseph would bring everyone back there along
with him.

Jacob had tried to settle in Canaan, but at the end of his life,
here he was, going down to Egypt–and God's words to him had
a bittersweet ring:

אַל־תִּירָא מֵרְדָה מִצְרַיְמָה כִּי־לְגוֹי גָּדוֹל אֲשִׂימְךָ שָׁם:

Do not fear going down to Egypt, for I will make
you a great nation there (Genesis 46:3)

It seems almost as if God is commenting on the initial promise
He had made to Jacob, all those years before. *Yes, I will still make*

---

59. This, indeed, is what the Sages of the Midrash seem to have had in
mind when, commenting on the verse's words "Jacob settled," they added: "Jacob sought to settle down in tranquility... but [was foiled], for then,
the troubles of Joseph [and his sale] descended upon him" (see *Rashi* to
Genesis 37:1).

you a great nation, just as I said before. But you won't become a great nation in the Land of Canaan. Instead, your progeny will multiply in exile, in the Land of Egypt. The nation will be built outside its ancestral land.

More than the King Must Know

The lingering aftertaste of Jacob's dream may account for something puzzling in the biblical text. When Jacob arrives in Egypt, Joseph introduces him to Pharaoh. Jacob blesses the king, and Pharaoh engages Jacob in what one might call polite small talk; he asks Jacob how old he is. And here is Jacob's astounding reply:

וַיֹּאמֶר יַעֲקֹב אֶל־פַּרְעֹה יְמֵי שְׁנֵי מְגוּרַי שְׁלֹשִׁים וּמְאַת שָׁנָה מְעַט וְרָעִים
הָיוּ יְמֵי שְׁנֵי חַיַּי וְלֹא הִשִּׂיגוּ אֶת־יְמֵי שְׁנֵי חַיֵּי אֲבֹתַי בִּימֵי מְגוּרֵיהֶם:

And Jacob said to Pharaoh: The years of my sojourning are 130 years. Small and disappointing have been the years of my life. They have not even equaled the years of the lives of my fathers in the days of their own sojourning (Genesis 47:9)

Why is Jacob in such a bad mood? Why say all that to Pharaoh, who seemingly was only trying to be nice, complimenting Jacob on having lived to an advanced age?[60]

Something is on Jacob's mind as he stands before Pharaoh. It is a sense that somehow, he has not lived out his dream. He is in the sunset of his life, and still only a sojourner like his forefathers.[61] Wasn't he meant to settle in Canaan and begin the work of nation-building? But he just couldn't do it. Yes, he and his family would survive here in Egypt; they would not starve. *But is this really where he was supposed to be?*

---

60. This question is also advanced by *Ramban* to Genesis 47:9.

61. Cf. *Rashi* and *Seforno* to Genesis 47:9.

When Making It Better Makes It Worse

Immediately after Jacob exits his audience with Pharaoh, the text tells us something curious. The brothers had told Pharaoh that they had come to sojourn in the land (Genesis 47:4). And yet Joseph gives his brothers and father something that no sojourner or stranger could ever have:

וַיּוֹשֵׁב יוֹסֵף אֶת־אָבִיו וְאֶת־אֶחָיו וַיִּתֵּן לָהֶם אֲחֻזָּה בְּאֶרֶץ מִצְרַיִם

Joseph settled his father and brothers, and gave them
ancestral holdings in the Land of Egypt (Genesis 47:11)

Ancestral holdings are the deepest type of land ownership described in the Bible. Later, this particular word, *achuzah* (אֲחֻזָּה), will be used to characterize Israel's possession of the Land of Canaan (Numbers 32:22). But Joseph is providing this kind of land ownership to his family–in Egypt.

Joseph seems keen to ensure that his family *won't* be mere sojourners in Egypt. They will feel like they *belong* here (*Ramban* to Genesis 47:11). It does not seem coincidental that Joseph makes this small adjustment in his family's immigration status immediately after he overhears his father complaining to Pharaoh about living the life of a sojourner at the end of his years. Joseph wants his father and brothers near him, but he certainly doesn't want them to feel like displaced persons. He wants them to feel at home, so he gives them an *achuzah* in Egypt.

And so it happens. The family of Joseph takes possession of land in Egypt, and, over time, they prosper and become numerous there. As the text expresses it, they "take hold" (וַיֵּאָחֲזוּ) of the land they were given (Genesis 47:27)–a play on the Hebrew *achuzah*, the word used above for the "ancestral holding" Joseph had given them. On the face of it, the family is now secure. They are living near Joseph. Everything should be wonderful.

In Joseph's eyes, making his family into landed gentry in Egypt was a great privilege. But there is at least one man who understands the dark side to all this—Jacob. The family's destiny lies in Canaan, not Egypt. *But how will they ever get there?* They came down to Egypt with seventy souls. But as Jacob nears death, years later, there are hundreds of family members. The family is wealthy and privileged. They are landowners. Children have grown up here; Egypt is all they know. What will make them leave?

This is the background for Jacob's fateful talk with Joseph.[62] Seventeen years after he first set foot in Egypt, Jacob summons his son for a crucial discussion. It is a discussion Jacob had avoided until now. But finally, as he approached death, there was no choice. He would say what needed to be said. And it will be up to Joseph to choose with which father his deepest loyalty rests.

---

62. Tellingly, it is immediately after we are told that the family "took hold" of the land "and were very fruitful" there (Genesis 47:27), ensconcing the family firmly in the land, that we hear of Jacob's decision to summon Joseph to discuss his burial arrangements (Genesis 47:29). As the Bible presents it, the former happenings are the final straws that catalyze the latter.

CHAPTER TWENTY-FOUR

The Fence of Thorns

If Jacob cannot "take hold" of the Land of Canaan in life, he will at least be enveloped by it in death. He summons Joseph and asks him to bury him in the Land of Canaan, in the cave where his forebears are buried. Joseph says he will, but that's not enough—Jacob asks him to swear to it. Earlier, we wondered why a solemn oath would be necessary, but we can now understand why.

Joseph was like a son to two men—an actual, biological father, Jacob, and a figurative father, Pharaoh. That was all well and good as long as the interests of those two men, Jacob and Pharaoh, aligned with one another. *But what would happen if one day they didn't?*

Now is the moment when Pharaoh's and Jacob's interests diverge. There's just no way to make both men happy anymore.

Consider this: who, exactly, is Jacob, in Egypt's eyes? He is the father of Egypt's savior, Joseph—which means that Jacob is Egyptian royalty. When he dies, all of Egypt mourns him for seventy days. How would Pharaoh feel about a state funeral in a little backwater of the Middle East called Canaan? Imagine Queen Elizabeth dying and being buried in Madagascar. Things like that don't happen. To make such a request of Egypt's king would be a dicey thing to do, to say the least.[63]

---

63. Cf. *Ramban* to Genesis 50:6.

Joseph's Choice

Nevertheless, Joseph swears to Jacob that he will bury him in Canaan. And then Jacob bows to the head of the bed. Now we can appreciate what the Sages of the Midrash meant when they said that Jacob had bowed in gratitude:

יוֹסֵף מֶלֶךְ הוּא וְעוֹד שֶׁנִּשְׁבָּה לְבֵין הַגּוֹיִם וְהֲרֵי הוּא עוֹמֵד בְּצִדְקוֹ

Joseph was [Egyptian] royalty, and furthermore, he
had been captured [and lived] among heathens—and
yet he remained steadfast in his righteousness (*Rashi*,
from *Sifrei Va'etchanan* 31, *Sifrei Ha'azinu* 334)

We asked earlier why it took Jacob seventeen years of living in Egypt to realize that Joseph was righteous, that Joseph had not assimilated into Egyptian culture. Why did Jacob not realize this the moment he first set eyes upon him, when Joseph embraced him, cried, and promised to take care of the family's every need? *That* seems like the moment Jacob should have realized what a good son Joseph was. Why was it only *now*—seventeen years later—that Jacob understood this?

But it makes perfect sense. This really *was* the moment that Jacob knew that Joseph was a loyal son. Providing for the family was one thing. That choice did not really require him to put his relationship with Pharaoh under any strain. But a state funeral in Canaan? Trying to honor *that* request could come at a real price for Joseph. When Joseph *swore* he would do it, Jacob understood what that meant. In a contest between competing fathers and their respective interests, Joseph had just chosen Jacob.

Where Is Home?

In truth, burial in Canaan wasn't just about the disposition of his body—it was about the destiny of the family. What Jacob was really telling Joseph was something like: *Look, Son, Egypt is nice, and Pharaoh is very gracious—but, at the end of the day, Egypt is not our place. Home is Canaan, the land God promised to us. That is where our family has an achuzah waiting for us, an ancestral holding.*

The Israelites weren't meant to become God-fearing Egyptian aristocrats; they were meant to serve God as a sovereign nation in their own land. Jacob's real question for Joseph, his child who ruled over Egypt, was: *Are you on board with that vision?* Will you publicly back our family's allegiance to another homeland, to a larger national mission that doesn't include Egypt as a place of residence?

Joseph answers in the affirmative. He understands the family's destiny, and despite the personal sacrifice it might entail, he will do his part to uphold it—which helps us understand the conversation that ensues.

A Deathbed Conversation

The Torah records that, after Joseph swore to Jacob that he would bury him in Canaan, Joseph came back to Jacob for a further audience, and brought along his two sons, Ephraim and Manasseh. Jacob tells them about a promise God made to him long ago, a promise about the Land of Canaan:

קֵל שַׁדַּי נִרְאָה־אֵלַי בְּלוּז בְּאֶרֶץ כְּנָעַן וַיְבָרֶךְ אֹתִי: וַיֹּאמֶר
אֵלַי הִנְנִי מַפְרְךָ וְהִרְבִּיתִךָ וּנְתַתִּיךָ לִקְהַל עַמִּים וְנָתַתִּי
אֶת־הָאָרֶץ הַזֹּאת לְזַרְעֲךָ אַחֲרֶיךָ אֲחֻזַּת עוֹלָם:

The Lord appeared to me in Luz, in the Land of Canaan, and blessed me. He said to me: I will greatly multiply your progeny, and will make you into a multitude, a nation; and I shall give this land to your descendants after you, as an ancestral holding (Genesis 48:3–4)

Jacob is letting Joseph and his sons in on the backstory behind his desire to be buried in Canaan. *God made two promises to me: children and land. Here, in Egypt, the promise of progeny is being fulfilled. But the promise of land is still outstanding. Canaan will yet be our homeland, the place of our achuzah. In consenting to bury me in Canaan, this is what you have consented to...*

Ephraim and Manasseh

Jacob then says something about the two children standing before him. At first glance, what he says about them seems unconnected to the point he has just made about Canaan. Here are Jacob's words:

וְעַתָּה שְׁנֵי־בָנֶיךָ הַנּוֹלָדִים לְךָ בְּאֶרֶץ מִצְרַיִם עַד־בֹּאִי אֵלֶיךָ
מִצְרַיְמָה לִי־הֵם אֶפְרַיִם וּמְנַשֶּׁה כִּרְאוּבֵן וְשִׁמְעוֹן יִהְיוּ־לִי:

And now, your two children that were born to you in Egypt, before I ever came to you in Egypt—they are mine. Ephraim and Manasseh—like Reuben and Simeon [my own children] they shall be to me (Genesis 48:5)

At the simplest level, Jacob seems to be telling his son, Joseph, that he considers Joseph's two children, Ephraim and Manasseh, to be as dear to him as if they were his very own. To be sure, that is a touching sentiment for a grandfather to express. But Jacob seems to be saying something more...

Unfinished Business

Look how Jacob characterizes the birth of Ephraim and Manasseh. He calls them the two children "that were born to you in Egypt, before I ever came to you in Egypt." Why did he have to say that? Was he helpfully reminding Joseph how old Ephraim and Manasseh were, in case their father had somehow forgotten?

No, Jacob was after something else entirely. Before he died, he was acknowledging, and lovingly redeeming, something painful in Joseph's past, something symbolized by the birth of these two children.

Who *were* Ephraim and Manasseh? What did their births mean to Joseph? These are the offspring that were born when Joseph was just reaching the height of his powers in Egypt, when it perhaps seemed to Joseph that he had been thrown out of the family. The possibility of ever reclaiming his past life with his father and brothers had seemed virtually nonexistent when these kids were born. A benevolent Pharaoh had become a replacement father, giving Joseph a new name and a wife. And with that wife he had sired these two sons—sons he named for his sense of pain and alienation from his family, and for his hope of starting a new life in this foreign land: Manasseh, "for God has allowed me to forget all my travail, all of my father's house"; Ephraim, "for God has given me children in the land of my oppression."

If those names seem haunting to *us*, reading about this, how much more might they have haunted Jacob. These truly *were* children "born to you in Egypt, before I ever came to you in Egypt." Ephraim and Manasseh represented Egypt as it *used* to be for Joseph, before Jacob was back in Joseph's life: a foreign land that had once enslaved a seemingly-orphaned Joseph, but had then taken care of him, just as he took care of it. All the while, Jacob was a world away. These two children were symbols of a seemingly unbridgeable gulf that had existed between Jacob and Joseph.

One might think that the best Jacob could do, with regard to these children, would be to benignly tolerate them, to politely smile at them as they passed in the hallway. He could try his best not to notice the deep alienation they represented. He could adopt a cool and standoffish attitude toward them.

But that would not, in fact, be Jacob's stance. Jacob wanted Joseph to know that he would embrace his grandchildren fully and without reservation. Joseph, with his oath to bury Jacob in Canaan, had bridged the divide that separated him from his father, and now Jacob would reciprocate. Joseph had accepted his father's future, in which Egypt would fade away, and now, Jacob would accept his son's past, in which Canaan, tragically, had seemed to fade away. These children that had once been symbols of Joseph's alienation from his father's house–Jacob would hold them as dear as his very own.

A Second Seventeen Years

Jacob's words concerning Ephraim and Manasseh seem to contain one more layer of significance. In saying that he regarded these grandchildren as if they were his very own children, he was in effect elevating them by a generation. In so doing, he was giving them a special status that would have long-lasting implications. If Ephraim and Manasseh really *were* like Reuben and Simeon, then they, like Jacob's children, would become tribes, with their own distinct territories in the Land of Canaan.[64] And that's exactly what happened. For, indeed, Israel's tribes include Reuben, Simeon and Levi–but they do not include Joseph, because Ephraim and Manasseh, "elevated by a generation," represent Joseph among the tribes.

When we add it all up, this means that, through Ephraim and Manasseh, Joseph accounts for *two* of the tribes of Israel, whereas every other child of Jacob only accounts for one. Those familiar with Deuteronomy might catch the allusion here: Joseph has a kind of "double share" in his father's legacy, a fact that resonates with later biblical laws regarding inheritance. The Torah entitles a *bechor*, a firstborn child, to a double share in his father's estate (Deuteronomy 21:16–17). It seems that Jacob's words about Ephraim and Manasseh constituted a kind of bestowal of status

---

64. See *Rashi* to 48:5; Cf. *Ramban* loc. cit.

upon Joseph–a confirmation that yes, he could finally be called a true *bechor*.[65]

Whether Joseph was biologically firstborn was no longer the point. Joseph had acted as *bechor* in this family, serving its interests selflessly. Years ago, Father had seemed to accord him this status with a special coat.[66] It was an open question whether Joseph deserved that coat–and it had perhaps fueled his brothers' resentment of him. But that was then, and this was now. In the intervening years, Joseph had saved the family from starvation. And now, as Jacob lay on his deathbed, Joseph had sworn to uphold Jacob's burial wishes, at great personal cost. He truly was, for all intents and purposes, a *bechor*, a child-leader in the family, devoted selflessly both to the welfare of his brothers, and to the vision of his father.

Like Father, like Son

In light of all this, the final verses of the book of Genesis, detailing Joseph's own burial wishes, attain a greater poignancy:

וַיֹּאמֶר יוֹסֵף אֶל־אֶחָיו אָנֹכִי מֵת וֵאלֹקִים פָּקֹד יִפְקֹד אֶתְכֶם
וְהֶעֱלָה אֶתְכֶם מִן־הָאָרֶץ הַזֹּאת אֶל־הָאָרֶץ אֲשֶׁר נִשְׁבַּע
לְאַבְרָהָם לְיִצְחָק וּלְיַעֲקֹב: וַיַּשְׁבַּע יוֹסֵף אֶת־בְּנֵי יִשְׂרָאֵל לֵאמֹר
פָּקֹד יִפְקֹד אֱלֹקִים אֶתְכֶם וְהַעֲלִתֶם אֶת־עַצְמֹתַי מִזֶּה:

---

65. See Appendix B, *One Coat, Two Coats* for an extended discussion of this passage in Deuteronomy regarding inheritance, and its implications for the early part of the Joseph saga.

66. According to the Sages, Joseph's coat carried that symbolism. He had been given a "double portion of coats," evoking the doubled portion in his father's estate that Deuteronomy (21:16–17) promises to a *bechor* (Genesis Rabbah 84:16).

And Joseph said to his brothers: I will die; but God will surely
redeem you, and bring you up from this land to the land that He
promised to Abraham, Isaac, and Jacob. And Joseph made the
Children of Israel swear, saying: [When] God indeed redeems you,
you shall bring my bones up from this [place] (Genesis 50:24–25)

God will "redeem" you. Redemption is a powerful word. Why
would the family need redeeming from this land of plenty? But
on his deathbed, Joseph, who brought his family *to* Egypt to
save them, has a premonition that his family will at some point
need saving in order to make it *out* of Egypt. Years before, Joseph
couldn't really leave. But now his family, his countrymen, can't
really leave either. For all its sweetness, Egypt's plenty has become
a veritable prison. In years to come, as the sweetness is replaced
by hostility, it will become a greater prison still.

Joseph's father had made him swear to bury him in Canaan.
Now Joseph imposes a similar oath upon his brothers. One day,
they will all leave. And they must promise that when they do,
even if it is centuries later, they will take his bones with them.
The land that God promised will once again be his home. If not
in life, then at least in death.

The Fence of Thorns

How Joseph negotiates the triangle involving Pharaoh, his father,
and him, forms the backstory to another strange comment made
by the Sages.

The biblical text tells us that before Jacob was buried, he was
eulogized in a place on the east bank of the Jordan called *Goren
Ha-Atad,* which means "a threshing floor surrounded by thorn-
bushes" (*Rashi* to Genesis 50:11). The Talmud (*Sotah* 13a, cited by
Rashi) suggests that the place was named for something that
happened there during Jacob's funeral.

As the Sages of the Talmud tell it, during Jacob's burial procession, all the kings of Canaan and the Princes of Ishmael assembled to attack the Israelites, who had gathered at this spot to eulogize Jacob. But then, the would-be attackers saw something that made them halt in their tracks:

כֵּיוָן שֶׁרָאוּ כִּתְרוֹ שֶׁל יוֹסֵף תָּלוּי בָּאֲרוֹנוֹ שֶׁל יַעֲקֹב, עָמְדוּ כּוּלָן וְתָלוּ בּוֹ כִּתְרֵיהֶם, וְהִקִּיפוּהוּ כְּתָרִים כְּגוֹרֶן הַמּוּקָף סְיָיג שֶׁל קוֹצִים

Joseph's crown was hanging on Jacob's casket, and when they saw this—all [these kings and princes] stood up, [put down their weapons] and hung their own crowns on it, and surrounded his casket with crowns, like a threshing floor surrounded by a fence of thorns (Sotah 13a, in Rashi to Genesis 50:10)

What do the Sages mean to say with their cryptic story? Why were these kings attacking? And why did the sight of Joseph's crown make all these kings halt their attack—and join their crowns to his?

Consider this: who, exactly, do the Sages say were attacking the children of Jacob? They weren't just random attackers. They were the kings and princes of Canaan and Ishmael.

Think back to the founding fathers of these nations, Canaan and Ishmael; what was the common denominator between them?

They were both dispossessed children.

Thrown Out of the Family

Canaan was the cursed grandson of Noah, who was thrown out of the family. Ishmael was the son of Abraham, also thrown out of his family. Both of these dispossessed children now come to attack other children—children their own fathers had loved and legitimized.

Shem was accepted by Noah. Isaac, a descendant of Shem, was accepted by his father, Abraham, too. And now, generations later, as the descendants of all the accepted children gather for

Jacob's funeral, the kings of Ishmael and Canaan come to attack them. But then something halts them in their tracks: the crown of Joseph, hanging over the coffin of Jacob.

Joseph was a child who thought himself dispossessed, too. But Joseph didn't, in the end, turn around to attack. He clawed his way, somehow, back into the family. It took years, but he made it. When the fateful moment came for him to choose–*are you, with all your wealth, power, and prestige, a son of Pharaoh, or a son of Jacob? Whose family do you call your own?*–Joseph chose his own family, the family of Israel, with all the difficulty this choice entailed.

Joseph buried Jacob in Canaan. In so doing, he put his crown, as it were, on his father's casket–Joseph had put that crown at risk for his father. As the Midrash puts it, when the Kings of Canaan and Ishmael saw that crown, they stopped their attack, and with humility, joined their crowns to Joseph's.

Only Joseph holds the moral force to take the venom out of an attack of dispossessed children. And remember: not only does he fend off these kings, he wins them over; they join their crowns to his. One wonders if the Talmud is painting a picture not only of the past, but of a possible future, gilded with hope for reconciliation within the extended family of Israel. If, after all the pain, anger, and misunderstanding in his past, Joseph can solemnly give Jacob honor–if, after everything, he can wed his destiny to that of his family–then perhaps other fragments of dispossessed families can find in Joseph an example to emulate. If Joseph can make it back, perhaps there is hope for them, too.

Unexpected Heroism

In our look at the triangle of interaction between Joseph, Pharaoh, and Jacob, we have come to appreciate the significance of Joseph's promise to honor his father's request to be buried in Canaan. Still, it is one thing to make a promise, and another to carry it out. How, in practice, did Joseph manage to approach

Pharaoh with news of the state funeral that would have to be held in Canaan? And how, in the end, did Pharaoh respond to that outrageous request? The answers to these questions reveal that Joseph was not the only one who acted honorably and heroically in the affair of Jacob's funeral. Heroism also came from unexpected quarters...

CHAPTER TWENTY-FIVE

A Conversation, Delayed

Jacob dies.

Joseph weeps over the body of his father, and then he gets up (Genesis 50:1). One would assume that if Joseph had not yet spoken to Pharaoh about his father's peculiar burial request, right about now would be the time to do that. And yet Joseph does not. Here is what happens next:

וַיְצַו יוֹסֵף אֶת־עֲבָדָיו אֶת־הָרֹפְאִים לַחֲנֹט
אֶת־אָבִיו וַיַּחַנְטוּ הָרֹפְאִים אֶת־יִשְׂרָאֵל:

Joseph commanded his servants, the doctors, to embalm his father. And so the doctors embalmed Israel... (Genesis 50:2)

Instead of speaking to Pharaoh about the special burial needs of his father, Joseph proceeds with what was apparently standard operating procedure for the death of a member of the royal family: he directs that Jacob's body be embalmed. The embalming process takes weeks–and still Joseph remains silent. He seems to be procrastinating, delaying the inevitable conversation. The possible repercussions of that conversation, if it does not go well, are dismaying indeed.

Journey to a New World

As for the embalming of Jacob's body, the Torah mentions exactly who is doing the embalming—the task falls to the *rof'im*—the "healers." At first blush, that seems odd. A doctor or healer cares for the living, not for the dead. What healing, after all, could one provide to a corpse? But in Egypt, that was the whole point: the dead *could* be healed. The Egyptians wanted to ensure that the body would not decompose; as they saw it, the body still had work to do after death. What that work was is hinted at in the time period the Torah gives us for the embalming process:

וַיִּמְלְאוּ־לוֹ אַרְבָּעִים יוֹם כִּי כֵּן יִמְלְאוּ יְמֵי הַחֲנֻטִים

And forty days were fulfilled for him; for so are fulfilled the days of embalming (Genesis 50:3)

Forty days is a familiar time period for the reader of the Torah. Earlier in Genesis, rain fell for forty days in the Great Flood. Later, Moses spends forty days atop Mount Sinai. It seems as if the elapse of forty days signifies something: transition, a passage to a new world.

When it rained for forty days and forty nights, that was a bridge between one world and another. The old world was closing down, and a new one coming into being. When Moses spent forty days atop Mount Sinai, he too journeyed to a new world: he left the terrestrial sphere, and entered a transcendent one. And, according to the Egyptians, that was precisely the point of embalming someone: it was to prepare the dead for a journey between worlds. The dead *could* be "healed," if the body could be preserved—for the spirit would ultimately ride that body on an odyssey to another world.

A Nation Mourns

The forty days elapse, and the embalming period for Jacob ends. But Egypt's response to Jacob's death continues well beyond that. In a sign of just how venerated Jacob was by the Egyptian populace, we are told that Egypt cried over the death of Jacob for seventy days (Genesis 50:3). If that sounds like a long time, it certainly is—even by biblical standards. By way of comparison, the Children of Israel only mourned the death of Aaron, and later, of Moses, for thirty days (Numbers 20:29; Deuteronomy 34:8). Egypt cried over the loss of Jacob for more than twice that long.

And it wasn't even Jacob's own people that did this for him; it was a foreign nation that mourned him so! But if Joseph had perhaps regarded Pharaoh as a kind of adoptive father, it seems, remarkably, that Egypt reciprocated that sentiment with Joseph's own father. Joseph had saved them all from starvation, so the nation had "adopted" his father, Jacob, as one of their own. His death mattered deeply to them.

A Collision of Customs

Finally, the forty days of embalming are over, and the seventy days of mourning pass too (Genesis 50:4). Egypt dusts itself off, and gets ready to return to normal life. Having marked the passing of a great man with all the honor due to him, they are ready, finally, to put Jacob's death behind them.

But what the Egyptians don't realize is that it's not over. From the Israelite perspective, it hadn't even begun. All through those seventy days, Joseph still hadn't breathed a word of Jacob's burial request to anyone in Egyptian officialdom. Joseph hadn't had the heart to tell them that this was all *Egyptian* mourning. Awkwardly enough, from the perspective of the Israelites, they had not yet even begun to provide Jacob's body the only honor Jacob ever wanted for himself. They had not yet made good on their promise to bury him in the Land of Canaan.

To make things still more awkward, consider what Jacob want-ed done to his body: he wanted it buried in the earth. Contrast that with Egyptian embalming. Burial and embalming aren't just different ways of relating to a corpse–no, burial and embalming are *exact opposites*.

In the religion of ancient Egypt, one enters the afterlife with his physical body. The whole point of embalming a body is to preserve it from decaying, eventually, into dust. But burial is to *facilitate* the body's return to dust. "You are dust, and to dust you shall return!" (Genesis 3:19). Egyptians, then, would be horrified at the notion of *burying* the body of one of their royalty. Why would you do such a thing? You are destroying the king's vehicle to the afterlife!

The Courtiers

Joseph has really backed himself into a corner. By waiting to divulge his secret to Pharaoh, he may have only made matters worse. Had he at least told Pharaoh's court immediately about his father's insistence on burial, steps could have been taken, perhaps, to manage public opinion. A way could have perhaps been found to break the news to the Egyptian populace. But not now. In Egyptian eyes, the only thing worse than burying a beloved person of royal standing would be burying them *after* embalming them. To do so would seem to make a mockery of the whole embalming process.

So how does Joseph finally bring up his father's desire for burial?

וַיַּעַבְרוּ יְמֵי בְכִיתוֹ וַיְדַבֵּר יוֹסֵף אֶל־בֵּית פַּרְעֹה לֵאמֹר אִם־נָא
מָצָאתִי חֵן בְּעֵינֵיכֶם דַּבְּרוּ־נָא בְּאָזְנֵי פַרְעֹה לֵאמֹר:

*The days of the Egyptian mourning passed. And Joseph
spoke to [those in] the court of Pharaoh, saying: If I have
found favor in your eyes, please speak [on my behalf] in
Pharaoh's ears, and say [the following]...* (Genesis 50:4)

Notice who it is that Joseph addresses in that verse: people in the
court of Pharaoh. He wants them to carry a personal message to
the king for him. Moreover, look at the language Joseph uses to
address these lower-level courtiers: "If I have found favor in your
eyes, please..." Joseph outranks every last member of Pharaoh's
court. But he beseeches them in plaintive terms. The whole spec-
tacle must have seemed absurd, as if the Vice President were
beseeching the deputy Housing Secretary to deliver a personal
message on his behalf to the President.

In the past, Joseph has never had any trouble addressing
Pharaoh directly. When he wanted to settle his family in Goshen,
for example, he unhesitatingly brought that matter up directly
with the king. All of a sudden, though, Joseph seems to fear a
one-on-one audience with Pharaoh—and we can understand why.

If Joseph *finally* asks permission to bury Jacob in the ground
after forty days of embalming and seventy days of mourning, well,
he could expect Pharaoh—at the very least—to ask rather acidly
why Joseph didn't bring up this fine idea seventy days ago. *What
are we supposed to do now? Pretend all the embalming didn't happen,
all the mourning didn't happen? The honor and fanfare we gave your
father means nothing to you?* At best, Pharaoh might be incredulous;
at worst, rageful. Perhaps Joseph doesn't want to be around to
see Pharaoh's response. Perhaps this is an idea better broken to
him by others...

The Message

Here is the message Joseph asks those courtiers to deliver:

אָבִי הִשְׁבִּיעַנִי לֵאמֹר הִנֵּה אָנֹכִי מֵת בְּקִבְרִי אֲשֶׁר כָּרִיתִי לִי בְּאֶרֶץ
כְּנַעַן שָׁמָּה תִּקְבְּרֵנִי וְעַתָּה אֶעֱלֶה־נָּא וְאֶקְבְּרָה אֶת־אָבִי וְאָשׁוּבָה:

*My father made me swear, saying: Here, I am going to die. In
my grave that I've carved out for myself in the Land of Canaan,
that's where you must bury me. And so now, let me go up, please,
and bury my father—and I shall return* (Genesis 50:5)

The very first thing Joseph mentions to Pharaoh is his oath—and
Joseph's meaning is clear: *If it weren't for this oath, we wouldn't be
talking about this. I can't just break a solemn oath to my father; surely
you understand that.* The oath, Joseph hopes, will take some of
the sting out of it for Pharaoh. It is ironic, perhaps—and one
wonders whether Jacob anticipated this at the time—that the
oath Jacob made Joseph take, in the end, not only bound Joseph
to his promise, but became a tool Joseph used to help him *make
good* on the promise.[67] It gives Joseph just a little bit of distance
from a request that, were it to have simply originated in Joseph's
heart—*here's a nice thing I'd like to do for my father*—could have been
explosive.

Joseph's closing, "and I shall return," has a plaintive ring to it.
It seems strange that he would even need to say it, as if he needs
to assure the king that his loyal servant will faithfully return.
For the reader, though, who comes across these words with the
benefit of centuries of hindsight, Joseph's last phrase is chilling:
Oh, how they shall return! This, indeed, will be the last time for
generations that Joseph and Israel's children will set foot outside
Egypt. Soon, this benevolent Pharaoh shall die, and another
Pharaoh shall take his place. Soon, the Children of Israel will
not have the option of leaving. The terrifying specter of slavery
shall engulf them.

---

67. See *Ramban* to 47:31.

And so, with those final words, Joseph has finally said to the king what he must say. The die is cast. It is now up to Pharaoh to respond.

CHAPTER TWENTY-SIX

Honor Guard

Pharaoh says yes.

At first, it seems like a very reluctant yes, uttered through gritted teeth:

וַיֹּאמֶר פַּרְעֹה עֲלֵה וּקְבֹר אֶת־אָבִיךָ כַּאֲשֶׁר הִשְׁבִּיעֶךָ:

Pharaoh said: Go and bury your father, as
he made you swear (Genesis 50:6)

Those last words, "as he made you swear," seem to color the tone of the statement. As Rashi puts it, Pharaoh appears to be saying: *I'm not going to make you violate an oath you made to your father. Were it not for that oath, though, never would I allow such an outrage...* [68]

If you were Joseph in that situation, you'd take what you could get. If that yes from Pharaoh was halfhearted—well, a halfhearted yes is better than a no, you'd probably tell yourself.

And so, it would seem we've finally arrived at the end of the story of Joseph's interaction with Pharaoh over his father's burial. Joseph has the permission he needs, even if it *is* grudging permission. They can do what they think they have to—as long as they do it as privately and as discreetly as possible. As for Pharaoh, with his cold yes, he can simply wash his hands of this whole

---

68. See *Rashi* to 50:6; cf. *Ramban*.

awkward affair, and move on to more pressing affairs of state. The drama is over. Or is it? In the very next verse, something remarkable happens.

The Honor Guard

וַיַּעַל יוֹסֵף לִקְבֹּר אֶת־אָבִיו וַיַּעֲלוּ אִתּוֹ כָּל־עַבְדֵי
פַרְעֹה זִקְנֵי בֵיתוֹ וְכֹל זִקְנֵי אֶרֶץ־מִצְרָיִם:

*Joseph went up to bury his father—and with him
went up all the servants of Pharaoh, the elders of his
court, and all the elders of Egypt* (Genesis 50:7)

When it's time for Jacob's burial procession to get under way, it turns out that it is not just the family of Jacob going, quietly and unobtrusively, to do what they have to do in the Land of Canaan. An entourage from Egypt accompanies them—a delegation of such stature that it could only have been sent by the king himself. All of Pharaoh's servants set out with the family, along with the elders of the king's court.

And that's not all; the palace officials are joined by elders of Egypt—leaders of the general Egyptian populace. They are all going to accompany Joseph's father on his final journey.

And one last very special group will be coming along, too:

וַיַּעַל עִמּוֹ גַּם־רֶכֶב גַּם־פָּרָשִׁים וַיְהִי הַמַּחֲנֶה כָּבֵד מְאֹד:

*And along with [the family and the entourage], chariots and
archers went up, as well; the camp was very great* (Genesis 50:9)

Chariots and archers—what would *they* be doing here? There was no military necessity for them. This was a funeral, after all, not a campaign of war! But a moment's reflection settles that question: they were an honor guard. Pharaoh had sent them, too, to escort Joseph's father on his final journey.

Pharaoh's Choice

When the time comes for Jacob's burial procession to depart, Pharaoh's yes turns out not to be so cold after all: he sends the finest of Egypt, with pomp and circumstance, to accompany these Hebrews on their mission to Canaan. This was a state funeral, in all its glory. All the pageantry of Egypt accompanied a procession of Jacob's family on its way to a little Mesopotamian backwater called Canaan. What a peculiar sight that procession must have been! The text tells the reader as much; when the procession stopped to eulogize Jacob, it goes out of its way to say that the local Canaanites looked on in disbelieving wonder:

וַיַּרְא יוֹשֵׁב הָאָרֶץ הַכְּנַעֲנִי אֶת־הָאֵבֶל בְּגֹרֶן
הָאָטָד וַיֹּאמְרוּ אֵבֶל־כָּבֵד זֶה לְמִצְרָיִם

And the Canaanite inhabitants of the land saw the mourning in Goren Ha'atad, and they said: What a heavy show of mourning this is for Egypt! (Genesis 50:11)

A state funeral beyond Egypt's borders. A great figure of Egyptian royalty buried according to Hebrew, not Egyptian, custom. *What would other nations say?* For Pharaoh, it didn't matter. If this was how the family thought Jacob should be honored, then that's how he'd be honored–and Egypt would be a part of it. Public relations concerns were simply not going to be a factor. The loyalty of Egypt to its adopted father would not stop at Egypt's door.

Would there be some cultural awkwardness in all this for the royal courtiers and the captains of the King's Guard? Probably. The ceremonies and customs were unfamiliar, strange in Egyptian eyes. And burial after embalming? It certainly wasn't the easiest thing to get used to. But the Hebrews would lead and the Egyptians would follow. The Egyptian officials would watch for cues and make it up as they went along. *After all, this is how Father said he wants to be honored. It is not about us, it is about him.*

Two Heroes

The story of Jacob's burial, in the end, is the story of two heroes. The first is Joseph, who risked everything to bury his father according to his wishes. He risked the loss of power, prestige—and perhaps most of all, his good standing in the eyes of Pharaoh. But the second hero, unlikely as it may seem, is Pharaoh himself. He resisted the urge to impose upon the venerated Jacob an exclusively Egyptian identity. He allowed Jacob to be who he was—Israelite, not Egyptian—and still he and the populace would cherish him; still he and Egypt would regard Jacob as royalty. They would accord him all the honor of a king, notwithstanding Jacob's rather public decision that Canaan was his true home. The humility evinced by Pharaoh's stance is nothing short of remarkable.

And so, with the Torah's account of the splendor of Jacob's funeral procession, its account of the triangle linking Joseph, Jacob, and Pharaoh comes to an end—except that, in a way, it has not yet begun. For the story the Torah is telling us about Jacob's funeral has one more glorious act to it, an act that will take place centuries later. Everything we have seen thus far is a shadow of something much larger, a drama that will play out on the greatest possible stage.

CHAPTER TWENTY-SEVEN

Take the Long Way Home

Traveling in Circles

A hint that there is something larger afoot in the Torah's description of Jacob's burial comes from an easily overlooked detail in the story. It seems like a trivial thing, barely worthy of notice. It has to do with the location of *Goren Ha'atad*.

Goren Ha'atad, you will recall, is where the procession paused to eulogize Jacob before arriving at their ultimate destination. It was there that the Canaanites looked on and expressed their wonder at how great an expression of mourning all this was for Egypt. As it happens, the Torah makes a point of telling us where *Goren Ha'atad* was:

וַיָּבֹאוּ עַד־גֹּרֶן הָאָטָד אֲשֶׁר בְּעֵבֶר הַיַּרְדֵּן

And they came to Goren Ha'atad, which is on the other side of the Jordan River (Genesis 50:10)

The text goes out of its way to let us know that *Goren Ha'atad* was in *Ever HaYarden* (עֵבֶר הַיַּרְדֵּן), which is to say, on the east side of the Jordan River. But let's do a little reality check of the geography, here: what, exactly, was the burial procession doing on the east bank of the Jordan? Their starting point was Egypt; their destination, the tomb of Machpelah in Hebron. Both those points are *west* of the Jordan River. What were they doing, then, on the east side of the Jordan?

The shortest route from Egypt to Hebron is to head north-west in more or less a straight line. If the burial party traveled to Canaan via *Goren Ha'atad*, it means they went well out of their way. Leaving Egypt, they would have had to swoop down to the south of Canaan, traverse the Sinai desert, swing up and around the Dead Sea, travel due north for the entire length of that sea, and then hook left to cross the Jordan River, probably somewhere near Jericho. That's *really* taking the long way.

Now, I can't explain to you why they chose such a roundabout route. But the fact that they did is quite intriguing–for that particular route reminds the reader of another great journey. Ask yourself this: was there any *other* time in biblical history that a great procession of people took a similar roundabout route from Egypt to the Land of Canaan, crossing the Jordan River at the very end?

Yes, there certainly was. That was the route the Children of Israel took, centuries later, in the event we know as the Exodus from Egypt.

In the Exodus, God specifically had the people avoid the more direct route (Exodus 13:17-18). Instead, he led them into the wil-derness south of Canaan, where they traversed the Sinai desert. Eventually, the Israelites headed north, made a circuit around the Dead Sea, hooked left–and crossed the Jordan River, near Jericho, to enter the land.

Babysitting Arrangements

So the route of the burial party anticipates the route of the Exodus. Intriguing. What should we make of that?

Assembling some more data might help us figure that out. As it happens, the travel route is not the only thing about Jacob's burial procession that anticipates the Exodus. We noted, a few

chapters back, how the Torah goes out of its way to inform us
that the Children of Israel left behind their little children and
their flocks in the Land of Goshen, while everyone else traveled
to Canaan for Jacob's burial. We wondered why we needed to be
told of all these arrangements for the funeral. Of what lasting
significance is this information?

Consider this: in that apparently superfluous phrase about
the little children and the cattle, we hear an intriguing premonition of things to come. Where else in the Bible are Israelites
getting ready to leave Egypt en masse, when suddenly, the issue
of whether they bring along their little children, sheep, and cattle,
takes center stage? It happens during the story of the Exodus.

As you might recall from our survey of the Exodus story earlier in this book, child-care and animal-care logistics were part
of the final negotiations between Moses and Pharaoh over the
terms of Israel's three-day holiday in the desert. It is almost as
if Pharaoh, seeking to deny Moses's request for the children to
come along, is saying: *The last time you guys left for a little trip, for
Jacob's funeral, you didn't take the children and cattle. Why can't you
leave them behind this time?*

Of Chariots and Canaanites

And there are still other connections between the burial story
and the Exodus story. Isn't it interesting, for example, that, for
Jacob's burial, Pharaoh dispatches chariots and archers as escorts
for the procession on its journey from Egypt? When else do we
hear of Pharaoh's chariots and archers? The only other time in
the Five Books of Moses that we ever hear of them is in the story
of Pharaoh's pursuit of his former Hebrew slaves, in the episode
leading up to the Splitting of the Sea.[69]

---

69. It is intriguing, as well, that the chariots and horsemen accompany
the burial party to the shores of the Jordan River. Later, in the time of

And while we're at it, let's consider the Canaanite onlookers. In the burial story, the Canaanites gaze out at the burial procession and exclaim in wonder: "What heavy mourning this is for Egypt!" And in the Exodus story, the Canaanite onlookers are back again. This time, they appear in the ecstatic song of thanksgiving sung by the Hebrews after the victory at the Sea of Reeds:

שָׁמְעוּ עַמִּים יִרְגָּזוּן...נָמֹגוּ כֹּל יֹשְׁבֵי כְנָעַן:

The nations heard [what happened to Egypt]; the inhabitants of Canaan shrank away in fear (Exodus 15:14–15)

But What Does It All Mean?

It seems as if the connections between the Burial of Jacob and the Exodus are more than the product of mere coincidence. The Torah appears to be asking the reader to line up and connect these two journeys from Egypt. But why?

By *why*, I mean two things. First, *why* in the sense of *what*, if anything, *is the Torah trying to tell us* by creating these parallels between the two stories? What, if anything, is the reader meant to learn from all this?

But before we can even get to that, there's a more fundamental *why* we need to address: why should the Torah consider these two stories related? In other words: yes, I get it, both stories are about journeys from Egypt. Very nice. That doesn't seem like a good enough reason for the stories to be linked by so intricate a web of connections. The mere fact that both stories involve journeys and both stories start in Egypt seems like a tenuous—and

---

Joshua, when the Israelites arrive at the Jordan, the river splits as they pass through (Joshua 3:16), just as the sea did at the time of the Exodus. Thus, the chariots and horsemen in the burial story arrive, just as they do in the Exodus story, at a place where the waters will—one day—split.

frankly, a rather trivial—basis for connecting the two narratives this extensively. Indeed, if you had to pinpoint what each story is *really* about, they seemingly couldn't be further apart. One story is about a burial procession for a dead father, and the other story is about the escape of hundreds of thousands of former slaves. What does one have to do with the other?

But there's the rub.

Maybe we have been too hasty in characterizing what each of these two stories is essentially about. Yes, it *seems* like one is about a burial procession and the other is about an exodus of former slaves, but maybe that's not how the Torah sees it. Maybe the text sees the "burial" aspect of things and the "slaves leaving" aspect of things as just window dressing: in essence, the stories are exactly the same.

What does the text know about the essence of these stories that we don't?

CHAPTER TWENTY-EIGHT

Convergence

What is the essential thematic similarity between the Exodus and the burial of Jacob? How do these stories converge?

A burial procession for a revered patriarch and a mass departure from slavery for an entire nation do seem to be two entirely different kinds of events. But maybe that's because when we think of the Exodus, we think of the Exodus events as they actually came to pass. We think of the Ten Plagues, the destruction of the armies of Egypt at the sea—all overwhelming events. Those events can be distracting, because they tend to obscure a much less dramatic, but crucial, event at the very beginning of the story. To see the first event for what it was, we need to stop looking at the Exodus that actually was, and start looking at the Exodus that Might Have Been.

Earlier in this book, we theorized about different ways the Exodus could have taken place. We called them Exodus Plan A, Plan B, and Plan C. The Exodus that actually came to pass—that was what we eventually called Plan C. It involved the violent destruction of a recalcitrant Egypt and the complete defeat of a bullheaded Pharaoh. But Exodus Plan C didn't *have* to happen. It was a last resort, as it were, which came about because Pharaoh consistently refused to act in good faith. Pharaoh certainly *could* have chosen differently. For example, he could have internalized the lessons about the Creator-God that the plagues were designed to teach. Had he done so, Exodus Plan B would have succeeded, and Pharaoh, recognizing the existence of the Creator-God, would have set free his slaves in submission to the wishes of a Creator he was morally bound to serve.

But even before Exodus Plans B and C, there was another form of the Exodus that could have taken place, that *should* have taken place. It was God's ideal plan: Exodus Plan A. This truly was the Exodus that Might Have Been.

Plan A

The original hope for the Exodus was expressed in Moses's first speech to Pharaoh:

כֹּה־אָמַר יְקֹוָה אֱלֹקֵי יִשְׂרָאֵל שַׁלַּח אֶת־עַמִּי וְיָחֹגּוּ לִי בַּמִּדְבָּר:

Thus says the YHVH, God of Israel: Send out My people, and let them rejoice before Me in the desert (Exodus 5:1)

YHVH is God's Creator-Name. *The Creator has a relationship with a nation you are enslaving; they are His nation.* They are *Israel*, a special, covenantal name given to their forefather by this Creator-God. The Creator is directly addressing Egypt now, expecting Pharaoh, who has subjugated this nation, to allow them to leave for a while to celebrate with Him in the desert.

We all know Pharaoh said no, exclaiming with anger and evident impatience that he does not know this deity, YHVH, and will not listen to him. Pharaoh then hardened his stance still further, denying Moses's subsequent plea to allow a short holiday on grounds of religious tolerance for his slaves, if nothing else.

That's what *actually* happened. But what if Pharaoh *hadn't* reacted that way? We talked earlier about what might have happened had Pharaoh instead chosen to respond to Moses's plea in good faith.

The Journey

Had Pharaoh consented to the three-day work holiday, he would have allowed the people to go into the desert for just a short time and return. And why would they have been going? How did Moses phrase that purpose to him?

The people would be going into the desert to serve their God.

Who *was* that God? It wasn't one of the powers in the pagan pantheon. Moses had told him that it was a *new* god–YHVH, the Creator. They wanted to serve the Great Parent in the Sky.

It was Father.

Had Plan A worked, Pharaoh, in that moment right at the beginning of the Exodus, would have allowed the people to go into the desert, in a grand procession, for the sole purpose of honoring their Father, the way Father said He wanted to be honored.

Now do you see the connection between the Burial of Jacob and the Exodus?

Microcosm, Macrocosm

The stories of Jacob's burial and the Exodus really *do* converge; their essential theme is one and the same. In each, a grand procession was supposed to take place, to honor Father the way Father wanted to be honored. The only difference between the stories lies in *which* father we are talking about. In the Jacob story, we're talking about a procession honoring an earthly father. In the Exodus story, the procession honors the Heavenly Father.

Once we recognize this essential similarity, we can see the extent to which the Exodus story truly does echo the burial story, in many more ways than just the four or five points we mentioned last chapter (the exit route taken, the babysitting arrangements, the chariots and the archers). The tensions in each story, the kaleidoscope of reasons why key people make fateful choices—all of that echoes from one story to another, too. All these resonances combine to create two whole sagas, each revolving around a similar axis: will key people display the strength of will and humility to allow Father to be honored, the way Father wants to be honored?

Let me show you.

Microcosm

Once upon a time, a newly confirmed *bechor*, Joseph, would lead a family out of Egypt, in order to serve his father, Jacob, the way his father had said he wished to be served. Joseph's father wished to be buried in Canaan, where he knew the destiny of the family lay.

But there were many obstacles facing this *bechor* in making the trip actually happen. For Jacob was not the only one who looked on Joseph as his son—and the king of Egypt might not look kindly upon his adopted son leaving his side. He might not look kindly upon Joseph's overriding loyalty to his real father. He certainly wouldn't understand the kind of service Joseph wished to render to his father; burial would have seemed like the strangest of customs to the Egyptian king.

So there would have to be a moment of truth for this *bechor*. Which father would he choose to serve? It would not be the easiest of choices. The consequences for enraging his surrogate father might well be severe. Moreover, the choice was complicated by his haunted past. He had been abused, sold off into slavery—and, worst of all, he wasn't sure why. He wasn't sure whether Father was involved. He *thought* Father had loved him, back when he was a lad in Canaan, but now, it didn't seem so clear anymore. He wasn't sure whether he was a discarded child Father no longer loved or cared about.

So before this *bechor* could be expected to choose his real father's interests over those of his surrogate father, he would have to come to understand that his father truly loved him, that he had not been thrown out of the family. And this knowledge did, in fact, come to him. It came to him through a messenger.

One day, a messenger came to the *bechor* and told him the truth about his father. That messenger was Judah, one of Joseph's brothers. The messenger told the *bechor* about an emotionally fraught conversation he'd had with Father a while back, in which Father spoke of his son and his feelings for him.

Father had *always* loved him, this messenger had said. As difficult as it might be for Joseph to believe, Father had been crying over him every day of this long exile from Father's house. The grief Father experienced over this separation was unimaginable.

When the *bechor* heard this, something inside him *knew* it to be true. What he heard from this messenger did not answer all his gnawing questions, not by a long shot. He still didn't know why Father had sent him on that mission, so long ago, that ended so badly. That would remain a mystery. But one thing he *did* know: he had not been thrown out of the family. Father still loved him and wanted to be with him.

And that changed everything.

Armed with that knowledge, the *bechor* would be able to muster the strength and the courage to confront the very difficult choice that lay before him. He ultimately chose to publicly declare, in a way that even the Egyptian king would understand, that his father truly *was* his father. He would obey Father's wishes, as strange and as discordant as those wishes would sound to Egypt's ears. He made that clear to Pharaoh, come what may.

When he made that commitment to Father, something poignant happened. Father reciprocated that gift of love with a gift of love of his own.

Father confirmed Joseph's status as child-leader of his family. Although Joseph had occasionally been treated this way by his father earlier, he had not yet really deserved that designation; now he had earned it. Father acknowledged this, and designated Joseph as child-leader. Moreover, Father claimed the two children that had been born to Joseph in Egypt as his very own. Although these children had been born when Joseph felt his most profound alienation from Father–although they had been *named* for that alienation–still, Father claimed them as his own. Whatever distance from Father the *bechor* had experienced during his long years of exile would be healed through this act of paternal acceptance.

Let me now pause this retelling of Jacob's burial story, and take you to its "twin"–the events we know as the Exodus from Egypt. The correspondence between the stories now seems hard to miss.

Macrocosm

Centuries after this story involving Joseph and his father, there would be another *bechor* who would struggle with similar issues. But this time, the *bechor* was not a person, but a *people*. It was the nascent family-turned-nation called Israel.

This national *bechor* faced a choice. It had a Father in Heaven, and that Father was calling upon His child to leave Egypt to serve Him the way He wished to be served. In the short term, the Father in Heaven wanted His *bechor* to celebrate with Him in the desert for a few days; but ultimately, He wanted him to undertake a journey to Canaan. Heavenly Father was adamant that this is where the destiny of the people lay.

But there were obstacles that faced this *bechor* in making this trip actually take place. For God was not the only one who looked on Israel as his child. There was another father, too, who felt himself deserving of the allegiance of this people. As we've seen, the benevolent Pharaoh in the times of Joseph had treated Joseph like an adopted son. Ever since then, vestiges of that relationship had lingered. To some extent, the Egyptian throne continued to look upon Israel as its child, but that relationship had decayed. It was as if the loving surrogate father had become an evil and abusive caricature of his former self. He demanded the loyalty of his child, but extended none of the love a father would give one of his own. The Egyptian throne abused and enslaved its child, and brutally inured itself to the child's cries for mercy.

The king of Egypt would not look kindly upon his adopted son leaving his side. He would not look kindly upon the son's overriding loyalty to his "real" father. From the perspective of the king, that Father in Heaven didn't even really exist; He didn't deserve the title of *Father* at all. Moreover, he certainly would not understand the kind of service that Israel would wish to render to this Father. Celebrating with God in the desert seemed like the strangest of things to this king. Joy and closeness as a motivation for service? That's not the way anyone would serve a self-respecting deity.[70]

So there would be a moment of truth for this *bechor*. Which father would he choose to serve? Would he be willing to turn his back on his abusive surrogate father, risking his rage, so as to serve Heavenly Father? This would be the choice that faced the *bechor* when the time came to put the blood of Egypt's gods on his doors. It would not be the easiest of choices. The consequences for enraging the surrogate father might well be severe. Moreover, the choice was complicated by his haunted past: he

---

70. Thus, just as the Egyptians would have regarded Jacob's burial request as preposterous—*why turn your back on embalming?*—so the request of the Heavenly Father of Israel seemed preposterous, too. And this goes not just for the request to "celebrate" in the desert; it also applies to the longer-term idea, involving a trip all the way to Canaan, where the people would make a home for God in their own land. The notion of physical humans living together with a transcendent God is inherently a difficult one to wrap one's mind around. Nevertheless, Father wasn't bothered by this. He asked the people to make a place for Him, and He, transcendent as He was, would find a way to dwell with them (see Exodus 25:8).

had been abused, the victim of centuries of slavery. And, worst of all, he wasn't sure why. He wasn't sure whether Father in Heaven was involved. He *thought* Father loved him–God certainly had a close enough relationship with him back in Canaan, when he was much "smaller," back in the days of his ancestors, Abraham, Isaac, and Jacob–but now, it didn't seem so clear anymore. Slavery was painful and brutal. He wasn't sure whether he was a discarded child, a child Father no longer loved or cared about.

So before this *bechor* could be expected to choose his real Father's interests over those of his surrogate father, the *bechor* would have to come to understand something. He would have to come to understand that his Father in Heaven truly loved him, that he had *not* been thrown out of the family of "acceptable" children. And this knowledge *did*, in fact, come to him. It came to him through a messenger.

Moses and Judah

One day, a messenger came to the *bechor* and told him the truth about his Father in Heaven. That messenger was Moses. The messenger told the *bechor* about an emotionally fraught conversation he had, not too long ago, with Father in Heaven (Exodus 4:28–30). He had spoken directly with Father, he said, and in the conversation, the very first thing Father did was speak of his undying love for his enslaved child:

וַיֹּאמֶר אָנֹכִי אֱלֹקֵי אָבִיךָ אֱלֹקֵי אַבְרָהָם אֱלֹקֵי יִצְחָק וֵאלֹקֵי
יַעֲקֹב... וַיֹּאמֶר יְקֹוָה רָאֹה רָאִיתִי אֶת־עֳנִי עַמִּי אֲשֶׁר בְּמִצְרָיִם
וְאֶת־צַעֲקָתָם שָׁמַעְתִּי מִפְּנֵי נֹגְשָׂיו כִּי יָדַעְתִּי אֶת־מַכְאֹבָיו:

And [God] said [to Moses]: I am the God of your forefathers, of Abraham, Isaac, and Jacob... And YHVH said: I have surely seen the suffering of My people that is in Egypt, and their cries I've heard in the face of their oppressors. I know their pain (Exodus 3:6–7)

Father had *always* loved him, this messenger had said.[71] As difficult as it might be for this national *bechor* to believe, Father in Heaven had been grieving over him. The anguish Father experienced over his suffering was true and palpable. When the *bechor* heard this, he believed it to be true. Something inside him *knew* it to be true:

וַיֵּלֶךְ מֹשֶׁה וְאַהֲרֹן וַיַּאַסְפוּ אֶת־כָּל־זִקְנֵי בְּנֵי יִשְׂרָאֵל: וַיְדַבֵּר אַהֲרֹן אֵת
כָּל־הַדְּבָרִים אֲשֶׁר־דִּבֶּר יְקֹוָה אֶל־מֹשֶׁה וַיַּעַשׂ הָאֹתֹת לְעֵינֵי הָעָם:
וַיַּאֲמֵן הָעָם וַיִּשְׁמְעוּ כִּי־פָקַד יְקֹוָה אֶת־בְּנֵי יִשְׂרָאֵל וְכִי רָאָה אֶת־עָנְיָם

---

71. The way in which Father convinces his *bechor* of his love is similar in both cases. The last sure thing Joseph had to hold onto was his memory of a father who clearly seemed to love him back in Canaan. There was no denying that love of his youth. *But what of all this pain I've experienced since then? Does all that's happened to me mean Father changed his mind about me?* When Judah approaches Joseph (without knowing he is Joseph), he tells him specifically that Father has *always* been crying for him. He has been mourning incessantly since the moment he perceived Joseph was gone. Thus, Judah is able to seamlessly link the past with the present for Joseph: *The same father I remember as a child, he never turned his back on me. He loved me then, and loves me now.*

Something similar happens with God's first address to Moses at the Burning Bush. God first identifies Himself as the God of Abraham, Isaac, and Jacob—the God of this national "child," back when that child was young. Back then, it was easy to see that God loved the child. He spoke to the forefathers regularly, and assured them of great promises. Then, having touched upon that past as a kind of anchor, God moves to the present: *And now,* God says, *I have seen the pain of the people in their slavery...*

Judah had reached back to Joseph's earliest confirmed memories of father's love, and assured him that this love was still extant—and now, Moses would do the same for the people, the national *bechor*. He would reach back to their earliest collective memory of Father's love—the connection Father evidently had with Abraham, Isaac, and Jacob—and assure them that this love from the past was still extant.

*And Moses and Aaron went and gathered all the elders of
the Children of Israel, and Moses repeated all the words that
YHVH had spoken to Moses. And the people believed it; they
understood that God had come to take back the Children of
Israel, and that He had seen their anguish* (Exodus 4:29–31)[72]

What the Elders of Israel heard from Moses did not answer all
their gnawing questions. They still did not know why Father
in Heaven had allowed this descent into Egypt to take place, a
sojourn that had ended so badly. That would remain a mystery.
But there was one thing they *did* know, now: this incipient nation,
Israel, had not been thrown out of Father's family of children. It
was not a "discarded" nation. Father still loved them and wanted
to be with them. And that changed everything for them.

The Pesach Offering

Armed with that knowledge, this national *bechor,* the People of
Israel, would be able to muster the strength and the courage to
confront the very difficult choice that lay before them. They ultimately chose to publicly declare, in a way that even the Egyptian
king would understand, that their Father in Heaven truly *was*
their father. They participated in a Oneness offering, *Korban
Pesach*–proclaiming their allegiance to the Creator, their Parent

---

72. Note the emphasis of the text on what, exactly, the people understood. One might have supposed that it would be enough for them to
understand that God had committed Himself to saving them from their
suffering. That, after all, was their immediate need. The verse goes out of its
way, however, to add that they believed that God "had seen their anguish."
The implication seems evident: had they *not* also come to understand that
God was empathic toward their plight–emotionally moved, so to speak, by
their suffering–the people would not have been accepting God's assurances
about what He would do for them.

in Heaven. They would commit to obeying His wishes, as strange and discordant as those wishes would sound to Egypt's ears. They would "celebrate" with Father in the desert. They would follow Him to Canaan and make a home for Him there with them. They would try to be an example of a child who'd take Father's values, and make them come alive in the child's world. The *bechor* made that choice, come what may. And when he did, Father in Heaven reciprocated with a gift of His own.

Becoming God's *Bechor*

Father in Heaven responded to Israel's commitments, solemnly undertaken in their Oneness offering, by confirming Israel's status as child-leader of his family. Although Israel had previously been treated with favor when he was much younger, when God lavished promises upon Abraham, Isaac, and Jacob, the people—the masses who would now become the nation—had not yet collectively earned that favor in any way. Now they had earned it, and Father gratefully reciprocated by granting them the designation of *bechor*. The night they brought that offering, all *bechorot* in Egypt would die, save Father's own—and Israel survived.

Moreover, Israel's choice that night gave rise to one more poignant response on the part of Father. The Creator claimed the children that had been born to the nation in Egypt as His very own. In anointing Israel his *bechor*, in accepting the idea that Israel would represent His values in the world of children—this was, in a deep way, an echo of Jacob's acceptance of Ephraim and Manasseh.

Consider this: both *bechorot*—first Joseph, and centuries later, the nation of Israel—became numerous in Egypt.[73] Just as Joseph

---

73. Joseph names his son *Ephraim* because *hiphrani elokim be'eretz onyi* (הִפְרַנִי אֱלֹהִים בְּאֶרֶץ עָנְיִי), "God has made me numerous in the land of my suffering" (Genesis 41:52). Becoming numerous, for an individual, might

grew from an individual into a family while in Egypt, the People of Israel grew from a mere family into a nation in Egypt. The population explosion responsible for catapulting them from being a mere family into being a true people occurred when they all lived in, and were connected to, Egypt. The Israelites, we will recall, had been made into landed gentry; they had been granted an *achuzah* in a land not really their own. And with that gift of land had also come the gift of numbers. In the words of the text, "they took hold of the land, and they multiplied very greatly" (Genesis 47:27). So these children were the product, to some extent, of Israel's alienation from the Land of Canaan and their particular covenantal destiny. Nevertheless, just as Jacob had done with Ephraim and Manasseh once before, Father in Heaven would claim all these multitudes as His own. Whatever distance from Father Israel had experienced during their long years of exile, it would all be healed through this act of paternal acceptance.

Divergence

Up until this point, the stories of Jacob's burial and the Exodus more or less converge. But from this point forward, they will diverge dramatically. Jacob's burial story will express further heights of heroism, while the Exodus story will contain just a shadow of that, the empty shell of unrealized heroism. Why does the Exodus story diverge, at this point, from the promise of its

---

mean having two or more children—I was just one person, but a generation later, there are two or more. An individual is one thing; a bunch of kids is a qualitative leap forward. For a family, a qualitative leap forward means a dizzying number of progeny, enough that the family can be called a *people*. That is the sense of the verse when it states that, in Goshen, the people "took hold of the land and became very numerous."

predecessor? The answer lies where it almost always does when one searches for the root causes of unrealized heroism: in the simple vicissitudes of human free will.

Alas, free choice is a fickle thing. Children's decisions do not always conform to their father's hopes or dreams for them. And nowhere can this be seen more clearly than in the dramatic gulf that separates the choices of Joseph's Pharaoh and Moses's Pharaoh. In the gulf between those choices lies the difference between the Exodus that was, and the Exodus that Might Have Been.

CHAPTER TWENTY-NINE

Divergence

In the last chapter, we retold the story of Jacob's burial and the story of the Exodus from the "child's" perspective in each story: how Joseph acquitted himself in the great choice facing him, and, centuries later, how the Children of Israel made *their* choice in the decision facing them.

But now let's examine each story from a different figure's point of view. Let's look at the surrogate father in each story. How do the choices made by the Pharaoh in Joseph's day compare to those made by the Pharaoh of Moses's day?

The Pivotal Moment

In a very real way, the reaction of Joseph's Pharaoh created an opportunity, a precedent for how an Egyptian king might wrestle with a very particular challenge: *What do you do when the child you thought was yours expresses an allegiance to another, deeper, Father?*

Joseph's Pharaoh had acted heroically when confronted with that challenge. What would have happened if Moses's Pharaoh had responded with similar courage and integrity? What would that have looked like?

It would have looked like Exodus Plan A.

Let's go back to the moment Moses made his request of Pharaoh to allow the Hebrews to go into the desert for three days. They had asked to go celebrate with this God of theirs,

YHVH, this God who was their Father in Heaven. In an ideal world, what would have happened next?

The idea of a Creator-God was foreign to Pharaoh. Imagine that Pharaoh had asked for a sign by which Moses might demonstrate the truth of what he was saying, that he was the true messenger of the Creator of All. Interestingly, in the Exodus story recounted in the Torah, God had in fact provided Moses with just such a sign:

כִּי יְדַבֵּר אֲלֵכֶם פַּרְעֹה לֵאמֹר תְּנוּ לָכֶם מוֹפֵת וְאָמַרְתָּ
אֶל־אַהֲרֹן קַח אֶת־מַטְּךָ וְהַשְׁלֵךְ לִפְנֵי־פַרְעֹה יְהִי לְתַנִּין:

If Pharaoh should say to you: Provide a sign [to substantiate your words], then you shall say to Aaron: Take your staff, and cast it down before Pharaoh, and it will become a serpent (Exodus 7:9)

The verse seems to suggest that this sign would be *the* way Pharaoh could be brought to understand the truth, back at the beginning of the Exodus process, before any plagues had yet occurred. In the actual Exodus story, the sign happened: Aaron casts down his staff in full view of all Pharaoh's astrologers, sorcerers, and court, and it turns into a serpent. The sorcerers haughtily cast down their own staffs, and these become serpents as well. But then, let's recall what happens next: Aaron's staff goes and swallows all the other serpents in the room. *There's the sign.*[74]

---

74. As I suggested earlier, this was the first time Pharaoh had been presented with cold, hard evidence that there was a Creator-God in the world, and that Moses and Aaron were representing that Force. The natural world might appear to be populated with many sources of power—but there is One Power to rule them all. In the *actual* Exodus, of course, Pharaoh rejects the sign. As the text says, he hardens his heart, making himself stubborn and impervious to the evidence just presented to him. But what if he hadn't? *What if he had opened his heart instead?*

Now imagine that Pharaoh had fearlessly drawn the evident, logical conclusion from that sign, the only sign God had ever given Moses to establish the veracity of his words in Pharaoh's presence: one serpent swallows all the other serpents. *Yes, there are many powers out there—but there is one Power that rules them all.* Had Pharaoh come to understand that, how would he have responded to Moses's request that Israel be allowed to go serve its Father?

The realization that there *did* exist a Creator-God, and it was to this God Israel wished to show its allegiance—if Pharaoh had recognized *that* truth, it would have changed everything for him. It would have allowed him not just to grant Moses's immediate request for some time off to serve Father in the desert, but also to relinquish custody over the people he had brutally enslaved. *There's a deeper parent than me, and these Hebrews owe Him their allegiance. That parent wants them back, for His own purposes. How can I stand in the way of that?*

And of course, this Parent in the Sky—He was not just the parent of Israel; He was the parent of *all* humans, Egypt included. *Pharaoh included.* And that would have changed everything, too. All told, if Pharaoh had truly accepted the idea of a Creator and its attendant implications, he would, in all probability, not only have granted Moses's request for a procession into the desert to honor Father—he would have wanted Egypt to be part of the procession, too. He would have sent dignitaries and multitudes to escort the Israelites on their way, just as his predecessor, Joseph's Pharaoh, had done. He would have sent a military honor guard. He would have sent his chariots, horsemen, and archers. After all, if this is a procession to honor the Parent in the Sky—that parent is the father of all earthly children. *He's our father, too.*[75]

---

75. One might extrapolate still further from the connections between the stories. For example, one could imagine obstacles facing Pharaoh in carrying through on this plan. It was, after all, so unfamiliar. The Egyptian dignitaries sent along on the journey might grumble about it all: *The*

Two Pharaohs

It would have been difficult for Pharaoh to recognize the existence of a deeper Father he was bound to give honor to, but not impossible. It would have been difficult for him to accept an entirely new way of relating to a deity—*celebrating* with Him—but not impossible. The proof was that an earlier Pharaoh had done all this, centuries earlier. The great success of Joseph's Pharaoh serves as a bitter indictment of Moses's Pharaoh.

Joseph's Pharaoh had resisted the urge to look askance at an unfamiliar and seemingly-nonsensical Israelite custom (the burial of Jacob) that did not comport with Egyptian mores. Instead, he had allowed the Israelites to honor their father as they saw fit. On a deeper level, he was able to accept a far more threatening truth: *Joseph has another father, more deeply father to him than I am. Who am I to stand in the way of Joseph according him all due honor?*

In the end, Joseph's Pharaoh didn't just go along with the idea of the burial procession; he wanted Egypt to be part of it. He sent dignitaries, multitudes of Egyptians, a military escort of chariots and archers, to accompany the burial procession. It didn't matter that Israel wasn't doing things the Egyptian way. Jacob was *their* father, too.

The Dream

Moses's Pharaoh could have done that, too, but he didn't. Unlike his predecessor, he was unable to muster the honesty, humility,

---

Hebrews, they want to celebrate with their god? No one celebrates with a god. That's a ridiculous way to serve a deity! But, just as Joseph's Pharaoh might have done so long ago, this Pharaoh could have reassured his people. *Yes, this is unfamiliar. This whole Creator idea is new to all of us. But Israel, these former slaves, they are going to show us the way. If this is how Father has told them he wants to be honored, we are going to be a part of that, too.*

and courage necessary to change his view so radically and so fundamentally. He was not able to come to grips with the notion that there was a deeper Father than he.

And so, when the Israelites finally left Egypt, they left against Pharaoh's will rather than with his wholehearted assent. Instead of an Egypt that participated in the Exodus, there was an Egypt that resisted it. The Exodus as it actually transpired was a shadow of the Exodus that Might Have Been—for look at what could have been! Once again, there might have been crowds of Canaanites gathered in awe to watch the grand procession to honor Father. Once again, they might have looked on in amazement at Egypt's expression of honor to a Father they had only recently adopted as their own. Once again, they would have exclaimed: *What an extraordinary procession of honor on the part of Egypt!* [76]

Curiously, in the Exodus that Might Have Been, the role of Israel as child-leader would have been crucial, but almost transparent. Outside observers might miss seeing it altogether. Other nations would have perceived things just as the Canaanites did during Jacob's burial procession, exclaiming about the great honor being shown by Egypt to Father. Note that the Canaanites, back at the burial procession, didn't remark at all about the Israelites—they might not have even seen them. All that was visible was Egypt's great pomp and circumstance. Egypt was a great empire. What were they doing outside their borders, giving this kind of royal honor to someone they could not claim as exclusively theirs? Egypt was recognizing that it shared a father with

---

76. Indeed, the expression of the Canaanites, in the days of Joseph's Pharaoh was *evel kaved zeh lemitzrayim* (אֵבֶל־כָּבֵד זֶה לְמִצְרָיִם), "what heavy mourning this is for Egypt!" But *kaved* (כבד), the word for "heavy," also means "honor." The very words of astonishment uttered by the Canaanites, then, connote both the multitudes of Egyptians that accompanied the burial procession, but also, at least secondarily, the great "honor" Egypt was showing Father by virtue of their participation in the procession.

another family. There was a kind of universal father, and this nation was assigning him royal honors. That was impressive, indeed.

All that could have–should have–happened again. That was, after all, the role of a *bechor*. Not to be noticed, but to make a difference. The great honor that would be brought to Father would not come exclusively from Israel. In the ideal vision of what might have been, Israel, in that procession, was to facilitate a gathering of *all* God's children. It would have been, in the words of a more recent visionary, the realization of a great dream: "all of God's children... Jews and Gentiles," all joining hands and singing: "Free at last! Free at last! Thank God Almighty, we are free at last!"

Martin Luther King was on to something there. It was not a *new* dream he envisioned, but a very old one. It was the dream of the original Exodus.

The Chariots and Archers

Alas, when Israel finally did leave Egypt, they would leave alone. There would be no joyous cavalcade, no Egyptian multitudes escorting the Israelites out with pomp and circumstance. There would be no military escort. There would be no Egyptian horsemen and chariots, gloriously accompanying Israel all the way to the water's edge. There would be no Canaanite throngs exclaiming about the wonder of it all.

Except that there *would* be. The Master of the Universe would see to it that there would be. Centuries after their first appearance, the chariots and horsemen of Egypt would show up again. They would come to provide honor for God. It is not their *deaths* that would provide honor, as we had assumed before. No, the chariots and horsemen would once again be an honor guard–in life, as they were so long ago! It was as if God looked out at the scene, at Israel departing Egypt all alone, and said: *Something is missing in this picture. The first time around, there was pomp and circumstance;*

there was a military escort to honor Father. What happened to My honor guard? And so God would see to it that the honor guard came:

וַאֲנִי הִנְנִי מְחַזֵּק אֶת־לֵב מִצְרַיִם וְיָבֹאוּ אַחֲרֵיהֶם
וְאִכָּבְדָה בְּפַרְעֹה וּבְכָל־חֵילוֹ בְּרִכְבּוֹ וּבְפָרָשָׁיו:

*And as for Me, I shall hereby strengthen the heart of
Egypt, so that they shall chase after you. For I shall be
honored through Pharaoh and all his army; through his
chariots and through his archers* (Exodus 14:17)

If Pharaoh wished to be stubborn and to deny the coming into being of Exodus Plan A, then God would take that very stubbornness, and turn it into honor. It is intriguing, chilling even, that the word for the stubbornness evinced by Pharaoh, *kaved* (כָּבֵד), and the honor that God would take from Pharaoh's pursuing armies, *ikavdah* (אִכָּבְדָה) are simply different forms of one Hebrew root, כבד (*k-b-d*). One would quite literally be turned into the other: God would "strengthen" Pharaoh's heart, lending him courage to pursue his stubborn denial of the deeper Father, all the way to the very end.[77] And then, God would play with Egypt as if with a toy,[78] using the pursuing armies for His own ends instead of Pharaoh's:

וְאִכָּבְדָה בְּפַרְעֹה וּבְכָל־חֵילוֹ בְּרִכְבּוֹ וּבְפָרָשָׁיו:

*I shall be honored through Pharaoh and all his army; through
his chariots and through his archers* (Exodus 14:17)

---

77. In the verse cited above, in which God explains that he will provide the impetus for Pharaoh to pursue the Israelites, the word for God's involvement comes from the Hebrew root חזק (*ch-z-k*): וַאֲנִי הִנְנִי מְחַזֵּק אֶת־לֵב מִצְרַיִם. The reader will recall the significance of this root, as developed earlier in this book. It seems to signify "the lending of courage" to pursue an agenda.

78. See Exodus 10:1–2.

Pharaoh thought the chariots and archers were there to pursue his escaping slaves. In his blindness, he thought their purpose was to capture his adopted children so he could abuse them once more. But that wasn't really their purpose. God would appropriate those chariots and archers for different purposes, His own.

God would use them as His honor guard. There was going to be a parade when the Israelites left Egypt, and what would a parade be without a military escort? If Pharaoh wasn't forthcoming in providing an honor guard, then one would be taken from him. One way or the other, Egypt's finest would escort Israel, as before, to water's edge. One way or the other, as in days of old, Father would once again "be honored through Pharaoh and all his army."

And the Canaanite throngs would be back, too. Centuries before, they had exclaimed in amazement at the honor Egypt had given to a universal father. Now, they would exclaim in trepidation about the honor Father had taken, brazenly, from a recalcitrant Egypt:

שָׁמְעוּ עַמִּים יִרְגָּזוּן...נָמֹגוּ כֹּל יֹשְׁבֵי כְנָעַן:

The nations heard [what happened to Egypt]; the inhabitants of Canaan shrank away in fear (Exodus 15:14–15)

Those are the words of song Israel would sing at the sea after their Egyptian pursuers were vanquished. One way or the other, the Canaanites would look upon Egypt and be amazed. The only question was: what, exactly, would they see? Would they see Egypt's crowning moral achievement, or its destruction?

The Role of Egypt: the Ideal and the Shadow

Earlier, we spoke about God's words in the aftermath of the seventh plague, when Exodus Plan C seemed to first come into being. In the seventh plague, Pharaoh had consciously glimpsed the truth of God as Creator, but then turned his back on what he knew to be true. God then told Moses that a new plan would go into effect. God would perform further miracles, but for a different purpose:

לְמַעַן תְּסַפֵּר בְּאָזְנֵי בִנְךָ וּבֶן־בִּנְךָ אֵת אֲשֶׁר הִתְעַלַּלְתִּי בְּמִצְרַיִם
וְאֶת־אֹתֹתַי אֲשֶׁר־שַׂמְתִּי בָם וִידַעְתֶּם כִּי־אֲנִי יְקֹוָה:

*So that you should be able to tell your children and your children's children how I played with Egypt, **and the signs I place among them**. And you shall know that I am YHVH.* (Exodus 10:2)

The original plan had been for *Egypt* to come to the understanding that YHVH was a reality, that there was a Creator to whom they were subject. But Pharaoh and Egypt had shown themselves unwilling to accept this truth. So now, it would have to be enough for Israel to recognize it. *Now the miracles will be there so that you, at least, will know that I am YHVH, so that you shall tell your own children and grandchildren about your experience.*

The grand plan had been that Egypt's recognition of the Creator would stand as a testament to the truth of monotheism. *Now, you, Israel, will know this to be true. You'll tell your children and grandchildren what you've seen. Eventually, they will find a way to bring that idea to a larger audience.*

Either way, though, Egypt would have a role. The ideal was that Egypt would participate in the Exodus as a real player on the grand stage of history. The grand plan was that they and the Israelites, as once happened long ago, would form a single, joyous camp, enthusiastically partnering in paying homage to Father:

וַיַּעַל עִמּוֹ גַּם־רֶכֶב גַּם־פָּרָשִׁים וַיְהִי הַמַּחֲנֶה כָּבֵד מְאֹד:

And there went up with him chariots and archers;
and the camp was very great (Genesis 50:9)

To all eyes, there was but a single camp at Jacob's burial procession; the Israelites and Egyptians were united in a single purpose. That was the way it was supposed to be. The tragedy of the Exodus that actually was, is that there was not one camp, but two:

וַיָּבֹא בֵּין מַחֲנֵה מִצְרַיִם וּבֵין מַחֲנֵה יִשְׂרָאֵל

And [the divine cloud] came between the camp of
Egypt and the camp of Israel (Exodus 14:20)

The Egyptians had chosen to pursue the Israelites with malice instead of with joy, so Egypt and Israel had to be separated; they would be two camps, with the divine cloud between them, instead of one camp, with the divine cloud among them. And therein lies the tragedy brought about through Pharaoh's recalcitrance. In the end, the parade would happen, as a great divine drama began to unfold. One way or the other, Egypt's horsemen and chariots would be part of it all. The only question to be settled was: would their chariots and horsemen be willing, or unwilling, participants in the drama?

CHAPTER THIRTY

The Unfinished Journey

If the Exodus that Might Have Been did not actually occur, of what import is it to us? Generally, historians don't spend much time debating what could have happened but didn't. Why should we?

The answer is: because we aren't historians.

Judaism has always insisted that the Torah wasn't written to be merely a history book. Instead, the Torah is meant to be a guidebook. That is what the name *Torah* implies: *it teaches. It guides.*[79] Sometimes the Torah guides by telling us laws. Sometimes it guides by telling us stories about our past. The stories are relevant not just because they once happened. They are relevant because, like law, they can help shape us into our best possible selves.

The Exodus that Might Have Been is part of the Torah because it guides us. It is a story–or better, an implication that emerges from a close reading of *two* stories. And it exists, like much else in the Torah, to tell us about the meaning of what was, and the meaning of what can yet be.

---

79. The word *Torah* derives from *lehorot* (לְהוֹרוֹת), to lead, guide, or show the way (see Proverbs 1:8 and 3:1)–or perhaps even *yarah* (יָרָה), to guide the path of an arrow.

The Past

As regards what was–which is to say, the Exodus as it *actually* came to pass–the Exodus that Might Have Been gives us a yard-stick by which to assess those events. It confirms our suspicion that the events of the Exodus were never *only* about winning freedom for the enslaved Israelites, as much as this *was* on the agenda for Father in Heaven. It suggests to us that the Exodus was about other things as well. It was about a Father who, like Jacob long ago, needed to make His presence known to a child. It was about a potential *bechor*, who, like Joseph, had to summon reservoirs of strength to recognize that Father as his own, deepest parent. It was about a nation, Egypt, who had to recognize, like Joseph's Pharaoh long ago, that this was *their* Father, too, and act accordingly. It was about what kind of procession from Egypt to Canaan would ultimately ensue, and who would be a part of it.

The Future

The Exodus that Might Have Been teaches us about all that, but it also teaches us something about the future. It suggests to us that the Exodus, as it *actually* happened in history, did not accomplish everything it might have. There is work yet to do to complete its unrealized vision. The procession that departed Egypt was a shadow of what it might have been. It will be the destiny of Jew and Gentile to one day realize the promise of that journey as it should have taken place: to march side by side and join hands, proclaiming in unison the oneness of a Father they both share.

The prophets of Israel would speak often of that destiny. If we read the words of those prophets, we can't help but hear in them the longing to complete the Exodus's unfinished journey:

נְאֻם אֲדֹנָי יְקוִה מְקַבֵּץ נִדְחֵי יִשְׂרָאֵל עוֹד אֲקַבֵּץ עָלָיו לְנִקְבָּצָיו:

Thus says YHVH, who gathers in all the dispersed
people of Israel: I will gather still others to Him, beside
those [of Israel] that are gathered! (Isaiah 56:8)

Isaiah speaks of a time when God will gather in to the Land
of Canaan all the dispersed people of Israel, but when He does
so, He will gather others, too. They will all come in a grand
procession:

וּבְנֵי הַנֵּכָר הַנִּלְוִים עַל־יְקוָה לְשָׁרְתוֹ וּלְאַהֲבָה אֶת־שֵׁם יְקוָה...
וַהֲבִיאוֹתִים אֶל־הַר קָדְשִׁי וְשִׂמַּחְתִּים בְּבֵית תְּפִלָּתִי

Also the Gentiles, that join themselves to accompany
YHVH, to serve Him, and to love the name of YHVH... I
will bring them all to My holy mountain, and make
them joyful in My house of prayer (Isaiah 56:6–7)

The last time there was a procession like this, the Israelites had
traveled all alone. Israel had to be separated by the divine cloud
from those that pursued them. But in the procession of the
future, separation shall be a thing of the past:

וְאַל־יֹאמַר בֶּן־הַנֵּכָר הַנִּלְוָה אֶל־יְקוָה לֵאמֹר
הַבְדֵּל יַבְדִּילַנִי יְקוָה מֵעַל עַמּוֹ

Let not the child of a Gentile, who wishes to accompany
[those who are with] YHVH, say: YHVH has surely
separated me from His people... (Isaiah 56:3)[80]

---

80. The Hebrew here for "separate" is instructive. In the Exodus as it
actually came to pass, the Egyptians and the Israelites really were separated.
The cloud of the divine presence came between the camp of the Israelites
and the camp of the Egyptians to keep them apart. As we noted earlier,
echoes of the first few brushstrokes of Creation are evident in the events
of the Splitting of the Sea. One of those echoes was the divine cloud that

Once again, there would be a great procession, one overwhelmingly large camp, devoted to the honor of Father.[81] It would be a journey that would redeem the missed opportunities of Israel's first journey, the Exodus.[82] In the future procession, Israel, a

---

came between Egypt and Israel, providing light for Israel and darkness for Egypt. This, we suggested, echoed the original separation between light and darkness in the events of Creation. The word for the great separations of Creation is *vayavdel* (וַיַּבְדֵּל), which is echoed here, in Isaiah, by the Gentile's fear: *havdel yavdilani* (הַבְדֵּל יַבְדִּילַנִי). There is reason for the Gentile to fear separation, for that is the way things actually happened in the Exodus: a great separation between Israelite and Gentile. And yet, that separation was a corruption of the vision of the Exodus that Might Have Been. For at the burial of Jacob, there was no separation; there was but one camp.

81. In a chilling twist, Isaiah's word for "accompany" is *hanilvah* (הַנִּלְוָה). That is the same Hebrew word that would be used to describe one who accompanies a funeral procession.

82. Isaiah's vision is elaborated further by later prophets, such as Zechariah. Toward the end of the book of Zechariah, we hear of a similar vision–but one that specifically references the need for Egypt, of all nations, to join the procession, too. One of the sharpest of Zechariah's images portrays an event that seems to hark back to the Splitting of the Sea: בַּיּוֹם הַהוּא יִהְיֶה עַל־מְצִלּוֹת הַסּוּס קֹדֶשׁ לַיקֹוָה, "On that day, there shall be, inscribed upon the bells of all the horses, [the words] *Holy unto the Lord*" (Zechariah 14:20). In the original Splitting of the Sea, Egypt's chariots and horsemen had been used by God as tools. Now, in the future, the horses of Egypt would be back, but the horsemen and chariots would be willing participants this time. The bells that adorn the horses would be adorned with the same words that adorn the headpiece worn by the High Priest: *Holy unto the Lord*.

Lastly, the word Zechariah uses for "bells," *metzilot* (מְצִלּוֹת), is written with exactly the same letters as a fateful word that appeared in the Splitting of the Sea: *metzolot* (מְצוֹלֹת). Back at the Splitting of the Sea, the

national *bechor*, would lead, but they would be nearly invisible. Their numbers would be dwarfed by others who, with jubilation, would share Israel's purpose. They would all be there to honor the Father of All.

May we speedily see the day.

Israelites had sung about the horses of Pharaoh that "sank into the depths [*metzolot*] like a stone," תְּהֹמֹת יְכַסְיֻמוּ יָרְדוּ בִמְצוֹלֹת כְּמוֹ־אָבֶן (Exodus 15:5). Now, instead of being destroyed and sinking into the "depths," the "bells" of the horses would ring as part of the divine celebration.

God, Moses, and the Worst-Case Scenario

One of the arguments I make over the course of this book is that we should not succumb to the folly of reading the Bible with the end in mind. Although you and I know how the Exodus story actually turned out, events were *not* preordained, so to speak, to unfold the way they did. They *could* have–and perhaps even *should* have–unfolded along different paths. As I've discussed in the book, there are at least two crucial forks in the road where the Exodus could have developed differently.

As a general matter, the notion that events in the Torah need not have occurred precisely the way they did seems self-evidently true. The Israelites didn't *have* to sin with the Golden Calf; it would have been preferable for them *not* to have sinned. Moses didn't *have* to hit the rock when God asked him to speak to it. The mere fact that the protagonists in these cases were punished for their misdeeds seems evidence enough to indicate that things *should* have transpired differently. When it comes to the Exodus, though, the biblical narrative in several places does seem to convey a strong sense that, somehow, events were preordained. Several verses in particular give us this impression.

At the Burning Bush, before any confrontation between Moses and Pharaoh, God says to Moses:

וַאֲנִי יָדַעְתִּי כִּי לֹא־יִתֵּן אֶתְכֶם מֶלֶךְ מִצְרַיִם לַהֲלֹךְ וְלֹא בְּיָד
חֲזָקָה: וְשָׁלַחְתִּי אֶת־יָדִי וְהִכֵּיתִי אֶת־מִצְרַיִם בְּכֹל נִפְלְאֹתַי
אֲשֶׁר אֶעֱשֶׂה בְּקִרְבּוֹ וְאַחֲרֵי־כֵן יְשַׁלַּח אֶתְכֶם:

I know that the King of Egypt will not let you go, if not by a mighty hand. And I will stretch out my hand and smite Egypt with all of my wonders...and after that, he will let you go (Exodus 3:19–20)

Later, God will also speak to Moses and indicate to him that He will "strengthen" (Exodus 4:21) or "harden" (Exodus 7:3–4) Pharaoh's heart, and that God will ultimately have to take Israel out of Egypt *with a strong hand*–by force.

These verses seem to indicate that what we have called Plan C was a forgone conclusion. However, in this book, we marshaled evidence that suggests otherwise. God does seem to be after an "authentic" yes from Pharaoh, for example; moreover, as we argue in Part IV of this book, events in the Joseph story do seem to suggest that something along the lines of Exodus Plan A *ought* to have come to pass, and that Exodus Plan C is, by comparison, a tragedy. But how can we square this with the verses above, in which God foretells to Moses at the Burning Bush that Pharaoh will be recalcitrant, and that in the end, God will have to resort to force to free Israel from Egypt?

Foretelling the Worst-Case Scenario

By way of a response, I'd like to suggest that, strange as it may seem, the "mere" fact that the Almighty broadcasts a future occurrence to one or more human beings does not mean that those events *must*, of necessity, occur. Take, for example, the case of Jonah's prophecy. After much prodding, Jonah goes to Nineveh and prophesies, at God's behest, that Nineveh will be destroyed in forty days:

עוֹד אַרְבָּעִים יוֹם וְנִינְוֵה נֶהְפָּכֶת:

Forty more days and Nineveh will be destroyed (Jonah 3:4)

Of course, the foretold destruction never happens. The people of Nineveh repent from their evil ways, and God chooses to spare their lives (Jonah 3:8-10). What are we to make of that? Jonah delivered an unconditional prophecy: Nineveh *will* be destroyed! And yet, it does *not*, in fact, happen.

None of the classical commentators regard Jonah as a false prophet, though his prophecy didn't come to pass. Why?

The answer would seem to lie with a principle articulated by Rambam. In his *Mishneh Torah* (*Hil. Yesodei HaTorah* 10:4), Rambam speaks of the guidelines for establishing whether one who claims to have received prophecy is a genuine prophet. Rambam writes that if the prophecy the person delivers foretells some future act of compassion, mercy or beneficence on the part of God, and this event does *not* materialize, then the supposed prophet is surely a charlatan, because God would never renege on a promise of good tidings. If, however, the prophecy promises *bad* tidings–famine, destruction, or the like–then the failure of the prophecy to materialize cannot be taken as evidence that the prophet is a liar. This is so even if the prophecy of bad tidings was given unconditionally, because, Rambam argues, there is no such thing as an unconditional promise of bad tidings; the possibility of reversal *always* exists, even if the prophet doesn't explicitly state this.

In essence, Rambam seems to be suggesting that prophecies of bad tidings ought to be seen as cautionary warnings of a worst-case scenario that will take place unless steps are taken to avert it. Thus, when Jonah prophesied that in forty more days Nineveh would be destroyed, his prophecy must be seen as a warning to Nineveh that their destruction looms, unless it is averted by the force of human free will; in the event, it *is* averted, after the people of Nineveh choose to change their ways.

Rambam's guidelines, and the proof-case of Nineveh, open the possibility that something like this may have been going on in the Exodus, when God delivers a prophecy to Moses about the way events in Egypt will end. God's words to Moses seem to indicate, in absolute terms, the way events *will* happen, the way God *will* act in the face of Pharaoh's recalcitrance. But prophecies of this sort are *never* to be regarded as absolute—and thus, here too, it would seem that God is making clear to Moses some kind of worst-case scenario: here is the outcome that will ensue if Pharaoh acts as stubbornly as could possibly be imagined. *If that happens, I will deliver Israel by force.*

The same could be said about God's later words to Moses, forecasting that the time will come when God will "strengthen" Pharaoh's heart. Over the course of this book, we've made the argument that there were reasons God might choose to "lend Pharaoh courage" (or "strengthen" his heart). If, for example, Pharaoh would give in for the sake of expediency, but still hold fast to his denial of the Creator, God would lend him the courage to pursue his vision. However, when God forecasts to Moses that, in the future, the Almighty will do this—that, too, can be seen as the forecast of a worst-case scenario. If Pharaoh should choose poorly, if he should insist, in the face of all evidence, on denying his obligations to the Creator—*then, Moses, these are the steps I shall take to deal with that: I will encourage him; I will give him the strength to continue his struggle.*

Why Tell Moses All This?

Let us grant, then, that Rambam's principle establishes a framework that may be helpful for us: that God's forecast of bad tidings to a prophet can *never* be regarded as unconditional, and that humans, by exercising their free will, can always make positive choices that may alter the way divine justice prevails. However, we must still address one final question: why would God bother informing Moses about theoretical future events? Why would God tell Moses, at the Burning Bush and then again later, what He will do if Pharaoh should happen to make poor choices?

To see why God *does* have an interest in telling Moses what will ensue in a worst-case scenario, we must carefully read the Burning Bush narrative in its entirety.

God appears to Moses for the first time at the Burning Bush, and there they engage in a lengthy dialogue. That dialogue touches on many things, but has a central purpose: to indicate God's intention to free Israel from slavery, and to convince Moses to accept a divine mission—to be the person who helps actualize God's plan. Moses look askance at God's offer, and that's a gentle way of putting it. No matter what God says to him, Moses devises a reason why he can't do what God wants of him, why he's the wrong person for the job. Finally, all out of excuses, Moses simply tells God:

בִּי אֲדֹנָי שְׁלַח־נָא בְּיַד־תִּשְׁלָח:

Please, my Master, send [someone else] (Exodus 4:13)[1]

At this point, God becomes angry at Moses and dismisses him. The only concession he gives Moses is that Aaron, his brother, will be his partner, and will speak for him when necessary (Exodus 4:14).

All in all, it is an extraordinary conversation. If God appeared to you one day and asked you to do something, would *you* spend the conversation trying to convince the Lord that He had the wrong person? It seems astounding that throughout his inaugural conversation with God, Moses seems *this* close to just walking out on the whole idea.

Evidently, though, God has decided that, despite his reluctance, Moses *is* the man for the job. The Almighty parries every excuse offered by Moses, gently twisting his arm until Moses

---

1. Translation follows *Seforno*: Please send someone else who would be naturally gifted, already prepared for the task (see also *Rashi*).

sets off on his mission. We can debate why Moses is the only candidate God is interested in, why no one else will do—but the facts of the matter suggest that this is the case.[2]

It should not come as a shock, then, that in conversation with Moses at the Burning Bush, God would reveal to him a worst-case portrait of how the Exodus might unfold: *Pharaoh may well be stubborn enough to never recognize his Creator and to defy Me at every turn. But even if that happens, don't worry—I will not be thwarted. If necessary, I will free the slaves with a mighty hand. I will not hesitate to use force.*

To see this clearly, imagine the alternative: that Moses *isn't* made aware that God has a back-up plan, Plan C, in case Pharaoh remains stubborn to the end. Moses has already expressed extreme discomfort about going to Pharaoh; in all probability, he does not believe he has a chance of persuading Pharaoh of the reality of the Creator. Imagine that God had not conceded this possibility, and pushed Moses to go to Pharaoh anyway, demanding that Moses give Pharaoh the truth, come what may. And now imagine that Moses complies, and Pharaoh viciously rejects God's words—as in fact happened. Moses's resolve might break down. God has an interest in preparing Moses for the worst, at the Burning Bush. If God doesn't, Moses may not be willing to participate in the plan at all.[3]

The apparent contradiction, then, is resolved. God will soon ask Moses to seek Pharaoh's consent to free the slaves. God will give Moses the language to indicate to Pharaoh that there is a Creator, and a sign to back up those words. God will first ask Pharaoh to let the people leave just for a few days, in the name

---

2. For my thoughts on the reasons the Almighty was insistent on choosing Moses in particular, please see *Chanukah: Why Do We Celebrate?*, a series of short videos at alephbeta.org.

3. See *Rashbam* to Exodus 3:19 for a similar explanation.

of religious tolerance. All these are aspects of the hope for the realization of Plan A. If this fails, God will bring plagues that demonstrate, through cold, hard fact, His complete dominance of nature. God will do all that, and if Pharaoh acquiesces and acknowledges the Creator-God at any point, the Exodus can be brought to a neat and tidy conclusion quickly–Plan B. And yet, at the Bush, God only tells Moses what will happen if all else fails. Moses hears about Plan C. The message God is interested in communicating to Moses is: *Don't worry, I'll take care of it, no matter what. Even if everything else we try here fails, I have the ability to do this unilaterally. You need not fear a thing.*

A Corroborating Case: Abraham's Dark Prophecy

Are there other times in the Five Books of Moses in which a similar dynamic seems to be at work? Are there other situations in which the Master of the Universe chooses to reveal a worst-case scenario that might be brought about through some sort of human failing? Aside from the case we've just discussed at the Burning Bush, two other such situations come to mind.

The first is the covenant that God makes with Abraham known as the *brit ben habetarim*. In it, God gives Abraham a glimpse of a nightmarish future–that his progeny are destined to be "strangers in a land not their own, enslaved, oppressed, for four hundred years" (Genesis 15:13). Here, too, God seems to reveal a worst-case scenario, one brought about by human failing: ultimately, the brothers' decision to sell Joseph into slavery begins a chain of dominoes that will drag the family down to Egypt. And, indeed, it truly was a *worst*-case scenario. In the end, things don't end up quite as bad as the prophecy to Abraham "predicted": the people were *not* enslaved for four hundred years, but two hundred and ten (see *Rashi* to Exodus 12:40). Still, one wonders why God chose to tell Abraham any of this. Why haunt his dreams with events Abraham himself couldn't control?

But a similar divine rationale could be suggested for making such possibilities known to Abraham and his progeny. For what might happen if the people *weren't* forewarned about the possibility of slavery?

God had promised Abraham that his progeny would grow into a nation and enjoy sovereignty over the Land of Canaan. What if no one in the family ever had any inkling that the road to that sovereignty might be long and tortured? As it was, when Jacob came back from the house of Laban, there are indications that he thought his job was simply to stay in the Land of Canaan, have children and begin the process of nation-building.[4] How would the family have reacted to hundreds of years of Egyptian exile had they never heard a glimmer of warning? They might have concluded that God had forsaken them–or perhaps that God was not powerful enough to make good on His promises. One way or another, they were on their own. By the time the Master of the Universe came to redeem them, centuries later, there might not have been a distinct people left to redeem anymore.

Thus, the pattern seems to reassert itself: on rare occasions in biblical history, God may prophetically warn someone of a worst-case scenario, to help the prophet, or future generations, withstand that worst-case scenario, should it ever come to pass.

A Second Corroborating Case: *Shirat Ha'azinu*

One more case comes to mind: the events at the very end of Deuteronomy that precede Moses's death.

To set the stage for those events, consider this: if you were God and you were going to give a final goodbye speech to Moses, your faithful servant, before he died, what would you tell him? You might say *Thank you for your service*, or *You've been amazing*–something along those lines. But what does God *actually* say to Moses?

---

4. See *Rashi* and Midrash Rabbah to the beginning of Genesis 37.

הִנְּךָ שֹׁכֵב עִם־אֲבֹתֶיךָ וְקָם הָעָם הַזֶּה וְזָנָה אַחֲרֵי אֱלֹהֵי נֵכַר־הָאָרֶץ

You are about to die and to rest with your ancestors,
and this nation will rise and stray after the gods of
the land [of Canaan] (Deuteronomy 31:16)

God goes on to tell Moses that the people will worship false gods and abandon the Creator, desecrating their covenant with Him. But what kind of goodbye speech is this? *Dear Moses, I know you tried to build up this nation, instilling in them the importance of serving God, but I'm going to give it to you straight—it was all for naught. Everything is going to come catastrophically tumbling down after you die...*
Why would God tell Moses this?

God Himself provides the answer. In the verses that follow, God details the future that Moses least wants to hear: not only will the people rebel against God, they will fail to understand how to right themselves afterwards. And for *this*, God gives Moses an antidote: *Shirat Ha'azinu*, a poetic recounting of Israel's history and destiny, which will serve as an "eternal witness" to the people. In other words, it will be something they can always come back to—when there is no Moses or any other prophet to turn to—and understand the nature of what's happened to them, and what they must do to right their course:

וְהָיָה כִּי־תִמְצֶאןָ אֹתוֹ רָעוֹת רַבּוֹת וְצָרוֹת וְעָנְתָה הַשִּׁירָה
הַזֹּאת לְפָנָיו לְעֵד כִּי לֹא תִשָּׁכַח מִפִּי זַרְעוֹ

And it shall be, when terrible troubles befall them, that this
Song shall answer to them as a witness, for it shall never
be forgotten by their progeny (Deuteronomy 31:21)

Exactly how *Shirat Haazinu* might provide an antidote to future troubles is beyond the scope of this short essay.[5] But it is

---

5. For some insights, see the video series on *Nitzavim-Vayelech, Ha'azinu* and *V'Zot HaBracha*, created as part of Aleph Beta's parsha videos for year 5774, available at alephbeta.org.

clear that this is *Shirat Ha'azinu's* function. Just before his death, Moses is told about the worst-case scenario—the terrible happenings that may well befall the nation of Israel—not to cause him anguish, but because he can do something about it. He can, and must, write *Shirat Ha'azinu* for them. It will give future generations the strength and fortitude to persevere in the face of pain and troubles.

Thus, the pattern seems confirmed. In the Bible, on rare occasions, God seems to be willing to reveal worst-case scenarios to humans when it's necessary, in the Almighty's judgment, to steel them for the rigors that may well face them—or their descendants—in the future.

One Coat, Two Coats

Part I: The Mystery of the Doubled Coat

In chapter 24, *A Fence of Thorns*, I mentioned that a text in
Deuteronomy seems to confirm the idea that Jacob had, by the
time Joseph was seventeen, bestowed upon him the status of *bechor*,
the firstborn of the family. I want to explore that evidence with
you here. To set the stage, let's begin by noting a textual oddity in
the story of Joseph. The Torah relates that just before the brothers
cast Joseph in a pit and plotted to sell him as a slave, they stripped
him of his special coat, his *ketonet passim* (כְּתֹנֶת פַּסִּים).[1] The verse,
however, seems to unnecessarily repeat the point:

וַיַּפְשִׁיטוּ אֶת־יוֹסֵף אֶת־כֻּתָּנְתּוֹ אֶת־כְּתֹנֶת הַפַּסִּים אֲשֶׁר עָלָיו:

*And they stripped Joseph; [stripped him] of his coat, of
his special coat that was upon him* (Genesis 37:23)

---

1. *Ketonet* (כְּתֹנֶת) in Hebrew means cloak; *passim* (פַּסִּים) can be translated as "colorful" (*Radak*), "embroidered" (*Ibn Ezra*; *Ramban* on Exodus
28:2), or "striped" (*Radak*). According to some, *ketonet passim* denotes a
long garment, coming down to the palms of the hands (*Rashbam*; Genesis
Rabbah 84:11). Alternatively, *passim* denotes the fine wool out of which the
coat was made (*Rashi*).

Notice how the verse seems to mention twice that Joseph was deprived of his coat. The Sages of the Midrash are puzzled by this seeming repetition. Rashi paraphrases the Midrash:

אֶת כֻּתָּנְתּוֹ: זֶה חָלוּק אֶת כְּתֹנֶת הַפַּסִּים: הוּא
שֶׁהוֹסִיף לוֹ אָבִיו יוֹתֵר עַל אֶחָיו

[When the verse first states that they stripped him] "of his coat", it is referring to his cloak. [When it then states] "his ketonet passim," this refers to the [coat] that his father added for him, over and above the one that each of the other brothers possessed (Rashi to Genesis 37:23, from Genesis Rabbah)

In other words, the Midrash is telling us that the brothers stripped Joseph of two coats: an undercoat, which his brothers also wore, and a special coat, that his father had given only to him.

Rashi's comments seem astonishingly trivial. We are perched at one of the darkest moments in the Bible. Joseph's brothers are about to cast him in a pit and leave him, his fate hangs in the balance, the entire family of Jacob appears to be coming apart at the seams—and Rashi is reporting on exactly how many coats Joseph lost when his brothers stripped him, on whether Joseph was still wearing his undershirt as he was cast into a pit. Who cares about how many coats Joseph was deprived of?

But let's stop and play that favorite game of ours, Where Else Have We Heard This Before?—and it will become clear what Rashi is getting at.

Replay Rashi's words in your mind. *All the brothers, including Joseph, had one coat from their father. Joseph, though, was given an additional second coat by Father, above the one given to everyone else.* Where else in the Torah do we hear something like this? What does a special "double portion" of coats remind you of? The portion that a *bechor*, a first-born son, receives in his father's estate.

In the book of Deuteronomy (21:16–17), we are told that when a man dies, his *bechor*, his firstborn, is entitled to a "double portion," *pi shanyim* (פִּי שְׁנַיִם) of his father's possessions. That every brother received one coat from Father, but Joseph received two, suggests that Jacob was treating Joseph as his *bechor*.[2]

Now, the notion that Joseph would be treated as a firstborn by Jacob at first sounds laughable. In a technical, biological sense, of course, it couldn't possibly be true. Reuben, Simeon, Levi, Judah, and many others were all born before Joseph. And yet, as we've touched upon earlier, Joseph could be *seen* as Jacob's firstborn. He was the first child born to the woman Jacob always felt he was supposed to marry; he was the firstborn child of Rachel.

Part II: The Deuteronomy Cipher

If we doubt whether this interpretation, seemingly advanced by the Midrash, actually jibes with the story of Joseph, we must explore the biblical passage of *pi shnayim*, the double portion to which a *bechor* is entitled in his father's estate.

Four Unusual Phrases

The passage begins this way:

כִּי־תִהְיֶיןָ לְאִישׁ שְׁתֵּי נָשִׁים הָאַחַת אֲהוּבָה וְהָאַחַת שְׂנוּאָה

When a man has two wives, one whom he loves, and another whom he hates...(Deuteronomy 21:15)

---

2. Other commentators, such as *Kli Yakar*, clearly adhere to such a view. *Kli Yakar* states outright his presumption that the gift of the special coat to Joseph signified that Joseph was being treated as the *bechor* of the family. He adds that the brothers' language in response to Joseph's dream hints at this as well. The brothers' words had been laced with doublets, paired phrases. They had said: *hamaloch timloch aleinu, im mashol timshal banu* (הֲמָלֹךְ תִּמְלֹךְ עָלֵינוּ אִם־מָשׁוֹל תִּמְשֹׁל בָּנוּ), "shall you rule, yes, rule over us; will you subjugate, yes, subjugate us?" The paired repetition, according to *Kli Yakar*, is a veiled reference to *pi shnayim*, the *bechor's* double portion.

Stop right there. Before even hearing what happens next, the reader is taken aback by that phraseology. *A wife that he hates? Maybe he doesn't like her as much as his other wife, but does that mean he hates her?* Couldn't the Torah have expressed its point more politely by saying that the man loved one wife more than the other? As we go further in the passage, it turns out that the man with two wives ends up fathering children with each. And the oldest son—the *bechor*—just happens to be born to the unloved wife. The text continues:

וְהָיָה בְּיוֹם הַנְחִילוֹ אֶת־בָּנָיו אֵת אֲשֶׁר־יִהְיֶה לוֹ לֹא יוּכַל
לְבַכֵּר אֶת־בֶּן־הָאֲהוּבָה עַל־פְּנֵי בֶן־הַשְּׂנוּאָה הַבְּכֹר:
כִּי אֶת־הַבְּכֹר בֶּן־הַשְּׂנוּאָה יַכִּיר לָתֶת לוֹ פִּי שְׁנַיִם בְּכֹל
אֲשֶׁר־יִמָּצֵא לוֹ כִּי־הוּא רֵאשִׁית אֹנוֹ לוֹ מִשְׁפַּט הַבְּכֹרָה:

And it shall be, on the day that he apportions his estate to his children, he shall not be able to turn the son of the loved wife into the bechor, in place of the son of the unloved wife, the [true] bechor. Rather, the bechor-child of the unloved wife he must recognize to give him a double portion in all that is found to him for [that son] is the first of his strength; to him goes the right of the firstborn (Deuteronomy 21:16–17)

A few things seem unusual in that paragraph:

He must recognize: The addition of this phrase seems superfluous, and makes the text read in a somewhat stilted way. The Torah could have simply stated: *he must give to him a double portion... for to him goes the right of the firstborn.* What does the Torah add with "he must recognize *to give*"?

In all that is found to him: The Torah seems to be saying that the father must give his oldest son an extra portion in his estate, but wouldn't it have been clearer to say: *...give him a double portion in all that **he has**?* Why say: "give him a double portion in all that *is found to him*"? What does "found to him" mean?

The first of his strength: The phrase here in Hebrew is *reishit ono* (רֵאשִׁית אֹנוֹ)– a poetic expression whose exact meaning is not immediately apparent. Rashi (Genesis 49:2), whose translation I have followed here, surmises that the words mean "first of his strength," based upon comparisons with verses in the later prophetic works Hosea (12:9) and Isaiah (40:26, 29). It is a rare and obscure word, and its poetic overtones seem out of place in a section of legal text that is otherwise composed in very straightforward prose.

These oddities might strike you as unimportant. What enduring significance could there be in these nitpicky observations? But let's ask ourselves: where have we heard any of these words before? Let's read this text again, with our ear attuned to the language cues that remind us of bygone deeds:

The Man With Two Wives

The text opens with its portrait of a man married to two wives, one who is loved, the other who is hated. We found that word "hated"–*senu'ah* (שְׂנוּאָה)–abrasive, unnecessarily harsh. But the very abrasiveness of the term is what catches our eye and forces us to focus: where have you heard that word before? Do we ever find a particular person described this way in the Torah?

The answer is yes, only one person in the Torah is described as *senu'ah*–Leah.

וַיַּרְא יְהוָה כִּי־שְׂנוּאָה לֵאָה וַיִּפְתַּח אֶת־רַחְמָהּ וְרָחֵל עֲקָרָה׃

And God saw that Leah was hated, and he opened her womb (Genesis 29:31)[3]

---

3. Undoubtedly, it sounds harsh to speak of Jacob's feelings for Leah in such disturbing terms. The phrase does not, and cannot, mean that Jacob hated her in the conventional sense of the word–for the immediately pre-

Could the text in Deuteronomy, by its use of this term, be making an oblique reference to Leah? The correspondence could, perhaps, be coincidental. But let's play out the implications of this possibility:

If the "hated" wife of Deuteronomy covertly refers to Leah, to whom would the "loved" wife refer? That's easy: Rachel. She is the woman Jacob loved unreservedly, the one he had worked so hard to marry, the one whose hand in marriage he sought through seven long years of labor.[4]

So now: If the comparatively unloved wife alludes to Leah, and the loved wife to Rachel, we know the man Deuteronomy describes as married to these women—it must be an allusion to Jacob.

Indeed, if we continue to play out the implications of this line of reasoning, the correspondence between Jacob's family and the hypothetical family described in Deuteronomy becomes uncanny. Jacob, like the hypothetical man of Deuteronomy, has children from both his "loved" and "less-loved" wives, and, like that man, his first child is born to the "less-loved" wife—Reuben, the first

---

ceding verse excludes that possibility. It says that Jacob "loved Rachel, also, more than Leah," explicitly telling the reader that Jacob loved Leah—just that, comparatively, Rachel was loved more than she. Thus, when the very next verse goes on to state "and God saw that Leah was hated," it seems to be making a point: when, as a wife, you feel that you are loved less than another, for all intents and purposes, that feels the same as being "hated." The Almighty, in "seeing that Leah was hated," recognizes and acknowledges the truth of that perception (cf. *Ramban*, citing *Radak*, to Genesis 29:30).

4. By way of confirmation, the text in Genesis *does* use this term "love" to describe Jacob's feelings for Rachel. In the verse that directly precedes the description of Leah as *senu'ah* (Genesis 29:30), we are told:

וַיָּבֹא גַּם אֶל־רָחֵל וַיֶּאֱהַב גַּם־אֶת־רָחֵל מִלֵּאָה

And Jacob married Rachel, also—and he loved Rachel, also, more than Leah...

of all of Jacob's children, the oldest child of Leah.[5]

Will the Real *Bechor* Please Stand Up?

Let us continue reading the passage in Deuteronomy, and see what happens next with this hypothetical man with two wives, and with his respective children from each:

וְהָיָה בְּיוֹם הַנְחִילוֹ אֶת־בָּנָיו אֵת אֲשֶׁר־יִהְיֶה לוֹ לֹא יוּכַל
לְבַכֵּר אֶת־בֶּן־הָאֲהוּבָה עַל־פְּנֵי בֶן־הַשְּׂנוּאָה הַבְּכֹר:
כִּי אֶת־הַבְּכֹר בֶּן־הַשְּׂנוּאָה יַכִּיר לָתֶת לוֹ פִּי שְׁנַיִם בְּכֹל
אֲשֶׁר־יִמָּצֵא לוֹ כִּי־הוּא רֵאשִׁית אֹנוֹ לוֹ מִשְׁפַּט הַבְּכֹרָה:

And it shall be, on the day [the father] apportions his estate to his children, he shall not be able to turn the child of the loved wife into the bechor, in place of the child of the unloved wife, the [true] bechor. Rather, the bechor-child of the unloved wife he must recognize to give him a double portion in all that is found to him—for [that child] is the first of his strength; to him goes the right of the firstborn (Deuteronomy 21:16–17).

---

5. See Genesis 29:32. Indeed, not only is there a correspondence between the Deuteronomy passage and Jacob's family insofar as the details of the family setup are concerned, but the *order* in which the Torah narrates these details corresponds precisely as well. Deuteronomy first tells us that there is a man who married two wives, then that one is loved and the other unloved, and finally that the unloved wife gives birth to the first child. We find precisely the same order of narration in Genesis, in the three verses (Genesis 29:30–32) that lead up to the birth of Reuben: *And Jacob married Rachel also...* [A man married two wives]...*and he loved Rachel, also, more than Leah. And God saw that Leah was senu'ah* [One is loved more than the other]... *and He opened [Leah's] womb, and Rachel was childless. And Leah conceived and gave birth to a son, and she called his name Reuben, because she said 'God has seen my suffering'* [The unloved wife gives birth to the first child].

If we continue to interpolate the Genesis narrative into the Deuteronomy text, the composite picture is astonishing indeed. The Torah is saying that Jacob, the man with two wives, shall not treat Joseph, the first child of the loved wife, as the *bechor* in place of Reuben, the first child of the unloved wife. Instead, he must recognize Reuben as his *bechor*, giving *him* the double portion that is due a firstborn.

The reader is left to contemplate the tantalizing implication: did Jacob himself try to do what the text in Deuteronomy is warning the anonymous man with two wives not to do? Did he try to make the child of his loved wife into the *bechor*? And as we contemplate that question, we are reminded, again, of the Midrash that speaks of Joseph's "second coat." The Midrash seemed to suggest that the special coat was a *bechor*-like "double portion" that Joseph received in Jacob's estate.[6] The Midrash had seemed so odd—but perhaps the Rabbis saw the very allusions that we see right now.

---

6. Some other *midrashim* appear to be even more explicit about the idea that Jacob was treating Joseph as a *bechor*. One of these is cited by Rashi in connection with Leah's naming of Reuben, her first child. Reuben (*Re'uven*), the Midrash suggests, can be read as a kind of shorthand for *re'u mah vein beni l'ben chami*—"See the difference between my son and the son of my father-in-law!" In this interpretation, the Sages have Leah contrast the behavior of her own son—Reuben—with that of Esau, her brother-in-law. In the words of the Midrash: "In Esau's case, he sold the right of the firstborn to Jacob, and Esau still protested [against Jacob assuming the status of firstborn]. My son, Reuben, never sold any rights to Joseph—and yet, he never protested [against Joseph's status]. On the contrary, Reuben was the one who saved Joseph when the other brothers were plotting against him!"

We will return to this Midrashic comment later. But for now, suffice it to say that it seems to take the position that Joseph was being treated as the *bechor*.

Look Before You Leap

But let's not leap to conclusions. It is at least possible that what we've seen is mere coincidence. Yes, it is true that this passage employs the term *senu'ah* to designate the man's less-loved wife—and yes, the only other time in the Torah we find that phrase again is when the text in Genesis designates Leah as *senu'ah*. But still, Deuteronomy's use of this phrase could, conceivably, be coincidental. Moreover, while the family described in Deuteronomy looks suspiciously like Jacob's—a man with two wives, one loved more than the other, with the first child born to the less-loved wife—that correspondence might also be coincidental. How do we know that these conclusions are anything more than chance?

We would need to see more evidence; the more parallels that can be shown to exist between two texts, the greater the likelihood that the Torah deliberately embedded these connections, and that we are meant to view one text in light of the other. Let us ask: are there other parallels between the Deuteronomy passage and the Joseph narrative?

One Down, Three to Go

The search for such parallels brings us right back to the four unusual phrases we identified in the Deuteronomy passage. We suggested earlier that the first of these phrases—the reference to the *senu'ah*, the less-loved wife—might be a covert allusion to Leah. What about the other three?

If you recall, they were the phrases *yakir,* "he must recognize," *yimatzei lo,* "that is found to him," and *reishit ono,* "the first of his strength":

כִּי אֶת־הַבְּכֹר בֶּן־הַשְּׂנוּאָה יַכִּיר לָתֶת לוֹ פִּי שְׁנַיִם בְּכֹל
אֲשֶׁר־יִמָּצֵא לוֹ כִּי־הוּא רֵאשִׁית אֹנוֹ לוֹ מִשְׁפַּט הַבְּכֹרָה:

*Rather, the bechor-child of the unloved wife, **he must*** *
recognize to give him a double portion in all **that is found** *
*to him. For [that child] is **the first of his strength**; to him* *
goes the right of the firstborn (Deuteronomy 21:17)

Let's start with the last phrase, "the first of his strength." As it
turns out, this phrase appears in only one other place in the entire Five Books of Moses—at the very end of the book of Genesis,
when Jacob blesses, of all people, Reuben, his firstborn son from
Leah. Jacob addresses him with the title *bechor*:

רְאוּבֵן בְּכֹרִי אַתָּה כֹּחִי וְרֵאשִׁית אוֹנִי

Reuben, you are my bechor, my power, the first *
of my strength [reishit oni] (Genesis 49:3)

And so the pattern continues. We have here yet another telltale
phrase from the story of Jacob's family adopted, in Deuteronomy,
as part of the Torah's description of the laws of the firstborn.
The anonymous man in Deuteronomy must award the double
portion to his true *bechor*, born of the *senu'ah*, for he—just like
Reuben, in Jacob's family—is "the first of his father's strength."

Finding Recognition

Let us turn to the two remaining unusual phrases we identified
in the Deuteronomy passage:

כִּי אֶת־הַבְּכֹר בֶּן־הַשְּׂנוּאָה יַכִּיר לָתֶת לוֹ פִּי שְׁנַיִם בְּכֹל אֲשֶׁר־יִמָּצֵא לוֹ

Rather, the bechor of the unloved wife, [the father] *
must recognize to give him a double portion in all *
that is found to him (Deuteronomy 21:17)

Is there another time in the Torah where we encounter these
two phrases—"recognize" and "found"—appearing together in

close proximity to one another? Is there another time in the
Torah where a father is asked to "recognize" something that is
"found"? It turns out that there is. As we might expect by now,
it is in the story of Jacob and his children:

וַיְשַׁלְּחוּ אֶת־כְּתֹנֶת הַפַּסִּים וַיָּבִיאוּ אֶל־אֲבִיהֶם וַיֹּאמְרוּ
זֹאת מָצָאנוּ הַכֶּר־נָא הַכְּתֹנֶת בִּנְךָ הִוא אִם־לֹא:

*[The brothers] sent [Joseph's] special coat [covered in blood]
and brought it to their father. And they said: 'This, we found;
recognize, please: Is it your son's coat, or not?'* (Genesis 37:32)

Well, then. Joseph's brothers had asked their father to "recognize" something they had "found"–the special coat he had been
wearing, now smeared with blood.

What are the implications of this? On one level, the Torah confirms the suspicion we've had all along: the text in Deuteronomy
is painting its laws about the right of the firstborn in colors
borrowed from the palette of Jacob's family. But there is a deeper,
more shocking implication to this as well, for in aligning its laws
of the firstborn with the words spoken by Joseph's brothers as
they present the bloody coat to their father, the Torah seems to
be illuminating a message the brothers dared not convey to their
father directly, but that was hidden, implicit, in their declaration
nevertheless. Centuries later, we can discern the icy imprint of
that message in the subtlety of the brothers' words.

How do we discern that message? The answer is: we must
read Genesis while letting Deuteronomy tell us the meaning of
its words. We must understand what the words "recognize" and
"found" mean when they are used in Deuteronomy, and then
keep these meanings in mind as we read Genesis.

Here, again, are the phrases in Deuteronomy. In context, what
particular meaning do these phrases have?

כִּי אֶת־הַבְּכֹר בֶּן־הַשְּׂנוּאָה יַכִּיר לָתֶת לוֹ פִּי שְׁנַיִם בְּכֹל אֲשֶׁר־יִמָּצֵא לוֹ

> *Rather, the **bechor**-child of the unloved wife **he must***
> ***recognize** to give him a double portion in all **that***
> ***is found** to him* (Deuteronomy 21:17)

"He must recognize" means that a father must recognize who his true *bechor* is. "Found to him" means "that which a father possesses and will hand down to his children"–his estate. Now, bring these meanings back with you into Genesis. Read what Joseph's brothers are saying to their father, one more time:

וַיְשַׁלְּחוּ אֶת־כְּתֹנֶת הַפַּסִּים וַיָּבִיאוּ אֶל־אֲבִיהֶם וַיֹּאמְרוּ
זֹאת מָצָאנוּ הַכֶּר־נָא הַכְּתֹנֶת בִּנְךָ הִוא אִם־לֹא:

> *They sent [Joseph's] special coat [covered in blood] and brought*
> *it to their father. And they said: This we found. Recognize,*
> *please: is it your son's coat, or not?* (Genesis 37:32)

On one level, the brothers are saying to their father that they found a bloody coat–might it perhaps belong to Joseph? On another level, however, they are saying something of far greater import:

> *This is what we found.*
> This, father, is your estate.

> *Recognize it, please.*
> Please recognize who your true *bechor* is.

> *Is it your son's coat...?*
> Does the doubled coat, by rights, belong to Joseph?

> *Or not?*
> Or maybe it doesn't belong to him at all.

But to whom else could it belong? The bitter implication of the verse is clear. *Maybe it really belongs to Reuben!*